Managing information resources in libraries

collection management in theory and practice

Managing information resources in libraries

collection management in
theory and practice

Peter Clayton

and

G. E. Gorman

Bibliography compiled by Adela Clayton

LIBRARY ASSOCIATION PUBLISHING
LONDON

© Peter Clayton and G. E. Gorman 2001

Published by
Library Association Publishing
7 Ridgmount Street
London WC1E 7AE

Library Association Publishing is wholly owned by The Library Association.

Peter Clayton and G. E. Gorman have asserted their rights under the Copyright
Designs and Patents Act 1988 to be identified as authors of this work.

First published 2001

British Library Cataloguing in Publication Data

A catalogue record for this book is available from the British Library.

ISBN 1-85604-297-9

Typeset in 9.5/13pt New Baskerville and Franklin Gothic Condensed by Library
Association Publishing.
Printed and made in Great Britain by MPG Books Ltd, Bodmin, Cornwall.

Contents

About the authors

Peter Clayton BA DipLib GradDipArts InfStudies MA PhD AALIA AFAIM MACE is Associate Professor in Information Management and Program Director for Information Studies at the University of Canberra, Australia. Dr Clayton has published well over 100 items, including more than 20 monographs and research reports. With G. E. Gorman he published *Qualitative research for the information professional: a practical handbook* (Library Association Publishing, 1997). This has been twice reprinted and will come out in a second edition in 2003, along with a companion volume, again with Dr Gorman, *Quantitative research for the information professional* (also Library Association Publishing). His other published titles include *Implementation of organizational innovation: studies of academic and research libraries* (Academic Press, 1997), and *Academics online: a nationwide quantitative study of Australian academic use of the Internet* (with Ann Applebee, Harry Bruce, Celina Pascoe and Edna Sharpe; Auslib Press, 1998). He is editor of *Australian academic & research libraries*. He has held various offices in the Australian Library and Information Association, including President of the ACT Branch and of the University, College and Research Libraries Section. For five years he was President of the ACT Acquisitions Section of ALIA.

G. E. Gorman BA MDiv STB GradDipLib MA ThD FLA FRSA is Professor of Library and Information Management in the School of Information Management at Victoria University of Wellington, New Zealand. Dr Gorman has written widely in the field of collection development/collection management and also has undertaken a number of research projects in this area. His books have been published in the UK, the USA and Australia, with translations in Russian, Korean, Chinese and Thai. He is founding general editor of the *International yearbook of library and information management* for Library Association Publishing, editor of

Online information review (MCB), associate editor of *Library collections, acquisitions and technical services* (Elsevier), reviews editor of the *Australian library journal*, and is actively affiliated with a number of other journals. He is also engaged in information-related development projects in Vietnam, Thailand and Lebanon, and is managing a major New Zealand government-funded information programme in Vietnam. He is actively involved in IFLA, especially the Regional Section for Asia and Oceania.

Adela Clayton BA AALIA is a reference librarian in the Research Centre of the Australian War Memorial in Canberra. Her previous positions have included Director, Curriculum Resources Centre, University of Canberra, and Distance Education Librarian, University of South Australia. She has had wide experience in collection management in state, public and academic libraries.

Preface

The new electronic world, which is transforming not only libraries but also the organizations that they serve, makes the role of every information professional more complex; all of us now need additional knowledge and skills. New entrants to the profession simply must be up to date in this area – it is, after all, one of the few realms in which they may be able to compete successfully for a job against their more experienced colleagues. As a result, every library school now offers online and internet units which expose and train students in this area.

Several library educators have pointed out the problems involved when library school curricula are constantly added to, but nothing is taken away: over-teaching and over-assessment on the one hand, or superficiality on the other. Unfortunately, when looking for something to omit, many schools have chosen collection management. Isn't this, after all, now being superseded by the very electronic information sources being taught in its place? We beg to differ – and know that we have good company in doing so – but the fact is that many new graduates have had little or no exposure to this traditional component of information education, despite its ongoing, even growing importance. This book is for them.

It is also for two other categories of librarian: those who did indeed study collection management (or 'acquisitions' or 'collection development'), but so long ago that little of what might have been taught remains; and those who know that their own knowledge desperately needs to be updated to take account of the ubiquity of electronic information sources.

It follows that we, the authors, see you, our readers, as our professional colleagues, either now or in the immediate future. We believe that the management of information resources in libraries is of increasing, not decreasing, importance in an increasingly digital world; and that librarians are well placed to provide leadership in this new century. But to do so they must see how their traditional skills of analysis, evaluation, synthesis and communication are no less relevant than they ever were.

Definitions

At this point, we need to clarify some of the terms that we will use throughout this book. 'Selection' involves the identification of information resources appropriate to a particular field, and the choice of what to acquire or provide access to from within it. 'Acquisitions' staff then take these selections and employ a range of methods to provide access to this information for clients. Both selection and acquisitions, then, are processes, the former with a strong professional component, the latter usually needing only professional direction.

'Collection development' is a wider term. It involves the formulation of a systematic general plan for the creation of a library collection which will meet the needs of that library's clients. The American Library Association defines collection development as

> A term which encompasses a number of activities related to the development of the library's collection, including the determination and coordination of selection policy, assessment of needs of users and potential users, collection use studies, collection evaluation, identification of collection needs, selection of materials, planning of resource sharing, collection maintenance and weeding.[1]

By 'library collection' we mean an assemblage of physical information sources combined with virtual access to selected and organized information sources. A 'collection development policy' is thus a statement of general collection-building principles which delineates the purpose and content of a collection in terms relevant to both external audiences (such as readers and funders) and internal audiences (or staff).

Following normal usage, 'collection management' is the all-embracing term. It has been defined as 'the systematic management of the planning, composition, funding, evaluation and use of library collections over extended periods of time, in order to meet specific institutional objectives'.[2] As Prytherch emphasizes, collection management is concerned with 'keeping the needs of users a priority objective, and considering alternative means of document and information supply to supplement local holdings'.[3] It therefore includes:

- collection development
- selection
- acquisitions
- provision of access
- maintenance
- evaluation
- preservation
- weeding.

This book is about collection management in a digital century. Hence it touches on all these topics, although a particular focus is upon what is new or different from traditional approaches to collection management.

It should be seen as part of a suite of recent titles from Library Association Publishing about aspects of collection management. David Spiller has given us *Providing materials for library users* (2000), which covers much of the same ground as the present work but from a different perspective, and is especially useful on the selection components of collection management. Liz Chapman has provided us with *Managing acquisitions in library and information services* (2001). This clearly relates to acquisitions management, which we treat in just one chapter. Her book, then, is a logical extension of the present volume and should be used by those who are seeking the acquisitions perspective. Taken together, Spiller, Chapman and now Clayton and Gorman give Library Association Publishing the leading edge in works on collection management.

Arrangement of this volume

Chapter 1 sets the scene and the context for this volume. In it we consider the role of the library in dealing with digital data, and the balance that must be established with more traditional print sources. Collection management must be an integral part, not just of the library as a whole, but of the wider organization that a library serves. In Chapter 2 we turn to policies for collection management and collection development: why have them, since it is apparent that so many libraries do not? And if they are valuable, how can and should they be created?

In these and every chapter we have included 'focus questions' which both indicate the principal issues to be covered, and invite readers to think about the chapter's content. At the end of the chapter, following a review or summary of it, we suggest you return to these focus questions and see if you can now answer them. We then ask, Where to now?, and include some further questions designed to link the chapter's subject matter to your existing knowledge and work experience. While these questions are intended for individual reflection, if you are using this book as part of your professional development in a library you may have a 'mentor' with whom you could usefully discuss these points. Finally, each chapter concludes by suggesting further reading on the topics covered.

Conspectus has been widely proposed as the vehicle for relating a collection development policy to the collection that it both reflects and serves, yet again only a minority of libraries worldwide have adopted it. In Chapter 3 we consider what should be its role, and how it might be updated more adequately to reflect the digital age.

In Chapter 4 we consider the range of co-operative collection development and access ventures in which libraries are now engaged, asking not only why they do this but what factors contribute to (or may hinder) their success.

Chapters 5 and 6 address issues of selection. In the first of these we look at the balance that is needed between acquiring the material that clients say they want, and material that library staff believe their library should provide; at censorship and intellectual freedom; place selection in the context of the selection environment – whether libraries are public, school, academic or special; and consider a range of selection strategies and criteria. In Chapter 6 we look at the resources drawn upon for selection, including reviews and online sources.

Chapter 7, on acquisitions, asks why most libraries use vendors to obtain material. It then considers the issues involved in acquiring serials, electronic resources, gifts and out-of-print material. Chapter 8 focuses on budget management, including budget planning and control, the internal allocation of material funds, and audit and stocktake.

In Chapter 9 we cover collection evaluation, including the steps involved and types of evaluation – both user-centred and collection-centred. Chapter 10 focuses on the final components of effective collection management, preservation and weeding.

This volume concludes with a select and annotated bibliography of the literature of collection management. This both complements the suggestions for further reading that end each of the chapters and also notes some areas – such as the problems associated with theft – which space prevented us from covering in the text proper. Although any such listing will inevitably date, most of the resources included are likely to be of enduring value. By consulting the journals and websites listed, readers will be able to keep abreast of future contributions in this area.

Acknowledgements

A theme of this book is that electronic sources of information alone cannot substitute for all the wealth and richness of the conventional library. Both are needed, now and in the future. As authors we have discovered an intellectual corollary: while we could communicate via e-mail and send draft chapters to each other as electronic documents, we could not in the end complete a satisfactory book this way. We actually had to meet.

This book has had both a long gestation and a protracted delivery. In part, this reflects G. E. Gorman's move from Australia to New Zealand and the non-monetary costs associated with this. To a greater extent it also reflects the increasingly hectic academic lives we both lead – with promotion have come increased demands on our time that, ironically, make productivity in terms of research and scholarship more difficult to maintain.

At another level, the appearance of this book reflects the professionalism and commitment of Library Association Publishing, who stayed with us throughout, asking about progress but never badgering and never questioning the worth of the final product. In fact, because final publication was delayed until many trends were clearer and additional published resources were available it is, we believe, a stronger work, yet one just as relevant to the profession as when first conceived. As always, Helen Carley, Helen Vaux and Lin Franklin of LAP deserve our gratitude for making the publishing enterprise relatively painless and trouble-free. We also wish to thank our copy editor, Alison Worthington, and indexer, Garry Cousins, for their professionalism.

Peter Clayton wishes to thank his wife, Del, who has also provided the annotated bibliography for this volume. She has contributed in many ways to this book, not least as an ever-available sounding board. He also wishes to express his appreciation to many colleagues at the University of Canberra. In addition, the University contributed by allowing him study leave to commence this project. Lastly he would like to thank his friend Gary Gorman, who has finally managed to stay in one place and one country long enough to enable this work to be completed.

G. E. Gorman wishes especially to thank the several generations of students who have enrolled in his collection management course, and particularly those who have been stimulated to undertake their own research in this area or seek employment as collection managers. He also expresses his gratitude to colleagues at Victoria University for their insights at various stages in the writing of this book – one of the joys of academic life is the rewarding professional relationships that develop, and in Wellington these relationships are especially productive and amiable. He extends a warm 'thank you' to Liz Chapman for her long-distance insights and absolutely evil wit – 'I laughed until I cried'. But above all others he wishes to thank his good friend, reliable colleague and ever-patient co-author, Peter Clayton, for his friendship and scholarly co-operation over the years. Very often collaborations of this sort are relatively short-lived, but this is our second book together, with three more in the pipeline – concrete evidence that Peter's friendship and wine collection are standing the test of time.

Notes

1   American Library Association, *ALA glossary of library and information science*, American Library Association, 1983, 45.
2   J. A. Cogswell, 'The organization of collection management functions in academic research libraries', *Journal of Academic Librarianship*, **13** (5), 1987, 269.
3   R. Prytherch (comp.), *Harrod's librarians' glossary and reference book*, 9th edn, Gower Publishing, 2000, 163.

1

Managing information resources in context

Focus questions

- What is the role of the library in dealing with electronic information?
- What is the place of the library in the information transfer process?
- What links should a collection management area have with other areas of the library, and with the wider organization?
- What changes in the publishing industry are impacting on collections management?

Our world is being transformed by the increasing availability of electronic information. Whether one is seeking the complete works of William Shakespeare or the latest perinatal statistics, these are now available electronically – somewhere. As a result, libraries everywhere are shifting their focus from building up collections to providing access to information. Many colourful phrases have been devised to describe this shift: from the collection which includes a particular item 'just in case' it may be needed to the document delivery service which provides it 'just in time'; or from the 'warehouse' to the 'wherehouse' approach.

The popular perception is that this growing availability of electronic information both renders traditional, primarily paper-based resources – and the libraries that house them – increasingly irrelevant, and that the new electronic information resources themselves offer simplicity and transparency in access and use. Both perceptions are wrong. Throughout history, there have been many examples of new communication technologies complementing rather than supplanting their predecessors. The invention of the printing press did not lead to the demise of the handwritten letter. When radio was first introduced it was expected that it would lead to the demise of the telephone: why talk to simply one other person, when you could talk to many at the same time? Ludicrous as this suggestion now seems, the point is that both radio and telephony best serve differing purposes. The same applies to electronic and paper-based media.

We are now living through a period of change when questions of which communication media are best suited for what purposes are still being assessed through a process of global trial and error. What is certain is that both paper and electronic forms will survive. Among the leading advocates of this view are Crawford and Gorman, who in their *Future libraries: dreams, madness and reality* offer several reasons for the future co-existence of print and electronic media, among them the following:

> As long as people prefer to read from the printed page, electronic distribution with on-demand printing will be ecologically and economically disastrous as a replacement for circulating print collections and print publishing.

> Cost models for electronic distribution that do not include the cost of printing each long text that is to be read are defective and a cover for the shifting of costs from the institution to the user. For libraries, this abandons the tradition of freely available common goods.

> Without strong public libraries and continuing print collections, electronic distribution will cause further disadvantage to the already disadvantaged.[1]

No one who has attempted a simple search using a popular term on the world wide web needs to be persuaded that simplicity does not equate to effectiveness. We tried searching for items on 'health' using AltaVista, for example, and found 17,075,546 matches.[2] The search engine's 'Tip: Do not worry about a large number of results: the best ones come first!' is hardly reassuring. While more sophisticated search capabilities exist, few inexperienced searchers know of them. Apart from the overwhelming quantity, a principal argument of those opposed to the digital tide is that 'most of what is on the web is rubbish', an argument that could equally well be applied to much that is printed. What is needed is expert evaluation of these myriad sources and the development of guides to them. Yet although these are tasks for which information professionals have been trained, and which they are now starting to undertake for electronic information sources, many people assume that both informational professionals and libraries will in time be superseded by the web. If libraries are to retain their traditional roles as entry points and guides to resources that support society's need for information, education and recreation, they must do more – and be seen to be doing it.

Those who advocate such an all-online, electronic world, in which collection management principles and tasks are irrelevant, are in fact suggesting that everything can (and probably should) be on the internet, or some bigger, better and faster successor to it. In such a world all this information will, of course, be instantly and forever available so there will be no need to save anything: if some materials needed to be saved, then the selection of those items would require special skills. No one will need to look through all that is available, choosing useful and relevant material for particular groups, such as schoolchildren: this, too, would require special skills. Everything that is put into this global database will naturally be accurate and up to date, for evaluation also needs some skill. Finally, we presume that all of this material is either free of charge, or priced fairly, because negotiations about pricing for individuals and special groups again is far from straightforward. All of this is, of course, the stuff of science fiction. It is because we do see a present and continuing need for selection of materials, for their acquisition – or for adequate electronic access to them – along with their evaluation and possible eventual deselection, and for negotiation in the best interests of information users, that this book exists.

Over 20 years ago, libraries responded to the increasing availability and sophistication of audiovisual media – now called multimedia: film and sound recordings, especially in the educational area – by incorporating them into their collections. Libraries then and now provided information to their users, whatever the format in which it came – and in whatever format best suited their needs.[3] Electronic information is in essence no different to information in other forms: libraries need to provide organized access to worthwhile digital information alongside the organized access they provide to worthwhile paper-based information and to worthwhile multimedia information.

In fact, of course, this understates the problems in at least two areas. First, multimedia information, like paper-based information, comes in discrete 'packages' which may be purchased, processed and stored in a book-like way. Much electronic data is not 'purchased' but leased, and some is available free. Such data cannot be processed and accessed in a book-like way; and longer-term storage and preservation are still unanswered problem areas. Second, electronic data are not merely some of the objects a library must now provide access to, but also and increasingly the means of identifying, ordering and obtaining that access, as clumsy printed bibliographic listings are superseded, written orders give way to electronic communication, and physical packaging becomes virtual.

For all that, the principle remains: libraries now, as always, provide organized access to worthwhile information, and they do this in order to meet the needs of those they serve. With this new mixture of print and electronic resources in mind, they are now frequently referred to as 'hybrid' libraries.

Meeting user needs

Libraries exist to serve the needs of their users. This service philosophy has always been a basic tenet of our profession. In the management of information resources, too, librarians must seek to serve the needs of their users. The difficulty is that, while some needs of current users are explicit, those of would-be or of future users may not be – and even current users may not even know of the existence of all that they need to have, or have access to. Hence, serving the needs of users is not a passive but an active role.

One model widely recognized depicting the flow of information in society is of the information life cycle (see Figure 1.1). In this model, starting at the top, the author or researcher will usually communicate informally with his or her colleagues – the so-called 'invisible college'. Eventually, however, if the information is scientific or academic in nature it is likely to be published as a report or journal article, and copies will go to the library as well as direct to potential readers. This

Fig. 1.1 *The information life cycle*

cycle is repeated up to three times, with different publishers (and frequently different authors, as each draws upon earlier work), but with the library at the centre of the cycle. Eventually new authors draw upon known information as part of a new cycle. By 'information', in this context we mean a full range of library resources, including educational and recreational materials. Of course, if the publication is a novel, primary publication will be in novel form, not as an article – but it will still be listed in secondary publications (such as *Books in print*) and, if well regarded, will eventually be referred to in textbooks and literary encyclopedias.

Looking at Figure 1.1, it is apparent that at each stage of the cycle the readers will be different and have different needs. For their research needs, school pupils, for example, will mostly draw upon tertiary publications. Thus one cannot meet the needs of users without also asking the question, who are our users? Most libraries are part of a wider organization: a university or a school, a government department or a law firm, or perhaps a local authority. While a special library may think it is able to identify its primary users relatively easily (they are the staff of the organization that it serves), even here there may be ambiguities. Are consultants attached to the organization also potential users? What about the organization's customers? And of the staff of the organization, are non-users also library clients? Similar questions arise with a school library: as well as the teachers and pupils, what about the parents? What about the wider community, if this is the only library in a small and remote area? Many libraries, particularly public or national ones, have much greater difficulty in defining their user population – and also in gaining constructive feedback from them.

In fact almost all libraries, however tightly defined their primary clientele, inevitably have two other, hidden user groups:

- The families and friends of the primary clientele. Almost all special libraries, for example, at times receive requests for information to be passed to family members (such as for children's school projects). A library's reputation is likely to be nearly as much influenced by its success in meeting the needs of the second group as of the first; and there is little doubt that reputation is ultimately linked to funding.
- The clientele of other libraries. If libraries are serious about resource sharing – and the imperatives of the digital age demand this – then we need to lift our eyes from immediate local needs to the library's place among its network of co-operating institutions.

One of the reasons we advocate the formulation of collection management and development policies is that they encourage objective and factual consideration of just such issues as who these various user groups are (see Chapter 2).

Having established who one's users are, perhaps through formally profiling the user community, it is easy to underestimate the great variety in skills and knowledge they may possess, and variety of needs they may have. The varying impact of technology makes this task even more complex. Universities have been in the forefront in providing their staff with access to the internet, and to electronic information more generally. Academics have had earlier, sometimes better, often faster access to this technology than have other users, and they are, for the most part, intelligent, highly motivated information consumers. For example, a major survey of the teaching staff of every university in Australia found that over 95% had desktop access to the internet.[4] There is good reason to believe that we are now witnessing an explosion in general access to the internet. Yet only 28% of academics used the world wide web on a daily basis, and a further 39% at least weekly. Over 7% never used it. Why? Shortage of time and lack of training were the most frequently cited reasons.

The other side of the coin is that it is too easy to assume that, because users have access to the latest technology, they will use it. Some will, and a library needs to be able to support that use. Others will rely on traditional library materials, so these too will continue to be needed. Finally, many will require training – an issue perhaps outside the scope of this volume, but which will again impact on the type of collection and type of services users require.

Equally relevant, especially in developing countries, are problems of equipment availability and infrastructure. In a country like China or Vietnam, for example, the telecommunications infrastructure simply does not exist to permit electronic data transmission. Even basic telephone lines do not reach all rural areas (only about 60% of Vietnam's population has telephone access), and there is not always the will for this to change rapidly – for some governments telecommunications equates with uncontrolled access to information, which is not always in their interests. Traditional library resources have the great virtue of being technologically *in*dependent. Despite problems, however, the experience in many countries has been that internet technology, in particular, has been adopted more rapidly than was initially anticipated. There can be real advantages for a library in being seen to be in the forefront of worthwhile technological innovation. Many special libraries and many school libraries, in particular, have benefited from being seen as the organizational experts in this area.

Collection management as part of the larger organization

If Figure 1.1 illustrates some of the relationships between significant library functions and those undertaken by users, Figure 1.2 places these within an internal organizational context. Links between the acquisition of materials and its cataloguing, and the sections within libraries responsible for these functions, have always been seen as important. Hence, in larger libraries acquisitions functions (including for serial acquisitions) and cataloguing have traditionally been brought together into technical services divisions. However, more recently many larger libraries have chosen to develop closer, multifunctional teams in this area to further integrate these functions.

Links between the collection management function and other, internal, areas of a library are also important. These can be maintained and built upon without necessarily combining functions within a team, as did the library in Case Study 1.1 (p. 8). One of the most important of these internal areas in terms of potential links is the circulation or loans area, as:

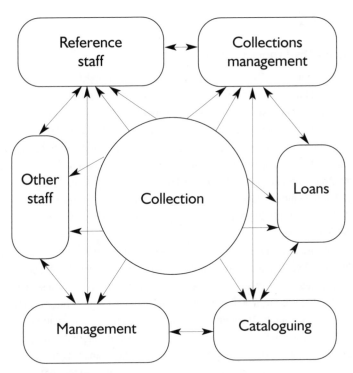

Fig. 1.2   *Links within the library*

- A user who has asked for an item to be acquired may well wish to use it on receipt.
- Circulation staff may well know which materials are in heavy demand.
- They will also handle material needing repair or rebinding (itself usually a function of a serials section).

Collections management staff will also need strong links to staff responsible for budgeting and accounts, not only within the library but also in the wider organization of which the library is part. This is dealt with in Chapter 8. Finally, as with other sections of any library, good working relationships need to be maintained with staff responsible for library-wide functions such as automation, and with organization-wide functions such as human resources.

Links between the library and the organization it serves are equally, if not more important. The institution's purposes, or mission, and the library's users must be kept as the principal focus of collection management. What are the basic institutional activities served by a collection? This is a key question.

Case study 1.1

The flow and ebb of subject teams

At one newer regional university, formerly a polytechnic, the incoming university librarian decided to restructure the library. The traditional readers services and technical services divisions were abandoned and almost all staff, professional and clerical, grouped into seven 'subject' teams which matched the seven faculties of the university. Each team had a middle-level professional librarian as leader, and was responsible for selection, acquisition, cataloguing and reader education for the faculty they served. The information desk was staffed on a roster basis by all seven teams. Apart from senior management, only loans, finance and human resources remained centralized. Team members were 'multiskilled': given training in any areas – such as cataloguing – about which they had no prior experience, and expected to be able to share in all the tasks appropriate to their level.

The results were a mixed success. The academic staff in the faculties greatly appreciated having a single point of contact for all their library queries, and regarded the subject teams as an outstanding success. Some of the teams were able to build up real levels of subject expertise. On the other hand, the library's book and serial suppliers were totally confused, now having not one but seven contact points. The library gradually reduced the number of its suppliers not for reasons of economy or service quality, but in order to simplify its internal and external communications. Cataloguing backlogs grew, until almost all cataloguing was outsourced: handed over to an outside commercial cataloguing operation. Staff complained that, far from feeling multiskilled, they were being deskilled – losing the special skills they once had – and many left. Team leaders and senior management seemed to spend all their time in internal library meetings. Eventually, academic staff who had welcomed the restructure began to query the library's internal budget allocations when comparisons with other institutions showed a much higher than usual proportion being spent on staffing rather than information resources.

In time, the university itself was restructured and the former faculties were amalgamated into three 'superfaculties'. The library promptly reduced its subject teams to three, whose members would hardly be able to claim much subject expertise over very large disciplinary groupings. However, some staff were released to recentralized functions, and others were able to begin to specialize in particular areas, such as selection, within the larger teams.

Links between a library and the particular users it serves are unquestionably important, and the university library described in Case Study 1.1 managed to establish close and strong links with its principal users, the teaching staff. Unfortunately, this was at the cost both of links with its suppliers and of its internal efficiency, and it is now seeking to alter the balance while maintaining its academic links.

Publishers and publishing

Libraries are also part of a wider information dissemination network or system – as suggested by Case Study 1.1 and shown graphically in Figure 1.3. Systems theory views an organization as a unified, purposeful interrelationship of component parts, which is in turn part of a larger system. Thus a public library is itself a small system, but also often part of a local authority, which is in turn a part of the system of government and ultimately the country. This approach emphasizes that organizations are not self-sufficient, living and working on their own, but instead belong in a bigger picture. A library exchanges resources with its outside environment: taking in money, information materials and educated staff, as well as electricity, water, telephone and postal services – the list is almost endless – and in return providing information, and usually training its users how to make better use of library services and of the information provided. Following general systems theory, then, changes in the wider system and in particular in networks of information provision will inevitably affect libraries.

In Figure 1.3, the library is shown as an important part of its parent organization. It has formal and informal links with other libraries, and with its publishers and suppliers. The parent organization also has links with other organizations, as do the other libraries, the publishers and suppliers. There is an integrated network of formal and informal linkages within the system as a whole.

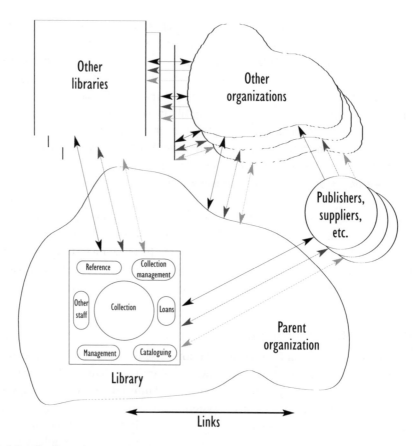

Fig. 1.3 *The library in a systems context*

It would be wrong to assume that the digital revolution is the only major change affecting library collection development. Equally important are changes in the worldwide publishing industry – itself also adapting to the increasing availability of electronic information. As far as libraries are concerned, publishing and publishers are involved with five elements of information: the *material*, which is expressed in a *mode* and packaged in a particular *medium* and then distributed by an appropriate *means* to a *market*. These are the value-added aspects of information which are the publisher's, and the consumer's or library's, particular concern. Some examples of this are given in Table 1.1.

Table 1.1 *Elements of information products*

Material	Mode	Medium	Means	Market	Example
Information	Text	Book	Retail	Professional	This book
Information	Text	Magazine	Electronic	Educational	*EdRev*
Information	Code, Visual	CD-ROM	Retail	Business	*Windows 2000*
Entertainment	Text	Book	Retail	Consumers	*Memoirs of a Geisha*
Entertainment	Visual	Videotape	Retail	Consumers	*Titanic*

Material is really at the core of these elements, which could also be visualized as a series of concentric circles with 'material' as the centrepiece, as shown in Figure 1.4. It is the choice of mode/medium/means/market that combine in various permutations with the material to create a product or service. In a sense the rings can revolve in an almost infinite series of combinations, and this is the opportunity given to publishers in the electronic age – an opportunity for them, a potential problem for libraries.

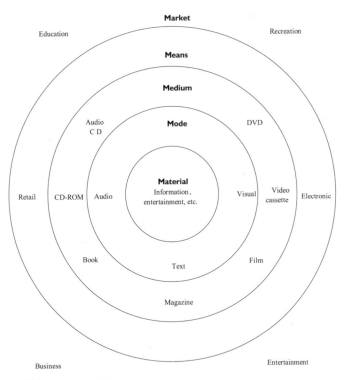

Fig. 1.4 *Publishing opportunities*

Universities have been particularly concerned about changes in the pattern of scholarly publishing, with organizations such as the Association of Research Libraries (ARL) and the Australian Academies sponsoring conferences which have examined the implications of these developments for scholars and the system as a whole, as well as on libraries.[5] Questions of public interest have been raised alongside concerns about the outcomes of university- and government-funded research being sold (or given) to commercial publishers, who then re-sell this back to universities at greatly increased prices.

Perhaps surprisingly, and despite increasing numbers of electronic publications of all kinds, the trend is not for a decrease in the number of printed books and journals being published: instead, the volume of traditional publishing output continues to rise. This has a triple impact on libraries:

- Library budgets are unable to keep pace with the increase in publishing output, and so libraries are collecting a diminishing proportion of the material that may be relevant to their users.
- As prices rise more swiftly than library budgets (in part because of ever shorter print runs), this trend to the acquisition of a smaller proportion of the whole is exacerbated.
- This is worsened again as libraries divert increasing proportions of their acquisitions budgets to electronic rather than traditional media.

ARL, for example, publishes annual figures showing 'Supply and demand in ARL libraries' which demonstrate the effects of these trends: usage continues to increase while the numbers of books and serials drops – and there is consequent dramatically increased interlibrary loan activity between libraries.[6]

The combined effect of these trends is not simply to increase pressure on library budgets: rather, what a library *does* choose to acquire needs to be demonstrably of continuing value to its users, and the balance between print, multimedia and digital resources needs to be the subject of conscious decision and continuing evaluation. Thus, a second-order effect of any decrease in library purchasing power is that more staff time and effort is devoted to selection, and the balance of expenditure between staff and materials moves towards staff unless other actions are taken.

Less dramatic changes in the wider environment will also have an impact. If authors increasingly cite electronic sources, then their readers will need access to these. If on the one hand, large publishers are increasingly the subject of amalgamations and takeovers, tending to reduce the number of players in the global marketplace, other new start-up publishers are filling the gap and providing a diversity of viewpoints. To keep track of where the publishing industry appears to be going, it makes sense to scan the industry newsletters: the *Bookseller* (UK: Whitaker), *Publishers weekly* (USA: Bowker), and similar national journals. Local factors are also likely to be of importance in particular countries – especially if the national language is not English, and most especially if, as for example with Thailand, yours is the only country using that language.

To be successful, the collections manager needs to take an active, outgoing role, keeping right up to date with the latest developments in technology, staying in constant touch with users, with publishers and the book trade, with colleagues in the library's own organization and with the wider professional community. Like so many other positions in today's libraries, this is not a job for the reclusive, bookish librarian of popular stereotype – and never was.

Review of Chapter 1

This opening chapter has sought to place the management of information resources in libraries in a broader context. It has argued that the traditional role of librarians in acting as entry points and guides to information resources has not changed with the advent of electronic information. Libraries exist to serve the needs of their users, and to support their information needs librarians must identify who these users are and appreciate the diversity of their needs.

The collections management area within a library needs to have strong links not only with cataloguing but also circulation, and with organization-wide functions such as budgeting and accounts. Externally, there needs to be an appreciation of changes taking place within the publishing industry and the impacts these are likely to have on libraries. The role of a collection manager is thus an active, not a passive one.

Where to now?

Before moving on to Chapter 2, you may wish to review the focus questions at the start of this chapter. Then see if you can answer the following questions:

- Can you think of any additional examples of communication technologies that have complemented rather than replaced earlier technologies? What impact have these technologies had on libraries?
- Other than the primary clientele of your own library, who else might its users be? Have their likely information needs been recognized?

- Again thinking of your own library, what links within the wider organization of which it is part may be of special importance?
- Can you think of any special factors that may influence the book industry in your country?

If you do not, at present, work in a library, then ask yourself these library-related questions of a library that you know well – perhaps one in which you have studied, or one you visit regularly as a user.

If libraries are to address their information management responsibilities seriously, and in a way that is fully and properly accountable, then this must be on the basis of written policies and procedures that have been agreed to by all the relevant stakeholders. Accordingly, in the next chapter we consider the value of collection management and development policies.

Further reading

There has been an avalanche of material on the impact of electronic information sources on libraries generally. One possible starting point would be W. Crawford and M. Gorman, *Future libraries: dreams, madness and reality*, American Library Association, 1995. Alternatively, almost any recent issue of most general professional journals will have some observations on the topic.

Rather fewer people have considered the impact of electronic information on collections management; indeed, this is a principal reason for the appearance of this volume. A complementary viewpoint to our own is provided by Samuel Demas, 'What will collection development do?', *Collection Management* **22** (3/4), 1998, 151–9. Another writing in this area is O. G. Norman, 'The impact of electronic information services on collection development: a survey of current practice', *Library Hi Tech*, **15** (1–2), 1997, 123–31. A more popular overview is provided by G. Nunberg, 'Will libraries survive?', *American Prospect*, **41**, 1998, 16–23.[7]

Meeting user needs in a comprehensive way may well involve surveying them in some way. Again, there is a substantial literature on undertaking user surveys; one straightforward starting point is provided by Maurice Line, *Library surveys*, 2nd edn, Bingley, 1982. However, unless very carefully designed, simple questionnaires may yield rather less information than is hoped. An alternative to quantitative research methods is presented in our own *Qualitative research for the information professional: a practical handbook*, Library Association Publishing, 1997.

Many who work in the collection management area develop a genuine interest in publishing. While one recent view is provided by Gordon Graham, *As I was say-*

ing: essays on the international book business, Hans Zell, 1994, we would also recommend such classics as Sir Stanley Unwin, *The truth about publishing*, Allen & Unwin, any edition – a title known to all who are interested in publishing, and surely part of the education of any new entrant to this arm of the profession. Perhaps a biography of Sir Allen Lane, such as J. E. Morpurgo, *Allen Lane, King Penguin*, Hutchinson, 1979 could complement this. Another worthwhile reference, more from a practitioner's perspective, is D. K. Kovacs (ed.), *Library Hi Tech*, **17** (1), 1999 – a theme issue on electronic publishing available on the internet at **http://epn.org/prospect/41/nunb.html**. Of particular value here are the papers on electronic journals, on virtual universities and publishing, and on publishing and technology.

Notes

1 W. Crawford and M. Gorman, *Future libraries: dreams, madness and reality*, American Library Association, 1995, 103.

2 **lowpages.com.au/** [31 December 2000].
    AltaVista simple search of 'the world, any language', **www.altavista.yellowpages.com.au/**

3 P. McNally, *Multimedia information resources*, Macmillan, 1997.

4 A. Applebee et al., *Academics online: a nation-wide quantitative study of Australian academic use of the internet*, Auslib Press, 1998.

5 M. A. Butler and B. R. Kingma (eds), *The economics of information in the networked environment*, Association of Research Libraries, 1996; J. Mulvaney and C. Steele (eds), *Changes in scholarly communication patterns: Australia and the electronic library*, Australian Academy of the Humanities, 1996.

6 For a summary of the 1996/7 ARL statistics see J. Blixrud, 'Still paying more, still getting less', *ARL* (bimonthly newsletter) **199**, 1998, 5. Data files are also available at **www.arl.org/stats/arlstat/mrstat.htm** [10 April 2001].

7 Other contributions noted include P. Bluh, who writes for law librarians (and others) in 'The winds of change: acquisitions for a new century', *Law Library Journal*, **88** (1), 1996, 90–5. Another, unfortunately too brief to be of more than limited value, is I. K. Ravichandra Rao, 'Impact of recent advances in information technology on collection development', *DESIDOC Bulletin of Information Technology*, **17** (1), 1997, 3–6.

2
Collection management and collection development policies

Focus questions

- What is the distinction between collection management and collection development?
- What are the advantages and disadvantages of having written collection management and collection development policies?
- How should such policies be affected by the increasing availability of electronic information?
- What sections might be included in collection management and collection development policies?
- How should a library go about formulating such policies?

Collection management, collection development or both?

In the 1960s and 1970s, in many countries libraries and library collections experienced unprecedented growth. This was a time of staff expansion to cope with the growing challenge of creating larger collections. It was also the era of subject and area studies specialists: professionals appointed specifically to develop collections in their own areas. The growth of physical collections necessitated the appointment of staff with particular commitments and expertise to build and develop well-tuned collections. Today the overall level of resources going to libraries is in decline, and certainly shrinking in comparison with the overall availability of information, and one wonders whether staff expertise and skills are keeping pace with this change. As noted in the previous chapter, technology that gives readers access to information without relying on a specific collection is also changing the shape of what we do. 'Collection development' has been replaced by 'collection management' as the approved professional term, but in fact the two components continue to exist.

In some of the most widely used literature in this field there seems to be considerable confusion about the distinction between the two concepts. Thus Edward Evans, whose views are generally to be respected, has inadequately defined collection management as the activity that 'relates to a library environment (in the traditional sense) where the emphasis is on collecting materials produced by other organizations', as distinct from 'information resources management', which deals with both internally and externally produced resources.[1] While in our view this is an incorrect definition, Evans' gloss helps to recover some ground: 'both terms incorporate all aspects of collection development . . . plus such managerial aspects as budget planning and control, staffing and physical facilities'.[2]

Less complex, and therefore more adequate in our opinion, is the definition suggested by Jenkins and Morley:

> Collection management is a more demanding concept, which goes beyond a policy of acquiring materials, to policies on the housing, preservation, and storage, weeding and discard of stock. Rather than selection and acquisition, collection management emphasizes the systematic management of a library's existing collection: 'the systematic management of the planning, composition, funding, evaluation and use of library collections over extended periods of time, in order to meet specific institutional objectives'.[3]

Morley and Jenkins go on to state that effective collection management should be based on an agreed collection development policy – perhaps this is a chicken and egg situation. In our view collection management may be driven in part by collection development needs, but at the policy level a collection development policy clearly resides within the broader objectives of a collection management policy. Collection development, in other words, is a subset of collection management, and both have a clearly defined policy role.

This distinction is reflected in how the two types of policies, collection management and collection development, are defined. A *collection management policy* has been defined as 'the systematic management of the planning, composition, funding, evaluation and use of library collections over extended periods of time, in order to meet specific institutional objectives'.[4] It is thus a global statement about a library's collections, of which the collection development aspect is but a single component. A *collection development policy*, on the other hand, is a statement of general collection-building principles which delineates the purpose and content of a collection in terms relevant to both external and internal audiences. It would not normally include the procedures necessary for the implementation of these policies – which should, of course, be detailed in a separate, internal procedure manual. This is where the wider collection management policy fits in.

It is fair to say that this whole area is one where there is not only considerable confusion about the terminology, but also considerable confusion and overlap in practice between what we have just described as two distinct types of policy. We may illustrate this with a figure, based on a Venn diagram (see Figure 2.1). Some libraries have a collection management policy (at various levels of comprehensiveness), others collection development policies, still others combine some of the features of both. Many, of course, have none. We know of no library that has integrated a fully developed collection management policy with a fully detailed collection development policy, but no doubt during the life of this volume some such policies will appear.

Why have these policies?

Today all institutions are involved in formal planning to cover most aspects of their activities and libraries are no exception, whether they are standalone entities such as public libraries or institutionally linked entities such as university and government department libraries. Contemporary requirements for accountability oblige institutions such as libraries to be able to justify decisions, especially concerning

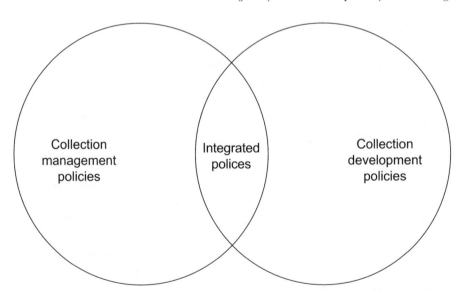

Fig. 2.1 *Types of policies*

monetary expenditure. In the discussion that follows, we concentrate first on collection development policies, because these have been in existence over a longer period of time and there has developed an extensive literature about them. With this as background, we then go on to consider collection management policies.

Any institution would be justified in expecting its library to be able to state broadly (1) how selection decisions are made, (2) what is to be acquired, (3) what is to be preserved, and (4) what is to be relegated or withdrawn. This is the essence of a collection development policy.

Cassell and Futas have suggested that collection development itself consists of a number of distinct, interrelated processes:

- Learning about institutional goals, objectives and priorities.
- Learning about the existing collection and how it relates to the community of users.
- Developing policies for selecting, acquiring, discarding, maintaining and evaluating collections.
- Learning how and what to select for an existing client base.
- Learning to recognize what needs to be looked at, to ensure that the client base has not changed.
- Developing procedures for handling the policies.
- Developing procedures for evaluating and revising the policies.[5]

It is apparent that all of these imply some kind of written document – and that document has conventionally been the collection development policy. A written policy is a contract between a library and its users; in our view this is a useful way to summarize the whole exercise, as it demonstrates to users what they can expect of the library. It should be noted, however, that such a contract is not immutable, but rather a 'notional' document that constantly evolves, setting parameters rather than once-for-all benchmarks. If a policy falls within the institutional planning cycle, then it will naturally be revised and updated in the normal course of events in response to changing institutional requirements and needs. Such a policy must not be conceived in static terms, but rather as a flexible document, constantly under revision and giving the institution room to manoeuvre. A collection development policy provides a framework, a set of parameters, within which an institution, library staff and readers can operate.

Two decades ago, Richard Gardner suggested that developing a written collection development policy had several advantages. For the most part these suggestions remain valid today. In his view a written policy:

- forces staff to think through library goals and commit themselves to these, helps them to identify the long- and short-range needs of users, and to establish priorities for allocating funds
- helps assure that the library will commit itself to serving all parts of the community, both present and future
- helps set standards for the selection and weeding of materials
- informs users, administrators and other libraries of collection scope, and facilitates co-ordination of collection development among institutions
- helps minimize personal bias by selectors, and to highlight imbalances in selection criteria
- serves as an in-service training tool for new staff
- helps assure continuity, especially in collections of any size, providing a pattern and framework to ease transition from one librarian to the next
- provides a means of staff self-evaluation, or for evaluation by outsiders
- helps demonstrate that the library is running a business-like operation
- provides information to assist in budget allocations
- contributes to operational efficiency in terms of routine decisions, which helps junior staff, and finally
- serves as a tool of complaint-handling with regard to inclusions or exclusions.[6]

All of these claims have been disputed. Perhaps the most telling argument against having a written collection development policy is that so many libraries do *not* have one – indeed, most of the great library collections in the world were originally created without such policies. However, there is no doubt that they (and the collections of any major library without a written collection development policy) have been guided by a well-understood, unwritten policy that is part of the institution's 'oral tradition'. Today, fewer major libraries choose to leave such an important aspect of their operation undocumented and therefore subject to collective amnesia, intentional or otherwise.

There are, of course, other reasons for deciding against (or putting off) such a task. It is unquestionably time consuming, taking both a great deal of senior staff time and, if adopted as the result of a genuinely consultative process involving library stakeholders, taking a considerable amount of elapsed time. There is also a perception that the world of information is changing so rapidly that long-term planning of this kind is less appropriate than it once was – a perception that is totally at odds with the even longer-term planning that is implicit in deciding to purchase information resources for use over an indefinite future.

Whatever the arguments in favour of having such a policy, its creation still involves diversion of attention from actually doing the job to thinking about the task that is to be done. By now, our own prejudices should be apparent: we believe that a major task like this is going to be done better and attract stronger support from outside a library if all involved in it know both what is to be done, and why. In summary, we see the advantages of having a collection development policy as:

- to enable a planned response to upward and downward changes in funding
- to enable a planned response to technological change
- to facilitate rationalization of resources between libraries
- to communicate with clients, colleagues and staff.

Essentially similar arguments apply to collection management policies.

Collection development policies or collection management policies?

Differences between collection development policies and collection management policies are best illustrated by discussing what may appropriately be included in each. There are emerging two distinct approaches to the documentary relationship between collection management and collection development policies, and to the content of the former. There is a trend for the collection management policy to subsume a somewhat truncated collection development policy as part of its content. This is increasingly apparent in Britain, where detailed collection development policies have never taken hold to the extent that they have in North America. Thus the division of a collection management policy into two major components is common, as seen for example in the *Collection management policy* of the University of Central Lancashire Library and Learning Resource Service at **www.uclan. ac.uk/library/libdoc1.htm#Coll_Man**, where the two parts are:

- a series of general policy statements, providing an introduction to the library and its information resources – the collection management policy
- statements of specific collecting and access intentions in various subject areas – the collection development policy.

Such a division is sensible, as the first group of statements is likely to be of interest to a wide audience, while the second will function more like a dictionary or encyclopedia, with only particular, relevant sections being consulted by those with a specific interest. The following discussion assumes this approach has been adopted.

Policy content

Content of a typical collection management policy

Our analysis of a number of evolving collection management policies suggests that typically they cover 12 to 14 main concerns. These are reflected in the template offered below.

1 Relationship to mission

A library's collection and access policies must be seen to reflect the needs and objectives of its parent body. The collection development (or information or resource development) policy should be placed in the context of the library's mission and that of the wider organization. If mission statements are available, it is appropriate to reproduce them in the policy, together with goals and objectives relevant to the collection.

2 The purpose of the collection management policy

Why has the policy been created? Remember that every policy should be prepared for a specific purpose, and this purpose should determine all that follows. Farrell has given the most comprehensive statement of possible policy functions, and any library's policy will fall into one or more of these:

- To establish priorities for collection development.
- To describe collection strengths and weaknesses for the library's staff, administration and constituencies, and support funding proposals and requests, as well as accreditation or performance evaluations.
- To provide information for establishing library-wide collection management policies.
- To educate librarians responsible for collections and assist in establishing staffing needs and priorities.
- To communicate between libraries for purposes of developing and maintaining co-operative collection development and resource-sharing programmes.[7]

To whom is it addressed? Many libraries see their information development policy as an expression of their accountability as well as an indication of their planning intentions. How is it to be used? Possible uses may include in discussions with funding bodies, to enlist support of stakeholders, to explain and justify to special interest groups the inclusion or exclusion of particular items, to provide information to network partners, and as a training tool for staff. What authority has it – has it been approved by the librarian, the library committee or chief executive, the council or the governing body?

3   Clientele served

It may be useful to refer to any unusual, distinctive or unexpected features of the clientele served. What are their needs? (See 'Meeting user needs' in Chapter 1.) Prison libraries, for example, serve two very different groups – inmates and staff – with very different needs. Some prisoners undertake distance education courses and make very substantial demands on all the libraries to which they have access. Is there differential treatment of those served? In an educational institution, for instance, pupils and teachers are rarely treated alike. Who is not served? Staff undertaking study that is not directly work related? Family members of the primary clientele?

4   Access

What access to the collection is available? This section should include the electronic access that clients and potential clients have now and should have to the library's own and to networked resources. This includes access to bibliographic records: is this via a network or local-area network, via a web-based OPAC? What are the provisions for personal access? Are all parts of the collection accessible throughout the opening hours? Some closed-stack libraries restrict retrieval at evenings and weekends. Are there any non-standard restrictions on interlibrary loan access? Are some client groups required to pay and others not? Is there provision for remote access to electronic media? Licensing agreements sometimes restrict off-site access.

5   Background to the collection

What broad categories of material are included in the collection – monographs, serials, audiovisual/multimedia materials, electronic media, archival materials? What is the history of the collection? How has this affected what is and is not included within it? For example, a collection based on a major donation may reflect the interests or background of the donor. Are there any unusual features that will affect the collection or its usage?

6   Budget

How is the acquisitions budget allocated? Specifically, is the budget divided by sub-ject or department or group? If it is divided using a formula, this should be quoted or referred to. Is there an expected ratio between expenditure on monographs and that on serials, between print and electronic media, between other categories of information resources purchased? This ratio should be specified, and a rationale provided for it. These considerations are dealt with in Chapter 8 of this book.

7   Selection principles and practices

Who is to undertake the selection? If users undertake selection, under what constraints do they operate, or do they merely order until all their allocation is committed? What control does the library exercise over their selection? Is one person permitted to com-mit the whole amount? Are unlikely-sounding titles queried? What principles are expected to guide those involved in selection? These should include:

- Selection criteria for purchased materials of all kinds. These will presumably include the traditional ones of currency, price, level, authority and accuracy, uniqueness, relevance, etc.
- Criteria for different types of media. What formats are collected? If items are available in multiple formats, which one or ones are collected, and what prin-ciples guide choice of format?
- As suggested by Norman, 'emerging criteria' for electronic resources including network capability, ease of use, strength of retrieval engine, hardware com-patibility, software compatibility, service implications, potential/actual use, remote accessibility, faithfulness in reproduction of print original and licence restrictions, among others.[8]
- Library policy on language. Libraries in anglophone countries may need to com-ment only if material other than in English is held or to be acquired; libraries in other countries will need to develop a policy on which languages are appro-priate to meet their needs. Variations in language policy by subject area will then be documented in the second half of the policy.
- Selection criteria for gift material. Are these the same as for purchased mate-rials? If not, why not? What happens to material that is rejected? Gift procedures are discussed in Chapter 7 of this book.
- Library policy on questions of intellectual freedom where appropriate. This may not necessarily be a matter of course, for in some situations it may be politi-cally unacceptable.

Many public and school libraries have found it helpful to quote professional association statements on censorship and have a formal procedure for handling complaints.[9] These could appropriately appear in the information development policy. However, note that many statements about censorship now need urgent revision to reflect the availability of public use internet facilities. Many of these considerations are dealt with in Chapter 5 of this book.

8 Special collections

History and background, special selection criteria, and possibly cataloguing, storage and access arrangements, may be relevant here. For example, a donated special collection may have a provenance worth noting, a printed catalogue and, if rare or confidential material is included, some limitations on access.

9 Limitations

What categories of material are *not* acquired? Exclusions are commonly decided upon taking into account such factors as physical or electronic format, price, age and language, among others.

10 Co-operative relationships with other libraries and information resources

External library collections and information resources may impact on collection-building decisions, especially where materials are located in close geographical proximity or are accessible through networking or formal co-operative arrangements. What is the impact of the availability of internet resources on local resources? These considerations are dealt with in Chapter 4 of this book.

11 Collection evaluation

Is the collection evaluated? How, and how often? Evaluation is covered in Chapter 9 of this book.

12 Preservation activity

What is the physical condition of the collection? If some material is at risk, what is being done about it? In particular, what measures are being taken to preserve electronic data? Preservation is discussed in Chapter 10 of this book.

13 Weeding

Is there a weeding policy? If there is it should address the following questions:

- Who weeds the collection?
- What criteria are applied?
- How regularly is weeding to take place?
- What is done with material removed from the collection?

Weeding is also dealt with in Chapter 10.

14 Review of the policy

If the collection management policy is to remain relevant, it will need constant revision so that it continues to reflect accurately the changing needs of the library and its clientele. Who is to review the policy? Unless unduly delayed, review should not involve the major effort of initial creation and so may not need the same type of committee or task force – but the revised document should receive the same level of endorsement. How often is this to be undertaken? Annual reviews are probably too frequent, but so much is changing, so rapidly, that a policy not re-examined for several years can easily become so out of date that it is no longer of real value.

The collection development policy: basic or detailed?

Discussion of the content of a collection management policy, and whether this incorporates the collection development policy component, suggests that the latter may range from a very basic statement to a rather more complex, usually standalone, document. Indeed, there seem to have emerged two distinct schools of thought about the extent of collection development policies. One, perhaps the more popular at the time of writing, advocates a brief document concentrating on a basic outline of the subject areas covered by a collection, approaches to collecting, etc. The major argument for this is that the more basic a document, the greater the flexibility for selectors who work within an ever-changing environment. With a less comprehensive document, it becomes unnecessary for it to undergo revision every time a new collecting direction is deemed necessary in response to evolving community needs.

The earlier approach, and one certainly the norm in North American libraries and in principal libraries in many other countries, prefers a much fuller, blow-by-blow recording of who was responsible for what, and why. Usually such a policy will also include subject-by-subject details of the strength of the present collection, the current amount of collection building being undertaken, and future collection intentions – all aspects often covered by a Conspectus description of a collection, discussed in Chapter 3.

The newer, leaner approach does have the advantage of flexibility and cost-effectiveness in terms of staff time and documentation, but it suffers from not requiring – or even encouraging – any real in-depth understanding of a collection and the institution or community it serves. The earlier approach, while extremely costly in most respects, certainly did require this depth of understanding, and was often preceded by a detailed collection assessment exercise for this very reason. The assessment was necessary so that staff could comment accurately on the strength of the present collection and current amount of collection building being undertaken in each subject area. Similarly, there might also have been a user evaluation exercise as a means of predicting more accurately future collection needs and emerging trends among key user groups.

Whatever the form, such a policy begins with an introduction to the library's collections, and details of the subject areas collected or to which electronic or other access is available. A fuller version of such a policy will cover past, present and proposed future resources, while even the briefest should give an indication in more general terms of collecting activity. Whatever kind is adopted, the creation of a collection development policy by a library should represent a serious, considered attempt to gain some consensus among its principal stakeholders – its clients, its funders and its staff – on what the library should be making available, and why.

In the recent past, collection development policies were in many ways a natural extension of the work of collection development librarians, whose task was to expand collections in areas relevant to their institutional requirements. As such, these policies were usually devised and monitored by collection development staff, with the intention of using them to guide further collection development. Today, however, both collection development and collection management policies are documents with strong political significance and therefore usually under the direct control of senior management (and in any case the 'collection development librarian' is often a creature of the past). In British universities, for instance, the Research Assessment Exercise often leads to new directions, or at least awareness of unexpected weaknesses in the institution. This impinges directly on the library, which may be expected to help overcome a weakness by building collections in areas previously not regarded as crucial. The question then becomes whether the library diverts funds from collection development in an area of acknowledged strength to an undeveloped area, thereby weakening a strength in order to overcome a shortcoming.

The collection development component of a collection management policy

As indicated, the second principal component of any collection management policy is typically a more detailed description of the subject areas in which the library collects. This, too, has to be reconsidered in the light of such factors as the varying availability of relevant electronic information in different subject areas, and the varying levels of competence, convenience and comfort of library clients who work in different subject areas.

A consistent theme of this book is that widespread access to electronic information does not reduce the need for a collection development policy. Instead, if a library is to consider and support the full range of its clients' information needs, and justify its allocation of limited resources, such policies are more necessary than ever.

As noted in the next chapter, we suggest that an appropriately modified form of Conspectus be used to describe a library's collections in each relevant subject category, as follows:

1   Subjects covered

It is usual to base these upon the classification scheme adopted. Special libraries may, however, prefer to describe their collections in terms of broad subject categories.

2   Present collection strengths

Use Conspectus Levels 0-5. For a library not wanting to undertake a full collection evaluation as part of the policy development process, at least initially, an alternative is to rely on intuitive assessment by staff with considerable experience of the collection. As already noted, collection evaluation is covered in more detail in Chapter 9 of this book.

3   Future acquisition intentions

Again, use Conspectus Levels 0–5. Be realistic – a 'wish list' is of little value inside or outside your institution. Note that in deciding to provide 'comprehensive' coverage of a topic, a library is also deciding that it will deliberately seek out items known to be of poor quality, incorrect or misleading as well as the useful information every library seeks. (Of course, all of this is of some value to the historian or PhD student.) Very few collections need to be comprehensive.

4 Languages

Libraries in anglophone countries should note only if material other than in English is held or to be acquired in each subject area; libraries in other countries may need to provide more comprehensive details of current and proposed language coverage.

5 Geographic areas

Use this where appropriate, noting, for example, if the library has unexpected strengths in non-national subject coverage. Regional or local studies strengths should also be noted.

Case Study 2.1

Changing collection emphases

The University of Wessex undertook the Research Assessment Exercise last year, and one outcome was that it was assessed as weak in the teaching of information technology (IT). The University had never felt it necessary to excel in this field and offers only a basic degree in IT, since most other universities have invested heavily in this emerging discipline. At the same time, however, the University was praised for its high standard of teaching and research in the fields of economic history and African economic development. These two disciplines were particular strengths in the library collection as well, with the collection long regarded as Britain's best in these areas. However, neither economic history nor African economic development attracted significant numbers of students, and the international market for African studies, which once had brought many fee-paying research students from North America, seems to have dried up.

Should the library stop investing money and talent in building collections in economic history and African economic development – areas of historic strength – and instead divert funds to IT, and any other areas of current academic weakness? Should the staff take resources from collections of historic strength in order to invest in creating collections for current academic weakness, but of significance, in an attempt to boost overall institutional ratings?

Take a few minutes to analyse each of the following questions:

- Would a collection development policy help in making or in justifying such decisions?
- Are such collection development issues internal library ones, or institutional decisions?
- What status and components would a collection development policy need in order to support such decision making?

- Would a collection development policy or a collection management policy be more effective in such a context?

Policy formulation

Formulating a collection management and collection development policy

Clearly, drafting such a policy from scratch will be no small undertaking. The conventional advice on this is that it is better to assemble as many existing policies as you can from other, comparable libraries: this preparation is a major part of the task. Critically assess these; at the very least, they should provide a checklist of issues to consider, and a range of possible approaches to these. Frequently recommended is some 'creative plagiarism'. Of course, if you want to make use of substantial components of another library's policy you will need to seek their permission; most will give this readily. One problem with creative plagiarism, however, which is becoming clear in the work of many who use the internet as their primary resource, is that the examples and ethos of existing policies is principally American (as is so much else on the internet). For many libraries elsewhere – and certainly in Britain – US policies tend to err significantly on the side of detail.

It is important to recognize that policies can and should vary significantly by type of library, and that there is no standard template that can apply to all. Thus the mission, the collecting objectives, selection criteria, community analysis and issues of intellectual freedom and censorship will all differ depending on the type of library community. Equally, these may also differ significantly from country to country, and libraries around the world need to recognize that what is appropriate in North America is probably not appropriate elsewhere – no library should slavishly follow what other libraries, either in the same country or elsewhere, regard as normative in terms of policy.

The literature on collection management policies per se is at present extremely limited in terms of volume and quality, and this is a serious limitation to anyone who wants to have a sound understanding of this type of policy. For collection development policies, on the other hand, the literature is extensive, but most of it predates the widespread availability of electronic information. To be of value in the electronic age a collection development policy should now in our view be more rather than less comprehensive. Note that 'comprehensive' is not the same as 'detailed', and in fact a more comprehensive policy may well be less detailed, as seems to be the emerging trend.

At the very least, to avoid the appearance that the library is still only a physical collection, a collection development policy should clearly acknowledge the importance of access to electronic resources – possibly even in its title. An 'Information Development Policy', 'Resource Development Policy', 'Information Resources Development Policy' or some variant along these lines might well be appropriate.

There are many collection management and collection development policies now available on the internet.[10] These have the advantage of already being in machine-readable form, thus simplifying our recommended approach, that of thoughtful electronic cut and paste. The problems will be:

- You will need to create genuinely new text for any unique features of your library.
- Most existing collection development policies are strong on their approach to traditional print materials but weak on electronic media – if, indeed, they are covered at all.

The first of these should not be a great problem, if these unique features are well understood and adequately documented. The second raises an important question of principle: should a library have one collection development policy for its traditional media, and a separate electronic information development policy? Guidance in drafting electronic information policies is in fact already available – on the internet, of course.[11] There are also some useful writings by Peggy Johnson on this topic.[12]

The whole thrust of our argument is that a library should take an integrated approach to the management of its information resources. Accordingly, we regard the development of separate policies to cover its traditional and its electronic resources as a quick and dirty stop-gap, one that is bound to cause a series of problems in co-ordination and execution. Many practitioners agree with us. Norman has found that 'many libraries currently are in the process of integrating internet resources into their ongoing collection development programs . . .' and notes that several libraries that had not begun this planned to do so in future.[13] We strongly advise libraries to follow these examples and adopt a single, integrated policy.

Earlier, we noted the importance of involving all a library's stakeholders in the formulation of an information development policy: how can this be consistent with the adaptation of large components from other, existing policies? And who should be consulted? The conflict between inviting input from a wide group and utilizing as much pre-existing text as possible is more apparent than real. Anyone who has attempted to have a document written by a committee knows this: the committee may set the parameters, and will certainly revise the final wording, but the real work of writing a draft document falls to an individual (or is divided between a small number of individuals). Formulating an information development policy is no different.

We recommend that a library establish a committee or task force to create or revise an information development policy. Larger libraries should probably establish at least two: an internal committee and an external, advisory committee. Membership should include representatives of the major stakeholders, internal and external. Internal stakeholders will include representatives of senior management, of the principal areas of the library directly involved in collection management, and also any individuals with special expertise in the area. External stakeholders should include users if appropriate, and representatives of a library's funders, of major donors, and of any areas with significant political influence on its development.

The steps through which the policy planning process should then go will be:

1 *Set the guidelines.* What is to be included in the policy? Who is to be consulted? Who is to do the drafting? How are the decisions to be made?
2 *Analyse community needs.* Consult the client community served by the library, possibly by undertaking surveys or interviews and certainly by inviting external and internal library input to the policy development process.
3 *Prepare the draft document.* Utilize as much pre-existing material as possible as well as any input received, and flag difficult or potentially controversial areas.
4 *Circulate the draft document.* Engage in discussion of the draft with knowledgeable stakeholders and others, and make revisions as necessary.
5 *Adopt the revised document.* Formally adopt and publish the document and engage in some positive publicity, possibly involving an official 'launch'.
6 *Provide for ongoing review.* Ensure that a major reassessment and review process and date are noted in the policy itself.

From this list, it will be apparent that who is to be consulted will depend very much on the library, and on the purposes behind the development of the policy. Our preference would be for consultation to be wider rather than narrower, including representatives of various stakeholder groups as noted above, as well as library staff. A policy produced and supported by such a group will be more useful to the library in a wider variety of contexts.

Into the future

Of course, the most significant recent change for policy formulation must be the advent of electronic media and their blending into traditional collections to form the hybrid library. The new mix of paper and electronic formats has left us with unresolved questions and hard choices in terms not only of collection building, but also of access and policy issues. As Strong notes, 'we no longer enjoy a single copy physical format environment. Many titles are now accessible several ways, better suiting the access needs of the user. Libraries must develop policies to incorporate these new access demands into their structures.'[14]

In 1996 Billings had already anticipated this need and highlighted resource sharing (or access) as the key ingredient in evolving policies.

> Libraries must modify and update collection development policies and procedures to recognize that the local collection will evolve into one enhanced and extended by digital technologies and electronic information sources. Policies for managing and sharing national and global mega-collections will emerge from the construction of co-operative programs on a stage that far transcends concerns for building the local collection.[15]

But how this replaces traditional collection-building emphases when policies are created has not yet been addressed satisfactorily.

Thus the truly integrated policy that caters for the hybrid library, combining ownership and access, must be the next priority for collection managers involved in policy formulation.

Review of Chapter 2

This chapter has covered a critically important topic: the content and formulation of collection management and collection development policies. Following an initial definition, the advantages and possible disadvantages of having written policies were considered, as was the content of each type of policy. We then outlined the process for developing a library's own collection management and collection development policies. This should involve wide consultation both within and outside the library, and where possible build upon the many policies already published (including on the internet). This chapter has not discussed the RLG Conspectus, a method of describing collection strengths in a standardized manner, as this is complex enough to warrant separate treatment in the next chapter.

Where to now?

Once again, we suggest you first review the focus questions at the head of this chapter. You might then think about some of the following questions:

- Do you know of a major library in your own country or region, well known for its strong collections, but which does not have a written collection management or collection development policy? What might be some of the reasons it has been successful despite this lack? Can you think of any ways in which the adoption of a written policy might assist it further?
- Again looking at the libraries in your own region, is there one that has separate collection development and electronic information policies? How successful is this arrangement, and have any problems been reported? If no library in your area has a pair of policies of this kind, search the internet to find some. Are any potential problems apparent?
- Looking at libraries comparable to your own, find some that have written collection development policies, either published or available on the internet. What features do these libraries and those policies have that might usefully be adapted to your own situation – regardless of whether you already have a collection development policy?

Further reading

As already noted, there is a relative paucity of integrated literature on collection management, and a rather significant corpus of documentation on all aspects of collection development and collection development policies. With regard to the last topic, however, much of this predates the widespread availability of electronic data and access to the internet. Most of the exceptions to this are themselves on the web, where one can find policies that take account of access to electronic resources. One example of this is the very thorough web-based collection development policy of the London School of Economics at **www.blpes.lse.ac.uk/ collections/cdp/general.html**. Because this is where exciting developments are taking place at present, it is worth keeping up to date with the latest changes and developments on the web.

More traditional print-based resources worth reading for more detailed views on the value and use of collection management and collection development policies may be found in chapters by F. J. Friend, 'Policy: politics, power and people', in G. E. Gorman (ed), *International yearbook of library and information management 2000-2001: collection management*, Library Association Publishing, 2000, 45–58; and by D. Law, 'The organization of collection management in academic libraries', in M. Morley and C. Jenkins (eds), *Collection management in academic libraries*, 2nd edn, Gower Publishing, 1999, 15–38.

Among published collections of collection development policies perhaps the best is Elizabeth Futas, *Collection development policies and procedures*, 3rd edn, Oryx, 1995, which includes four 'full' library policies and sections from many others, arranged by topic (such as 'selection criteria'). It also includes seven appendixes covering issues of censorship and confidentiality. Richard Wood also discusses collection development policies and provides examples, but his work is more useful for its discussion of the content of these documents: R. J. Wood and F. Hoffman, *Library collection development policies: a reference and writers' handbook*, Scarecrow Press, 1996.

Notes

1 G. E. Evans, *Developing library and information center collections*, 4th edn, Library Science Text series, Libraries Unlimited, 2000, 19–20.

2 Ibid.

3 C. Jenkins and M. Morley (eds), *Collection management in academic libraries*, 2nd edn, Gower Publishing, 1999, 2. Jenkins and Morley are in part relying on the earlier work of J. A. Cogswell, 'The organization of collection management functions in academic research libraries', *Journal of Academic Librarianship*, **13** (5), 1987, 268–76.

4 Cogswell, op. cit., 269.

5 K. Cassell and E. Futas, *Developing public library collections, policies and procedures*, Neal-Schuman, 1991.

6 R. K. Gardner, *Library collections: their origins, selection and development*, McGraw-Hill Book Company, 1981, 222–4.

7 D. Farrell, 'Policy and planning'. In C. B. Osburn and R. Atkinson (eds), *Collection management: a new treatise*, JAI Press, 1991, 55–6.

8 O. G. Norman, 'The impact of electronic information services on collection development: a survey of current practice', *Library Hi Tech*, **15** (1/2), 1997, 127–8.

9 Statements include The Library Association's *Intellectual freedom and censorship* at **www.la-hq.org.uk/directory/prof_issues/ifac.html** [10 April 2001]. The Office of Intellectual Freedom of the American Library Association has compiled not just a statement, but a book on the topic: *Intellectual freedom manual*, 5th edn, American Library Association, 1996, which in Part 5 advises librarians to prepare policies, procedures and publicity to deal with censorship problems before these arise.

10 One site that attempts to list collection development policies is **http://bubl.ac.uk/link/c/collectiondevelopment.htm** [10 April 2001].

11 For example, the ARL's *Checklist for drafting electronic information policies* at **www.arl.org/newsltr/196/checklist.html** [10 April 2001].

12 P. Johnson, 'Collection development policies and electronic information resources'. In G. E. Gorman and R. H. Miller (eds). *Collection management for the 21st century: a handbook for librarians*, Greenwood Press, 1997, 83–104; P. Johnson, 'Collection policies for electronic resources', *Technicalities*, **18**, 1998, 10–12.

13 Norman, op. cit., 123–31.

14 R. Strong, 'A collection development policy incorporating electronic formats', *Journal of Interlibrary Loan, Document Delivery & Information Supply*, **9**, 1999, 53–64.

15 H. Billings, 'Library collections and distance information: new models of collection development for the 21st century', *Journal of Library Administration*, **24**, 1996, 3–17.

3
Conspectus

Focus questions

- What is Conspectus?
- What is the role of Conspectus in a collection development policy?
- How might traditional approaches to Conspectus be updated to reflect the need to deal with electronic as well as print information sources?

Clearly, a collection development policy will be of little value if it does not say what a library has or intends to acquire or provide access to in any particular subject area. The Research Libraries Group (RLG) Conspectus approach has often been recommended to describe the collecting levels for various subject areas in a collection development policy. In fact it is the only widely acknowledged means of doing this. Despite its origins in research libraries, Conspectus is a tool relevant to many kinds of library. Accordingly, we need to describe Conspectus and give some indication of its strengths and weaknesses. Because the development of Conspectus predated the widespread availability of electronic information, in our view it needs to be updated to reflect this if it is to be of continuing relevance to the library community.

What is Conspectus?

Conspectus is

> . . . a system which enables information about the collections of libraries and their collection development practices to be recorded in a relatively standardised way and which allows

some detailed comparisons to be made between the collections of libraries involved. The term is used to refer both to the methodology involved in describing collections and to the database of standard collection descriptions that results.[1]

It was developed by the RLG in the USA to describe collection strengths and collection development intentions in a uniform manner. Analysis is based on a library classification scheme, and strengths and collecting intentions are assessed against a set of more-or-less universally agreed categories ranging from 0 (out of scope – the library does not collect in this area) to 5 (comprehensive – the library attempts to collect exhaustively); see Figure 3.1.

RLG collection level codes are used by collection managers to indicate their subjective assessment of:

- how a collection has been created in the past (Existing Collection Strengths, ECS)
- the current focus within the collection (Current Collection Intensity, CCI)
- how they intend to approach the collection in the future (Desired Collection Intensity, DCI).

A range of language suffixes indicates whether holdings are primarily in English or include foreign languages, and scope notes and comments are also incorporated. Storage of such descriptions on a central database is intended to facilitate meaningful interlibrary comparisons.[2]

Level 0	*Out of Scope*	
	The library does not collect in this area.	
Level 1	*Minimal*	
	A collection for which few selections are made beyond introductory/very basic material.	
Level 1a	*Minimal with Uneven Coverage*	
	Few selections are made and there is uneven representation of a subject.	
Level 1b	*Minimal with Even Coverage*	
	Few selections are made, but key authors, some core works, or a spectrum of views are represented.	
Level 2	*Basic Information*	
	A collection of up-to-date materials which serves to introduce and define a subject and to indicate the varieties of information available elsewhere. It may include dictionaries, encyclopedias, access to appropriate bibliographic databases,	

Fig. 3.1   *Conspectus descriptions for levels of collections*

standard and significant works, handbooks, manuals, films, sound recording and a few popular or major serials. A basic information collection can support general enquiries, school and some undergraduate instruction, and information at a popular level, but is not sufficiently intensive to support advanced undergraduate courses.

Level 2a   *Basic Information: Introductory*
The emphasis at this level is on providing resources that introduce and define a subject. A collection at this level includes basic reference sources and explanatory works, such as textbooks, historical descriptions of the subject's development, general works devoted to major topics and figures in the field, and selective major periodicals. This level is sufficient to support clients attempting to locate general information about a subject or students enrolled in introductory level courses.

Level 2b   *Basic Information: Augmented*
At this level, basic information about a subject is provided on a wider range of topics and with more depth. There is a broader selection of basic explanatory works, historical descriptions, reference sources and periodicals that serve to introduce and define a subject. This level is sufficient to support students in basic courses as well as supporting the basic information needs of clients in public and special libraries.

Level 3   *Intermediate*
A collection containing a broad range of resources adequate to support undergraduate and most graduate instruction, sustained independent study, work-based interests or specialized enquiries; that is, adequate to impart and maintain a knowledge of a subject in a systematic way at less than research intensity. It includes a wide range of basic works in appropriate formats, the fundamental reference sources and bibliographical works, a significant number of classic retrospective materials, complete collections of the works of more important authors, selections from the works of secondary writers, a selection of representative journals, and access to appropriate databases.

Level 3a   *Intermediate: Introductory*
A collection at this level provides resources adequate for imparting and maintaining knowledge about the primary topics of a subject area. It includes a broad range of basic works in appropriate formats, classic retrospective materials, all key journals on primary topics, selected journals and seminal works on secondary topics, the fundamental reference sources and bibliographical works and access to appropriate databases. The collection is adequate to support undergraduate instruction, as well as most independent study and work-based needs of the clientele of public and special libraries; it is not adequate to support postgraduate courses.

Fig. 3.1   *Continued*

Level 3b   *Intermediate: Augmented*
A collection at this level provides resources adequate for imparting and maintaining knowledge about the primary and secondary topics of a subject area. The collection includes a significant number of seminal works and journals on the primary and secondary topics in the field, a significant number of classic retrospective materials, a substantial collection of works by secondary figures, works that provide in-depth discussions of research, techniques and evaluation, the fundamental reference sources and bibliographical works, and access to appropriate databases. The collection is adequate to support all undergraduate and most postgraduate coursework, as well as the more advanced independent study and work-based needs of the clients of public and special libraries.

Level 4   *Research*
A collection containing both current and retrospective resources, with historical material retained. Such a collection supports postgraduate and independent research and includes the major published source materials required. It includes all important reference works, a wide selection of specialized monographs, a very extensive collection of journals and immediate access to bibliographies, abstracting and indexing services in the field, materials containing research findings and non-bibliographic databases. The collection will provide materials in all appropriate formats and languages, including original materials and ephemera.

Level 5   *Comprehensive*
A collection that includes, as far as is reasonably possible, all significant works of recorded knowledge (publications, manuscripts, other forms) in all applicable languages, for a necessarily defined and limited field. This level of collecting intensity is one that maintains a special collection; the aim, if not the achievement, is exhaustiveness.

Fig. 3.1   *Continued*

The role of Conspectus

A collection development policy needs to give specific details about what is in a library, as well as provide the general principles on which these resources are assembled. Conspectus permits the subject-by-subject description of a collection, using the standard descriptions outlined above. As noted in Chapter 9, in order to comment accurately on the ECS and CCI aspects of the policy a detailed collection evaluation exercise is usually undertaken, at least in larger libraries where the staff are not working with the collection on a daily basis.

It is equally important to be clear about what Conspectus is *not*. It is not a method for evaluating collections, although to arrive at a defensible Conspectus description of a collection at least some evaluation is needed. In particular, it is not a 'scientific' approach: it is subjective and therefore not impartial. Instead, it is a way of *describing* collection strength and intentions.

Most of the likely benefits of Conspectus have been well publicized. The Conspectus approach provides:

- a standard means of describing current collection strengths
- a standard means of describing future collecting intentions (in both cases, the Conspectus approach facilitates the provision of an automated database to share access to this information, and permit ready updating of it)
- assistance with collection rationalization by informing librarians who else is collecting in a particular subject area
- assistance with resource sharing by listing collection strengths for users who may then visit other libraries, and for library staff, as a guide to interlibrary loans
- assistance with the prioritization of material for preservation activity, and recording of these priorities
- for those librarians who participate in the process, enhancement of both their skills and their knowledge of the collection[3]
- the establishment or strengthening of links with teaching and research faculty in academic institutions[4]
- assistance with the development of detailed collection development policies[5]
- information that may be used to support budget requests[6]
- information that may be useful in academic institutions subject to external accreditation.[7]

These are significant benefits. However, despite its initially enthusiastic reception in several countries, others have been more wary. The British reaction to it, for example, has been described as 'generally cool'.[8] Gorman and Miller have recently suggested that 'the Conspectus approach continues to find favour in the professional community, particularly in the US, where even smaller libraries are now using this method'.[9] However, there seems to have been a substantial diminution of books and articles on Conspectus, suggesting that its time may now have passed. As noted above, this may well be because it does not make provision for electronic resources.

Both experience with Conspectus and a reading of the literature suggest the following limitations:

- The very large amount of work involved in collection assessment for individual libraries. When the costs of its adoption and maintenance in each participating library are included, it becomes a very expensive exercise, as the literature recognizes.[10]
- The North American bias of Conspectus, with several subject areas under- or over-detailed for other countries. Consequently, there may be a need to 'nationalize' it.
- The subjective nature of many of the assessments made – discussed in more detail below.
- The understandable tendency to measure the size of a collection rather than its quality.
- The uneven balance between different subject disciplines. Conspectus has been widely reported as being more successful in dealing with some subject areas than others.[11]
- The basis in a library classification scheme, whether Dewey or Library of Congress. Few would dispute that these tend to scatter some related subjects, reflect a 19th-century view of the world and become very much subject to adaptation in individual libraries.
- The general nature of the information recorded. The RLG Conspectus uses around 7000 subjects; especially in larger libraries, these may not provide sufficiently fine detail for specialist libraries or their clients.
- Perhaps surprisingly, its limited value in interlibrary loan work. What is required for interlibrary loan is the location of a specific item, which Conspectus does not provide. In any case, most library staff working in the interlibrary loan area soon acquire a very good idea of the other libraries whose collections are complementary to their own.

As one might assume, there has been considerable debate around several of these limitations. One American article, generally supportive of the concept, quoted Yale university librarian's conclusion that 'the Conspectus values are not data, but subjective expressions of opinion'.[12] Similar comments have been made in the UK.[13] The American article suggested that expensive verification studies were the only means of ensuring that data were meaningful. Even after verification studies, however, some American universities were unwilling to alter their assessments, 'apparently reluctant to admit publicly that they did not have research collections in subjects in which they offered doctoral programs'.[14] Several other authors have expressed doubts about the value or 'goodness' of Conspectus-based assessments.[15]

Case study 3.1

Conspectus in Canberra[16]

In Canberra, the national capital of Australia, the Australian National University Library (ANU) decided to prepare a collection development policy based on that of the University of California at Berkeley. As part of this, it was decided to use the Conspectus approach but with only around 1000 LC subdivisions – similar to the number used at Berkeley, but many fewer than the 7000-odd of the RLG Conspectus. Using the full 7000 items would have been extraordinarily difficult with about 120 departments, centres and schools to be consulted as part of the process. Reducing this to only 1000, care had to be taken to ensure that significant but narrow research interests were not lost in more general categories, and geographic subdivisions related to Australia and the Pacific given in adequate detail.

One problem was that LC classification was not used throughout the library system: law materials were classified using an idiosyncratic version of Dewey, East Asian vernacular materials using Harvard-Yenching, astronomy by UDC and a handful of older materials were still classified by Bliss. In terms of levels, it was decided that the University did not need to collect in any area at Level 5 (comprehensive), but almost always would require more than Level 0 (out of scope). Having decided this, staff were surprised by occasional collection strengths: on the shelves Hunting Sports, far from being 0 as anticipated, could credibly have been claimed at 5 for the hunting of tigers in Bengal. With substantial Asian vernacular materials in the collections, the language suffixes were modified by adding an 'A' for Asian language materials and 'C' for the relevant colonial language.

Three sources of information were drawn upon to prepare the policy:

- collection development staff themselves
- annual reports, handbooks and other internal data about the departments and centres of the University
- academic staff, via a survey that asked for suggested collection levels to be assigned, an indication of the languages required, geographical areas and time periods of interest, along with suggestions about areas not well covered at the time.

While this was very successful in many ways, it involved protracted discussions about appropriate levels. Indeed, 'The collection levels eventually assigned were based for the most part on departmental wishes . . . the Library Acquisitions Policy contains many more Level 3 and Level 4 designations than would be confirmed by an objective evaluation; the academics tending to equate their own research interests with Level 4 regardless of any objective criteria.'[17]

A final conclusion from this exercise was that, despite the effort put into the development of the policy, the academic staff who are responsible for almost all ordering do not appear to have made any use of it.

Given the cost of collection assessment and the subjectivities involved, not surprisingly there have been attempts to address these through automated products – principally from the USA. For example, OCLC and the AMIGOS Bibliographic Council developed a product called the *OCLC/AMIGOS collection analysis compact disc* to assist libraries in measuring their collections against those of other institutions.[18] Vellucci suggested this could also be used for course analysis, generation of desiderata lists and management information data.[19] WLN has also produced Conspectus software.[20] However, such products would appear to have limited application elsewhere in the world.

Whether Conspectus is of real value in locating specific collection strengths, either for users or as an aid to collection rationalization, has also been questioned. In Australia, for example, an art librarian attempted to use the RLG Conspectus to locate North American collections with strengths in three art areas: Picasso, Cubism or Minimal Art, and North American Indian art. This was to advise a researcher which collections might be worth visiting. The results were mostly unsuccessful, and at best 'really too general to be much use'.[21]

Lucas has commented that 'the goal of using the Conspectus as the basis of cooperative arrangements at a more general level than the individual title, and in broader areas of scholarship than the PCR [the RLG's Primary Collecting Responsibility programme], continues to elude the research library community'.[22] In academic institutions collection rationalization will normally require academic rationalization – and, as with the interlibrary loan area, the complementary strengths of adjacent institutions are usually well known. However important such reservations may be for attempts to secure nationwide co-oordinated collection development, though, they do not affect the central promise of Conspectus: that it offers a standardized way in which to describe current collection strengths and collecting intentions.[23]

Conspectus in an electronic age

Overall, it seems to us that many of the various benefits claimed for Conspectus are, if anything, further reduced by the widespread availability of online library catalogues on the web. Who now needs to consult Conspectus data to see which libraries have strong resources in an area when collection building? Who now needs these data for interlibrary resource sharing, or to direct clients to strong collections? All of this information is already available electronically – often via online public access catalogues (OPACs) on the web.

Indeed, the whole resource-based approach of Conspectus reflects a pre-digital age. Look at the descriptions of the various levels: arguably an experienced librarian with a PC and an internet connection could provide information to at least Level 2b (Basic Information: Augmented), and in some areas even to Level 3a (Intermediate: Introductory). Whether a typical library user could do as well in gathering current electronic information is, of course, another matter. Level 3a is supposed to describe the type of collection most undergraduates require. In fact, anyone working in higher education will know of some undergraduates who appear to be able to complete some courses quite satisfactorily with very much *less* than they could get from the web.[24]

Unfortunately, whatever one thinks of Conspectus there is still no viable, well-recognized or widely used alternative to it for describing the strength of a library's information resources in a subject area. What we now need is a re-worked statement of Conspectus levels which takes into account the availability of digital data. Note here that digital data has only to be available, not 'owned' in the sense that print resources must be in order for them to be available. In fact, with multiple access to digital data possible, it can be argued that it can be made more readily available than even the undergraduate short-loan print collections of old.

As no such revised statement of Conspectus has yet appeared, adapting it to the digital library, we offer this ourselves as Figure 3.2. For terminology such as 'The collection includes . . .', we have substituted 'The library provides access to . . .', and so on. Using this statement, or one adapted from it, we suggest that a Conspectus-like approach might be adopted for the description of the specific areas in which a library has and will acquire collections, or will arrange access to resources. Given that access to many electronic resources is ephemeral – the databases a library subscribes to today it may not have access to tomorrow, a cancelled CD-ROM set may have to be returned to the vendor – such an approach will have real limitations for describing ECS. However, it should prove more useful than statements around two decades old for describing CCI, and ideal for any library deciding upon its DCI.

This suggested revision of the Conspectus levels will, of course, itself need further revision as the balance of material availability shifts further and further towards electronic media. Despite the zealots on both sides of the debate, however, no collection is now adequate that does not provide access to at least some electronic resources. Nevertheless, it will be a very long time, if ever, before a collection can be considered adequate without providing access to at least some print resources.

The future of libraries is an inclusive one, where readers will use and expect resources to be made available to them in all formats. Collection management and development policies and collection assessment tools that ignore this will be

Level 0	*Out of Scope*
	The library does not collect or provide access to resources in this area; electronic access is limited to internet resources.
Level 1	*Minimal*
	A collection for which few selections are made beyond introductory/very basic material; electronic access is limited primarily to internet resources.
Level 1a	*Minimal with Uneven Coverage*
	Few selections are made and there is uneven representation of a subject; electronic access is limited primarily to internet resources.
Level 1b	*Minimal with Even Coverage*
	Few selections are made, but key authors, some core works, or a spectrum of views are represented; electronic access is limited primarily to internet resources.
Level 2	*Basic Information*
	Access to up-to-date materials, print and electronic, which serve to introduce and define a subject and to indicate the varieties of information available elsewhere. It may include dictionaries, encyclopedias, access to appropriate bibliographic databases (including on CD-ROM), standard and significant works, handbooks, manuals, films, sound recording, a few popular or major serials and access to internet resources. A basic information resource can support general enquiries, school and some undergraduate instruction, and information at a popular level, but is not sufficiently intensive to support advanced undergraduate courses.
Level 2a	*Basic Information: Introductory*
	The emphasis at this level is on providing resources that introduce and define a subject. A collection at this level includes basic reference sources and explanatory works, such as textbooks, historical descriptions of the subject's development, general works devoted to major topics and figures in the field, selective major periodicals, and access to internet resources. This level is sufficient to support clients attempting to locate general information about a subject or students enrolled in introductory level courses.
Level 2b	*Basic Information: Augmented*
	At this level, basic information about a subject is provided on a wider range of topics and with more depth. There is a broader selection of basic explanatory works, historical descriptions, reference sources (including on CD-ROM) and periodicals that serve to introduce and define a subject. This level is sufficient to support students in basic courses as well as supporting the basic information needs of clients in public and special libraries.

Fig. 3.2   *Revised Conspectus descriptions for levels of access*

Level 3	*Intermediate*
	Includes a broad range of resources adequate to support undergraduate and most graduate instruction, sustained independent study, work-based interests or specialized enquiries; that is, adequate to impart and maintain a knowledge of a subject in a systematic way at less than research intensity. It includes a wide range of basic works in appropriate formats, the fundamental reference sources and bibliographical works (including on CD-ROM), a significant number of classic retrospective materials, complete collections of the works of more important authors, selections from the works of secondary writers, a selection of representative journals, and access to appropriate online databases as well as the internet.
Level 3a	*Intermediate: Introductory*
	At this level resources adequate for imparting and maintaining knowledge about the primary topics of a subject area are provided. Access is to a broad range of basic works in appropriate formats, classic retrospective materials, all key journals on primary topics, selected journals and seminal works on secondary topics, the fundamental reference sources and bibliographical works (including on CD-ROM) and access to appropriate online databases as well as the internet. Resources are adequate to support undergraduate instruction, as well as most independent study and work-based needs of the clientele of public and special libraries, but not adequate to support postgraduate courses.
Level 3b	*Intermediate: Augmented*
	This level provides resources adequate for imparting and maintaining knowledge about the primary and secondary topics of a subject area. Access is available to a significant number of seminal works and journals on the primary and secondary topics in the field, a significant number of classic retrospective materials, a substantial collection of works by secondary figures, works that provide in-depth discussions of research, techniques and evaluation, the fundamental reference sources and bibliographical works (including on CD-ROM), and access to appropriate online databases as well as the internet. The resources are adequate to support all undergraduate and most postgraduate coursework, as well as the more advanced independent study and work-based needs of the clients of public and special libraries.
Level 4	*Research*
	At this level access is provided to both current and retrospective resources, including historical material. Information available supports postgraduate and independent research. Access is to the major published source materials required, including all important reference works (both print and electronic), a wide selection of specialized

Fig. 3.2 *Continued*

> monographs, a very extensive collection of journals (including electronic journals) and immediate access to bibliographies, abstracting and indexing services in the field, materials containing research findings and non-bibliographic databases. Resources available will include materials in all appropriate formats and languages, including original materials and ephemera.
>
> Level 5   *Comprehensive*
>
> Resources that include, as far as is reasonably possible, all significant works of recorded knowledge (publications, manuscripts, electronic media and other forms) in all applicable languages, for a necessarily defined and limited field. This level of collecting intensity is one that maintains a special collection, complemented by all available online resources; the aim, if not the achievement, is exhaustiveness.

Fig. 3.2   *Continued*

increasingly irrelevant, however useful they once seemed.

Review of Chapter 3

This chapter has introduced the RLG Conspectus, a method of describing collection strengths in a standardized manner. Introduced at the end of the print-only era, its promise has never been fulfilled and interest in it is clearly waning. Our view is that, while it has limitations as a tool facilitating co-ordinated regional and national collection development, it should still be useful in its primary role of collection description. However, in its present form it is collection-centred rather than resource-access-centred, and now urgently needs to be updated to take into account the availability of digital data.

Where to now?

Begin by reviewing the focus questions at the head of this chapter. You might then think about some of the following questions:

- Do you know of a major library in your own country or region that has adopted Conspectus? Has it publicly reported on its experience with it (for example, through publication, conference or seminar presentations)?
- Take an area of knowledge with which you are reasonably familiar. Examine that section in a library's collection, and attempt to assess it using the Conspectus terminology.
- Finally, consider the electronic resources that are now available in this subject

area. Does the library provide access to these? Could you describe this access using the revised Conspectus descriptions we suggested above in Figure 3.2?

Further reading

There is a large published literature on Conspectus, yet most of this is clearly now dated. As suggested above, this may well be because in its present form it does not make adequate provision for dealing with access to digital data. Now nearly a decade old, the book by R. J. Wood and K. Strauch (eds), *Collection assessment: a look at the RLG Conspectus*, Haworth Press, 1992, provides a comprehensive overview of the approach and includes an annotated bibliography. A more recent bibliography is provided by Miller in 'The recent literature', the last chapter of G. E. Gorman and R. H. Miller (eds), *Collection management for the 21st century: a handbook for librarians*, Greenwood Press, 1997.

Recent writers on Conspectus include M. S. Sridhar, who provides an overview in 'Role of Conspectus in collection management and resource sharing', *Library Science with a Slant to Documentation and Information Studies*, **34** (2), 1997, 91–9. B. Davis, in 'How the WLN Conspectus works for small libraries', *Acquisitions Librarian*, **20**, 1998, 53–72, argues that Conspectus assessment details are easier to manage in small libraries, suggests appropriate adaptations of the Conspectus structure and provides an illustration of the use of WLN Conspectus software.

The University of Birmingham has created a series of subject-based collection profiles using a Conspectus approach. Policy and other documents are available from the University website at **www.is.bham.ac.uk**, and J. Russell has written about the process in 'Collection profiling', *SCONUL Newsletter*, **16**, 1999, 26–30. D. Biblarz provides another European perspective in 'The role of collection development in a teaching library', *European Research Libraries Cooperation*, **7** (2), 1997, 397–422.

Notes

1 Australian Council of Libraries and Information Services, *The Australian Conspectus: National Task Force on Conspectus final report*, Australian Council of Libraries and Information Services, 1989, 8.
2 For further details see N. E. Gwinn and P. H. Mosher, 'Coordinating collection development: the RLG Conspectus'. *College & Research Libraries*, **44** (March), 1983, 128–40.
3 L. R. Oberg, 'Evaluating the Conspectus approach for smaller library collec-

tions', *College & Research Libraries*, **49** (May), 1988, 187–96.

4 Ibid., 195; A. W. Ferguson, J. Grant and J. S. Rutstein, 'The RLG Conspectus: its uses and benefits', *College & Research Libraries*, **49** (May), 1988, 197–206.

5 Ferguson, op. cit., 202.

6 Oberg, loc. cit.; Ferguson, op. cit., 203–4.

7 Ferguson, op. cit., 203.

8 A. Matheson, 'Conspectus in the United Kingdom', *Alexandria*, **1** (1), 1989, 51–9.

9 G. E. Gorman and R. H. Miller, 'Changing collections, changing evaluations'. In G. E. Gorman (ed.), *International yearbook of library and information management 2000–2001: collection management*, Library Association, 2000, 314.

10 See, for example, Oberg, op. cit., 194; *The Australian Conspectus*, 18.

11 For example, in A. Matheson, 'Co-operative approaches in Scotland'. In S. Corrall (ed.), *Collection development: options for effective management . . .* , Taylor Graham, 1988, 131.

12 M. D. Abell, quoted in T. A. Lucas 'Verifying the Conspectus: problems and progress', *College & Research Libraries News*, **51** (March), 1990, 199–201.

13 Matheson, 'Conspectus in the UK', 54; Matheson, 'Co-operative approaches in Scotland', 119–31.

14 Lucas, op. cit., 201.

15 M. D. Abell, 'The Conspectus: issues and questions'. In *Association of Research Libraries: Minutes of the 109th meeting. NCIP: means to an end*, Association of Research Libraries, 1987, 26–30; J. Coleman, 'The RLG Conspectus: a history of its development and influence and a prognosis for its future', *Acquisitions Librarian*, **7**, 1992, 25–43; S. E. Siverson, 'Fine-tuning the dull roar of Conspectors: using scaled bibliographies to assess collection level', *Acquisitions Librarian*, **7**, 1992, 45–64.

16 This case study is based on M. Henty, 'Library acquisitions policy by consultation out of Conspectus.' *Australian Academic & Research Libraries*, **20** (1), 1989, 47–50.

17 Henty, op. cit., 50.

18 J. Harrell, 'Use of the OCLC/AMIGOS collection analysis CD to determine comparative collection strength in English and American literature: a case study', *Technical Services Quarterly*, **9**, 1992, 1–14.

19 S. L. Vellucci, 'OCLC/AMIGOS collection analysis CD: broadening the scope of use', *OCLC Systems and Services*, **9**, 1993, 49–53.

20 D. Forsythe, 'OCLC/WLN merger provides new opportunities for libraries', *OCLC Newsletter*, **239**, 1999, 42–3. See also B. Davis, 'How the WLN Conspectus works for small libraries', *Acquisitions Librarian*, **20**, 1998, 53–72; and B. Davis,

'Using local marketing characteristics to customize the Conspectus for fiction assessment', *Acquisitions Librarian*, **19**, 1998, 29–44.

21 J. M. Shaw, 'Conspectus as a tool for art libraries in Australia', *Australian Academic & Research Libraries*, **21** (1), 1990, 37–8.

22 Lucas, op. cit.

23 A much more positive assessment is provided by R. J. Wood in 'The Conspectus: a collection analysis and development success', *Library Acquisitions: Practice and Theory*, **20** (4), 1996, 429–53.

24 The statement in the Dearing Committee report, *Higher education in the learning society*, HMSO, 1997, that undergraduates are heavily dependent on access to printed textbooks is, of course, normative. Research in several countries has found only limited or no correlation between library use and academic success. See, for example, J. Wells, 'The influence of library usage on undergraduate academic success', *Australian Academic & Research Libraries*, **26** (2), 1995, 121–8. That report also cites several earlier studies in the area.

4

Resource sharing and co-operative collection development

Focus questions

- What is the purpose of co-operation, and what are the benefits?
- What are the barriers to co-operation, and how might they be overcome?
- What are the principal characteristics of effective resource-sharing management?

Resource sharing and co-operation, especially co-operative collection development, are essential components in collection management – and this has been the case rather longer than these have been 'hot topics' among information professionals. In the USA, for example, it has long been a part of professional practice, as the Association of Specialized and Cooperative Library Agencies recognizes:

> Cooperation among libraries is not a new phenomenon and, indeed, over a century of co-operation among librarians in the United States makes up the heritage of present day practitioners. That libraries should be able to work co-operatively to find access to information in distant collections which is not available locally is a deeply rooted concept in librarianship.[1]

Resource sharing is the simpler of the two approaches discussed in this chapter, involving reciprocal access to the holdings of a group of libraries. Co-operative collection development is more proactive, as it involves actively influencing what is currently being acquired by other libraries in order to extend the range of materials available to groups of users, and permitting that same influence to be exercised by other libraries.

Co-operation occurs at many levels and in most areas of library service, from joint storage facilities and shared technical processing services to interlibrary loans (ILL) and reciprocal access for users. But this chapter is about co-operation at the level of collection development, with the intention of providing readers with access to a wider range of information resources.

Co-operative activities are becoming increasingly important for service delivery, primarily because of the ever-expanding availability of electronic data and improvements in telecommunications. Network access to online catalogues facilitates resource sharing at the item level – the only level of real interest to most clients. But having established that another library has what is wanted, how is it to be obtained? Network access to the electronic documents themselves poses a different set of problems. Some of these – including costs, access and preservation – were noted in Chapter 1. Book loans remain at the pace of 'snail mail' but journal articles, at least, can routinely be faxed to the requester. And there is good evidence that electronic service delivery results in greater usage of resources. For example, in the OhioLINK Electronic Journal Center, Sanville found that the downloading of articles not only increased exponentially as the Center became a familiar part of the users' normal information landscape, but also represented a significant improvement over the old system of hard-copy article access by means of ILL:

> The first 18 months of operation of the OhioLINK Electronic Journal Center (EJC) is an exemplary illustration of the dramatic benefits of expanded access. Patrons have executed over 535,000 article downloads. On average each Ohio university uses three times more titles than they previously held in print, and over 50 per cent of downloaded articles were not available in print on each campus.[2]

On the basis of this evidence Sanville concluded that users tend to seek expanded levels of use that suit their needs when user-friendly systems that deliver information rapidly are available. This improved service level is one consideration in co-operative library activity, but, oddly, not one of the principal considerations usually discussed by librarians.

Why do we co-operate?

In fact there are two other reasons most often advanced for co-operative activities in relation to collections. The more principled of these is a recognition that libraries can no longer hope to own all the materials that their readers need or want, and that we need to share in order to achieve maximum reader satisfaction.

But hardened campaigners are well aware that a more compelling reason for co-operation is financial, driven by a need to limit budgets more effectively. There seems little doubt that, at least in the short term, it is often cheaper for libraries to obtain individual journal articles on interlibrary loan than to subscribe to the journals themselves. McCarthy has quoted Columbia University figures showing that, for biology journals, even with the most-requested titles (ten requests per title) subscription costs outweighed access costs. For titles requested only three, two or one times, subscription costs outweighed those of access by factors of 7:1 to 21:1.[3]

Stemming from this overriding financial impetus are a number of more specific goals:

- to fill existing gaps in coverage of some specific area within the universe of knowledge, or to reduce duplication in holdings
- to achieve better understanding of collection management and development practices among related libraries
- to co-ordinate future collection development planning
- to establish mutually agreed collecting responsibilities for specific disciplines, formats, etc.
- to acquire joint site licences for shared databases[4]
- to co-ordinate collection management decisions related to preservation, storage, weeding, cancellations, etc.

Major barriers to co-operation

Edward Evans, in *Developing library and information center collections*, devotes some space to barriers to co-operation under six headings: 1) institutional, 2) legal, political and administrative, 3) technological, 4) physical, 5) human and 6) knowledge-based issues.[5] For those with a 'glass is half empty' view of co-operation, these pages may repay reading, but in our view they are unrealistically pessimistic and tend to give minor impediments the same level of significance as major barriers. In this section we prefer to focus on the major issues: the will to succeed, a desire for autonomy, a competitive environment, changing collection foci, and financial constraints.

For most information professionals the essence of effective co-operation is the will to succeed. In many situations such will simply does not exist, or cannot overcome an inbuilt resistance to co-operation founded on a desire to remain autonomous.[6] This is a powerful force based on the premise that what we own we also control. If we are not the owners, then we must be cognizant of the demands of other institutions and flexible in responding to them. In Branin's view there is a basic conflict between 'the local autonomy of the individual library and the shared responsibilities of the consortium or network'.[7] Just as you cannot be both single and married, if you join a co-operative or a network you have to relinquish some degree of independence. Those who do not, do not stay married for long.

On the one hand there are strong forces pushing libraries towards co-operation; on the other, powerful forces favouring local self-sufficiency. A most persuasive argument in the latter camp, for example, was advanced some years ago by Ballard. In relation to public libraries, he maintained that what users want is books on shelves here and now, not somewhere else at some other time, and that they will settle for second or third best rather than go to the trouble or waste the time in acquiring a first choice from somewhere else.[8] This argument has never been effectively countered.

Even if this basic impediment can be overcome, there are other barriers of a similar nature. For example, we live in an environment of increased competition among institutions for 'clients', and part of attracting clients is providing a library service that is better than anyone else's – so why should we share our hard-earned collections and information resources with libraries that belong to 'the opposition'?

Also, a resource-sharing arrangement may begin to falter when the collecting needs of an institution evolve in response to the changing profile of its members – when an academic major is downgraded, or a research focus wanes. And then there is the ever-present spectre of affordability; what we can afford today in terms of meeting obligations as part of a co-operative arrangement we may not be able to afford tomorrow. Closely allied to this, at least in academic institutions, is 'a fear among faculty that, over time, such programs of divided collection responsibility will diminish the lustre of their own program's reputation and could ultimately influence academic decisions regarding appointments, promotion, and tenure'.[9]

The argument that interlibrary loans, electronic document delivery services and other means of resource sharing can fill gaps in a library's collection has not been accepted by most users. Dougherty notes that many academics in his university were

... adamant in their view that performance of the existing document delivery systems – i.e., ILL – was 'woefully' inadequate for their needs. It is probably true that the attitudes of some users toward interdependence have changed; it is probably also true that others remain staunchly opposed to the proposition that access to collections should be dependent on document delivery. For this latter group, the memory of four- to six-week interlibrary loan delivery performance may never fade away.[10]

Dougherty's findings date back to the late 1980s in the USA, but academics in Britain, Australia, New Zealand and elsewhere continue to echo this largely negative attitude towards the practical consequences of co-operation. With so many users – public library readers, students and academics alike – not in favour of resource sharing, it is very difficult for the principal barrier to co-operation, the will to succeed, to be overcome.

Factors favouring co-operation

These barriers to co-operation are more than matched, in our view, by factors that facilitate the development of effective co-operative arrangements. As already indicated, the unending inflationary spiral in the cost of library materials is probably the principal factor in favour of co-operation. Chapter 1 pointed out that this is accompanied by increased output by publishers, and the escalating introduction of new or improved multimedia formats. Costs and volume will continue to be the principal motivators that push libraries into co-operative arrangements.

In some parts of many countries parity of access is a strong motivator for co-operation. Remote parts of Britain, for example, may be better served by co-operative information networks in which libraries are key players, allowing the most remote reader to have something akin to the resources available to a reader in central London or the Home Counties. This becomes increasingly possible with the advent of genuine virtual libraries and reliable electronic access to information. If this is true for Britain, how much more so will be it be in the northern reaches of Canada, the Australian outback or on a tiny island in the Pacific Ocean?

Information technology is playing a role in other ways as well. New techniques for storing, retrieving and preserving electronic formats are becoming more economical and reliable, making it feasible for resource sharing to utilize this technology. Digital imaging systems, for example, are becoming economical as a means of full-text delivery, as well as for preservation of brittle and visual materials.

Resource sharing

While the barriers to co-operation may seem rather more numerous than the favourable factors, the latter have the advantage of being in the ascendant for the foreseeable future, and this is most evident in resource sharing through consortial arrangements. Resource sharing is perhaps the simplest and most traditional type of library co-operation. By 'resource sharing' librarians mean the sharing of library collections through a variety of activities, including:

- sharing of information on the holdings of co-operating libraries
- reciprocal lending and borrowing of materials
- reciprocal services to users of the co-operating libraries.

At one time, in the early days of the SCOLMA (Standing Conference on Library Materials on Africa) scheme, for example, resource sharing tended to involve just one of these services: shared information on holdings. Today, however, resource sharing does not involve just 'improved bibliographic access, or better document delivery, or more co-operative collection development, but a combination of activities in all three areas'.[11] When long-standing programmes like the Farmington Plan in the USA failed to understand the need for co-operation to occur at all levels to ensure success, they eventually withered on the vine, to be replaced by the more business-like consortia that characterize the field today.

Co-operative collection development

When we speak of 'co-operative collection development' we are referring to the coordination of any component of collection building (specialization in collection profiles, selection, acquisition, etc.) between two or more libraries. According to Paul Mosher and Marcia Pankake, who compiled a seminal guide to co-operative collection development activities, co-operation in collection development involves the sharing of responsibilities among libraries for three purposes:

1 acquisition of materials
2 development of collections
3 managing the growth and maintenance of collections.[12]

In Branin's view these three purposes of co-operative collection development are accomplished through three sets of activities:

1 mutual notification of purchasing decisions
2 joint purchase
3 assigned subject specialization.[13]

To some extent, of course, neither these purposes nor the activities that follow on from them are discrete. Acquisition flows into development, and development into managing growth; similarly, purchasing decisions lead naturally into joint purchasing, which may be affected by agreed subject specializations. Nevertheless, these are useful categories with which to work, especially if one is either investigating the establishment of a consortium or considering whether to join an established co-operative entity.

From ownership to access to co-ordinated collection management

At the end of the 1980s collection managers became excited about the issue of access versus ownership, and what the former might mean for the quality and integrity of collections and collection services. We have already noted the change in rhetoric from the so-called 'just-in-case' library to one that provides access 'just in time'. If libraries choose between access and ownership, they will choose access because of their growing inability to own all that they require. The enduring problem with access, though, is that someone has to own the material in order for it to be accessed. In the words of Keller, 'access to what? All the money and attention showered on delivery systems and meta-information systems is money well spent, but in the end if we cannot deliver the stuff of scholarship, we will suddenly be in the museum business.'[14]

As this recognition took hold by the early 1990s, the issue evolved from an either–or scenario to a both–and preference, with libraries believing that they needed to rely on both ownership and access in order to service their users' needs and wants. Ownership became the priority for 'core' collections, leaving access as the option for more peripheral materials. The problem with this, however, as we are learning perhaps too late, is that:

- The core is shrinking as libraries apply 'slash and burn' tactics in response to reduced funding.
- A greater proportion is relegated to a periphery in which no one seems able or willing to collect.
- The core is remarkably similar across libraries of the same type, which means that collections focus on the same basic materials.

Some of these trends are inevitable, but it may be that co-ordinated collection management offers a solution worth attempting. This is a slight variation on the third category advanced by Mosher and Pankake – 'managing the growth and maintenance of collections'. In our view comprehensive and effective co-ordination might give access and ownership together a chance to succeed by encouraging us to think globally and act locally – to consider what we can do together in order to give our individual user communities what they require. For this approach to have any impact, however, it must mean the co-ordination of all components in collection management.

'All components in collection management' can be reduced to four sets of functions that are held together by the shared collections of a consortium. These functions, all of which must be shared, include:

- collection development
- bibliographic access
- storage and preservation
- document delivery.

If the components in each of these functions can be undertaken co-operatively, then resource sharing through a combination of access and ownership can become a genuine possibility. Without co-operation in collection development (including selection, weeding and maintenance) we fall back to the situation where everyone collects core materials, and no one looks after the non-essential, low demand items. Without shared bibliographic access, now an almost universal reality through electronic communications, we lack locational information about individual resources in a standard format intelligible to all partners. Without joint decisions about storage and preservation, we cannot ensure that items will continue to be available when wanted and in an agreed format. And without co-operative delivery arrangements, we cannot get the materials to our users.

The attributes of successful resource sharing

To talk about co-ordination as if it is something easily achieved through the sharing of key components or functions of collection management is all very well, but in practice it can be much more complex. There are many reasons for this complexity, and many reasons why co-operative ventures fail; but in the main these can be summarized under three headings, as in Figure 4.1: agreed priorities, value of service, and proactive co-ordination.

Perhaps the most important is to have a set of agreed priorities that do not result in conflict between global and local needs. One of the almost congenital defects of resource-sharing programmes is the reality that local priorities must take prece-

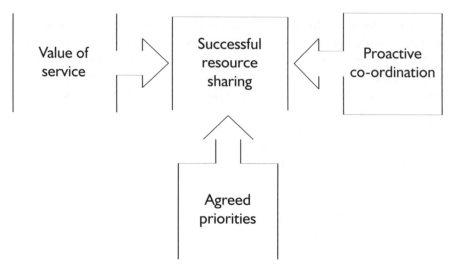

Fig. 4.1 *Components of successful resource-sharing programmes*

dence over collective priorities – each library, after all, exists to serve a discrete local community, is funded by or for that community, and so the needs of the community must come first. Libraries wishing to co-operate must make certain that the collective needs match local requirements as much as possible, and that the needs of individual partners are also broadly similar. There is little sense, for instance, in one library seeking to collect materials in order to preserve them for the needs of limited access, cutting-edge research and another seeking to service a large circulating collection of undergraduate course-related materials. Because local priorities must take precedence, it makes sense for these and the 'global' priorities of the consortium to match as closely as possible. Beyond this, however, as already noted, there must be some preparedness to compromise if resource sharing is to work.

The value of the service is equally important, for if co-operation does not result in substantial financial savings then its necessity will be questioned by managers both within and outside the library. It is increasingly the case that resource-sharing agreements need to result in considerable savings for participants: savings on the cost of individual items and subscriptions, savings in terms of material processing and maintenance, and savings in technology costs. If any of these savings does not exist – and even more so if additional expenses are incurred – then the programme is not successful. If it *is* successful, that success will be manifest in better services to readers than would otherwise have been possible.

The third attribute of a successful co-operative venture is proactive co-ordination among the participating libraries. Specifically, the co-ordinating organization established by the co-operating libraries must itself be an initiator of activities and not just a passive recipient of interactions initiated at the local level. If the organization itself is not seen to be actively involved, then it is not long before participants begin to question the reason for the organization. In fact, the real benefits of participation often come at the organizational level: the sharing and exchanging of ideas, ironing out of problems, initiation of consortium-wide ventures, etc.

Effective management of co-operative schemes

Any co-operative activity, whether resource sharing or collection development, requires a high level of managerial skill and commitment if it is to succeed. In our view successful co-operative ventures are characterized by six features: committed leadership, a formal governing structure, staff participation, staff training, adequate funds, and agreed collection description guidelines.

Committed leadership

The senior management of a library, the governing body and the parent organization's executive must all be fully committed to co-operation. Where senior management is not committed, there is a tendency not to share the decision-making process with staff and not to welcome input from others – both factors can result in lack of support by those staff who ought to be most directly involved in day-to-day co-operative work.

A formal governing structure

Closely related to commitment by senior management is the need for a formal governing structure in which there is broad staff involvement and clear lines of command. The level of formality will vary in accordance with local requirements, in some instances taking the form of a legal entity. The governing structure can be a library system, a network, an area authority, a consortium, or even a parent institution. Whatever the structure and degree of formality, the governing structure must have responsibility and authority to make and review policy, to review activities and to issue directives for management of the co-operative venture. It must have the political authority and managerial responsibility to deal with conflicts of interest, as well as the authority to administer programmes that operate over considerable distances and for an extended period of time.[15] In addition, it must facilitate the involvement of those staff with relevant expertise or experience. In practice, meeting these several requirements usually involves the creation of a series of interconnected committees.

Staff participation

Staff who are directly involved in day-to-day management of the co-operative activities must be represented in the governing structure's decision-making process. The less involved they are in decision making, the less likely they are to become committed to the programme.

Training of staff

Both managers and line staff need to have practical knowledge and skills in collection assessment, collection development and other aspects of collection management. This knowledge should extend from the operations staff up through the senior management of all participating libraries so that everyone knows precisely the amount of work that is involved in each activity. If librarians do not know the criteria for selecting quality materials, if they do not know how to determine which materials warrant preservation, then the consortium's collections will be the poorer. It should never be assumed that staff with collection development responsibilities know the criteria to be used for co-operative collection development purposes; rather, there must be on ongoing programme of training and induction in all aspects of managing a co-operative venture. The benefits of such a programme – and not only in terms of collection development – can be one of the greatest advantages of co-operation to participants.

Adequate funds

There must be adequate funds and a detailed budget for the acquisition of materials for the co-operative scheme, and there must also be funds for the additional management and associated costs of operating the joint activity. If funds are not sufficient, then the co-operative venture soon loses momentum, and the critics will justifiably become more vociferous. Management must be able to show that money and staff resources diverted from local acquisitions programmes to networking, meeting attendance, etc., is beneficial to the local institution.

Agreed collection description guidelines

A mutually agreed collection development and assessment framework and methodology are important criteria in a successful programme. In this regard the RLG Conspectus has become the preferred collection description language or coding method. If all participants have agreed to use Conspectus, then information on collections can be readily exchanged, making evaluation and monitoring a much simpler process.

From all of this it is apparent that the implementation of a co-operative programme is complex and time consuming and that it requires strong commitment in terms of planning, organization, staffing and funds. Underlying the commitment is clear understanding and detailed knowledge of five principal factors that underpin co-operative activities:

- the missions of the parent institutions, and how the libraries support these missions (ideally, these should be broadly similar – mission statements of universities, for example, ought not to be in conflict with one another)
- present and evolving information needs of the various user communities served by the libraries
- existing strengths and weaknesses of the respective collections – this is where a Conspectus-based analysis can be useful
- current collecting intensity and practices of the participating libraries
- statistics on the use and non-use of the respective collections (this will help ensure that substantiated utilization of the collections will not be damaged by future decisions by partner libraries, or by increased demands from users of those libraries).

It should be clear from the discussion of collection development policies in Chapter 2 that most of these requirements are met by a full and carefully written and researched collection development policy. Therefore, the sharing of these policy documents is often the starting point for discussions about co-operative arrangements. Such documents can become the touchstone for the development of co-operative agreements, in the sense that one refers back to a collection development policy to ensure that it is not being compromised by a subsequent co-operative agreement; or, if it is, that this can be justified and that the collection development policy can be amended to take account of this arrangement.

In most co-operative ventures there tends to be a more-or-less formal agreement that takes into account many of these points. Such an agreement will also cover practical day-to-day issues such as the processing and retention of materials, agreed procedures for determining what to do with materials not wanted for retention, restrictions on the use of materials (in-house only, borrowing periods, etc.), user fees, preservation criteria and standards. All of these factors need to be enshrined in a contract, a mutually agreed document signed by all participants. Changes need to be negotiated by all parties. The bottom line for all of this activity is to minimize the unwanted duplication of materials, to broaden the availability of and access to resources – and to avoid the potential for destructive conflict between the parties.

Consortia – the future for co-operation

Co-operative arrangements, whether for resource sharing or collection development, depend on sound local management and strong consortia. Local management has been treated in the preceding section, and we now close with some comments on the second important factor, consortia. To the extent that belonging to consortia is becoming the norm for libraries (or their parent organizations) in many countries, it appears that co-operation will become more effective in the future. Add to this the fact that increasing numbers of publishers, aggregators and vendors are willing to negotiate consortial agreements, even in once traditionally independent markets such as Taiwan, and the future looks brighter still.[16] There is, of course, still an undercurrent of resistance to co-operative arrangements from powerful interest groups such as the Association of American Publishers, but this is being somewhat countered by consortial agreements being made by many specialist publishers around the world.[17] Legitimate concerns persist about the sustainability of discount levels offered to consortia, declining quality of service, etc.[18]

In our view the factors that favour co-operation, and indeed can make it a necessity, are on the increase. Certainly there is no decrease in the volume of information being produced in print or electronic format, which is what prompted co-operative arrangements in the first instance. More libraries than ever before have developed well-articulated collection development policies and engage in the regular exchange of information on their collections. As both policies and practices are more clearly articulated, co-operation becomes easier. The secondary and tertiary resources that libraries need in order to serve their users effectively are experiencing spiralling production and subscription costs, and this as much as anything will continue to drive the need for co-operative collection development and resource sharing.

Behind all of this is the way in which electronic networks and linkages are developing and improving 'just-in-time' information delivery. Budd and Harloe have chronicled this development on more than one occasion, and indicate the exciting developments that lie before us. In the context of co-operative collection development and resource sharing, they see electronic networking as a way of moving beyond the 'access versus ownership' debate to the development of libraries that are not local physical entities but rather networks of collections. And the next step, in their view, is a future in which libraries will be less concerned with the management of artefacts than with the management of intellectual content – that is, not collection management, but content management.[19] In other words, co-operation is evolving from a focus on repositories of information to gateways to information, or portals, and this is changing the nature of both resource sharing and collection development quite dramatically.

What, then, is a consortium? In a very useful article, Michael Sinclair has suggested a typology of four kinds of library co-operatives: a bilateral exchange model (the earliest form); a multilateral pooling model; a dual service (all participants contributing) model; and a service centre (central facilitator) model.[20] Evans has included a diagrammatic representation of this in the fourth edition of his standard work.[21]

Sinclair thus establishes a typology for models of co-operative undertakings by libraries, which is useful for libraries wishing to understand the options open to them and which have been tried and tested. In any model the nature of the co-operative relationship may be relatively informal, or it may be of a legally binding nature, with numerous variations in between. There are various factors that determine precisely how a consortium within any model actually operates, and where it sits on the continuum from informality to legally constituted. This has been addressed by Wade in *Library consortium management*, who found that four factors emerge as keys in a consortium's move from informal alliance to legal recognition. These factors are

- joint ownership of infrastructure and assets
- funding and payment for services
- provision and staffing of joint services
- organization and legal structure.[22]

In Wade's view we have a continuum of service provision, ranging from limited activities to joint services. At the lower end of the continuum an informal arrangement may be quite sufficient, with libraries undertaking such activities as reciprocal borrowing, interlibrary loans, negotiation of database licences, training seminars, Z39.50 union catalogue linking and so on. These activities, which could exist within any of the models proposed by Sinclair, do not require a legally constituted entity. 'They represent arm's length cooperation in that each library operates independently and there is no handing over control of service delivery that otherwise would be the responsibility of the individual member library'.[23]

The provision of joint services, by contrast, means that the consortium is providing services to users on behalf of its members, and these services require detailed consultation at developmental and operational stages. Such services might include electronic database systems, shared library systems, shared interlibrary loan systems, shared storage facilities, etc. It should be obvious that these services are beyond the control of individual member libraries, and they in fact represent not only individual participants but also the consortium as a whole. When facilities and resources are shared (hardware, software licences, buildings), as tends to be the case with joint services, the consortium normally becomes involved in common ownership of assets. 'It is at this point that a consortium usually initiates the process of becoming a legal entity for, as much as anything else, the needs of perpetual succession and the need for accountability'.[24]

Developments in co-ordinated collection development are reflected at the national level by ongoing discussion of the concept of a 'national distributed collection'. This concept suggests that, rather than seeing the holdings of separate library collections as a set of discrete entities, which together amount to little more than the sum of their parts, instead we visualize these individual collections as part of a more or less unified whole. This whole is a single, national collection of resources, physically separated (and with much local duplication) but united through their common bibliographic database and accessible through traditional interlibrary loan arrangements, if not a networked ILL system. Thinking in such terms immediately suggests different collection development and management priorities – but also raises once again the same local barriers and concerns that we noted at the start of this chapter. As these barriers are overcome, in the course of this century we expect to witness the development of regional and finally international perspectives based on this concept. Here, the distributed 'resources' will of course increasingly be electronic. Indeed, it could be argued that the world wide web is another harbinger of just such a global information storehouse.

Case Study 4.1

OhioLINK[25]

In the mid-1980s the need for additional library accommodation led state-supported higher education institutions in Ohio to propose establishment of a co-operative network and a series of remote storage facilities. The network would include a shared central catalogue with local subsystems to permit end-user-initiated system-wide borrowing. It was hoped this would not only ease the ILL load but also increase the variety of resources available to students and staff, eliminate any unnecessary duplication, and give greater value for money.

Following the development of a very detailed 'request for proposal' including, as well as the usual requirements, collection management and development functions, Innovative Interfaces, Inc. was selected as the system supplier. From the beginning of the project there was a central OhioLINK management structure including an executive director and a systems director. However, despite the state funding, management – 'governance' is the usual term applied in consortia – remains with the universities.

Overall policy is the responsibility of a general advisory board composed of university administrators. In addition, a technical board and task force groups provide expertise in specific areas. A working group of library directors provides day-to-day management. This group is supported by four committees: database management (acquisitions, cataloguing and related services); collection management; inter-campus services, including circulation policies; and user services. All these committees include representatives from the consortium, and are serviced by staff at OhioLINK. In some cases, such as with the installation of databases, the work is undertaken by OhioLINK staff; in others, it is undertaken primarily by the members of the committee. This is true in the case of collection management and co-operative collection activities.

The collection management group is responsible for selection of databases, the establishment and implementation of co-operative collection development in particular subject areas using Conspectus, and the generation of statistical reports. As an example of its work, a state review of doctoral programmes in history reduced their number to two – and of course the two collections supporting these programmes will be of increasing importance to the other members of the consortium. At the same time, reallocation of the funding formerly devoted to history was also discussed by the collection management group.

OhioLINK has already affected local selection decisions. Consideration of large, expensive purchases increasingly takes into account the overall network's holdings, and decisions to purchase such materials are increasingly made only after consultation with institutions who hold complementary or supplementary collections. This procedure has become part of the approval process at the administrative level. If a member institution knows what other institutions hold and can count on the actual provision of materials to readers, decisions not to duplicate are more readily justified.

As originally envisaged, the system allows readers to request books held remotely, and planned enhancements will also provide for article requests and the ability to request microform materials, rather than using a 'preferred partner' ILL system.

In considering this case study, we suggest you ask yourself:

- Using Sinclair's typology, which kind of library co-operative is this?
- Which of the six features listed above under 'Effective management' can you identify in OhioLINK?
- What features of the OhioLINK governance structure seem likely to engender success?

Review of Chapter 4

This chapter has considered the range of co-operative ventures libraries have employed to develop and share information resources, some of which are of very long standing. At the informal end, these may consist of no more than interlibrary loans and reciprocal access agreements. But technology has enabled deeper levels of sharing and interactivity. More proactive arrangements involve formal networks and consortia, and are becoming increasingly important for service delivery.

Libraries co-operate now for the reasons they always have: to provide additional material for their readers, and to assist in containing costs. But such co-operation requires overcoming barriers of delay in document delivery if the material is not in electronic form, of competition between institutions, change in institutional priorities, and shortages of resources. Against these the ever-increasing costs of acquiring materials – and the ever-increasing quantity of material available – demands for equity of access to information, and increasing capabilities of information and communications technology serve to push libraries into resource sharing.

Co-operative collection development involves shared responsibility for acquisition, collection development and maintenance. Most libraries have moved on from 'just-in-time', access-based thinking to thinking in terms of both access and ownership of core collections, despite the problems associated with deciding what is core and what peripheral. The attributes of successful resource-sharing programmes are agreed priorities, value of service, and proactive co-ordination. In turn, effective management of such schemes will rely upon committed leadership, a formal governing structure, staff participation, staff training, adequate funds, and agreed collection description guidelines.

It seems clear that consortia are the way of the future for library co-operative efforts in all areas, including the management of information resources. Well-articulated collection development policies and electronic networking will increasingly enable co-ordinated access to information content, regardless of media, as part of wider co-operative service provision. At the highest level this is reflected in the concept of the national distributed collection.

Where to now?

Before moving on to the following chapter, you may wish to consider the following questions:

- Over the last few years, many new co-operative ventures between libraries have been founded, while others have died. Can you identify some of the reasons why a venture known to you was forced to cease operation? What could have been done to address these problems?
- Now consider a newly founded consortium in your region or country. Has it attempted to address the potential barriers we have discussed in this chapter? Does it appear to have the features we suggest are required if it is to succeed?
- Do you know of a library that belongs to more than one consortium? What benefits does it gain through this, and how do the two or more consortia complement each other?

Further reading

Early in this chapter we mentioned the first detailed guide to co-operation: Paul Mosher and Marcia Pankake's 'A guide to coordinated and cooperative collection development', *Library Resources and Technical Services*, **27** (4), 1983, 417–31. While this is readily available in most libraries, a newer American guide edited by Bart Harloe takes into account recent developments and is well worth consulting: *Guide to cooperative collection development*, ALCTS Collection Management and Development Guides 6, American Library Association, 1994.

Harloe, too, is becoming dated, and there is a need for a more current, less US-focused analysis of the situation. Some of this is available in three chapters in the inaugural volume of the *International yearbook of library and information management 2000–2001: collection management*, Library Association Publishing, 2000. In 'Library purchasing consortia: their activity and effect on the marketplace', David Ball and Jo Pye described the characteristics of British consortia in four sectors (pp. 199–219), while Alicia Wise discusses the big picture of the DNER (Distributed

National Electronic Resource) and how co-ordination of a range of collection-related issues is a key to its effective development: 'Managing national distributed collections: reflections on the British experience', pp. 267–90. This chapter concludes with a brief examination of national and international distributed collections initiatives in Morocco and through the International Coalition of Library Consortia. Clare Jenkins complements this in 'Collection management initiatives in Britain', a general chapter on changes to collection management in Britain, which includes many insights into the DNER and how this is affecting co-operative activities in Britain (pp. 243–66).

As we have seen in this chapter, co-operation in collection development has detractors as well as exponents. It is important not to discount the former, for they often point to weaknesses and shortcomings that must be addressed. In our view one of the most stringent, and therefore most telling, criticisms comes from Dan Hazen in 'Cooperative collection development: compelling theory, inconsequential results?' In *Collection management for the 21st century: a handbook for librarians,*: Greenwood Press, 1997, 263–83. While his views are coloured by long experience with a particular area studies programme in the USA, he nevertheless sounds a number of warnings that apply in any arrangement in any country. Similarly, in the same collection of essays Richard Wood looks in part at 'barriers' to effective co-operation, but overall focuses on the success factors and benefits of co-operative collection development: 'The axioms, barriers, and components of cooperative collection development' (pp. 221–48). These two complementary pieces usefully round off of this chapter.

Notes

1   Association of Specialized and Cooperative Library Agencies, *Standards for cooperative multitype library organizations*, American Library Association, 1990, 1.

2   T. Sanville, 'Use levels and new models for consortial purchasing of electronic journals', *Library Consortium Management: An International Journal*, 1 (3/4), 1999, available at **www.emerald-library.com/** [18 January 2000].

3   P. McCarthy, 'Serial killers: academic libraries respond to soaring costs', *Library Journal* (15 June), 1994, 41–4. However, this ignores several factors. First, all of us know the importance of browsing. Then there is the question of the longer-term economics of publication: fewer institutional subscriptions are already resulting in greatly increased subscription costs, and further cancellations. What is cost-effective for a single institution may not be so for the system as a whole – the classic situation where co-operative action is required.

4   See, for example, the article on site licensing at National Chiao Tung University in Taiwan by H. Ke and R. Chang, 'Resource sharing digital libraries: a case study of Taiwan's InfoSpring Digital Library Project', *Library Collections, Acquisitions and Technical Services*, **24**, 2000, 371–7. The InfoSpring Digital Library Project at National Chiao Tung University provides mirror sites in Taiwan for well-known reference databases and full-text electronic journals. By means of resource sharing, universities and industries in Taiwan can access the databases loaded in the InfoSpring Digital Library under certain subscription agreements. See also Y. Chen, 'Towards a new paradigm of resource sharing: the partnership between a mirror site and consortium in Taiwan', *Library Consortium Management: An International Journal*, **2** (8), 2000, 190–7.

5   G. E. Evans, *Developing library and information center collections*, 4th edn, Libraries Unlimited, 2000, 463–75.

6   See 'Challenge of the future: the Asia-Pacific experience [An interview with Dr Gary Gorman]', *Intelligence*, **3**, 1999, 7–12, which looks at this issue from the perspective of libraries in the Asian region.

7   J. J. Branin, 'Cooperative collection development'. In C. B. Osburn and R. W. Atkinson (eds), *Collection management: a new treatise*, Foundations in Library and Information Science, vol. 26A, JAI Press, 1991, 83. See also D. H. Stam, 'Collaborative collection development: progress, problems and potential'. In B-C. Sellen and A. Curley (eds), *The collection building reader*, Neal-Schuman Publishers, 1992, 201–7.

8   T. H. Ballard, 'Public library networking: neat, plausible, wrong', *Library Journal*, **107** (1 April), 1982, 679–83; T. H. Ballard, *Failure of resource sharing in public libraries and alternative strategies for service*, American Library Association, 1986.

9   R. M. Dougherty, 'A conceptual framework for organizing resource sharing and shared collection development programs', *Journal of Academic Librarianship*, **4**, 1988, 288.

10 Ibid.

11 Branin, op. cit., 82

12 P. H. Mosher and M. Pankake, 'A guide to coordinated and cooperative collection development', *Library Resources and Technical Services*, **27** (4), 1983, 419–20.

13 Branin, op. cit., 12.

14 M. A. Keller, 'Foreign acquisitions in North American research libraries', *FOCUS on the Center for Research Libraries*, **12** (4), 1992, special insert.

15 Branin, op. cit., 105.

16 See Ke and Chang, op. cit. One spin-off of the InfoSpring Project has been a consortium to decide which databases ought to be hosted in Taiwan and to negotiate competitive prices with information providers

17 The Association of American Publishers is on record as viewing sharing under ILL arrangements as 'systematic' copying and therefore illegal. See *Statement of the Association of American Publishers on commercial and fee-based document delivery*, Association of American Publishers, 1992.

18 D. Ball and J. Pye, 'Library purchasing consortia: their activity and effect on the marketplace'. In G. E. Gorman (ed.), *International yearbook of library and information management 2000–2001: collection management*, Library Association Publishing, 2000, 213–16.

19 B. Harloe and J. M. Budd, 'Collection development and scholarly communication in the era of electronic access', *Journal of Academic Librarianship*, **20** (2), 1994, 83–7; J. M. Budd and B. Harloe, 'Collection development and scholarly communication in the 21st century: from collection management to content management'. In G. E. Gorman and R. H. Miller (eds), *Collection management for the 21st century: a handbook for librarians*, Greenwood Press, 1997, 3–25.

20 M. Sinclair, 'A typology of library cooperatives', *Special Libraries*, **64** (4), 1973, 181–6.

21 Evans, op. cit., 458.

22 R. Wade, 'The very model of a modern library consortium', *Library Consortium Management* **1** (1/2), 1999, available at **www.emerald-library.com/** [18 January 2001]. See also G. E. Gorman and R. Cullen, 'Models and opportunities for library co-operation in the Asian region', *Library Management*, **21** (6/7), 2000, 373–84, available at **www.emerald-library.com/** [20 April 2001].

23 Wade, loc. cit.

24 Ibid.

25 This case study is based on G. N. Dannelly, 'Cooperation is the future of collection management and development: OhioLINK and CIC'. In G. E. Gorman and R. H. Miller (eds), *Collection management for the 21st century: a handbook for librarians*, Greenwood Press, 1997, 249–62. See Dannelly's chapter for full details of the project.

5
Selection: policies and procedures

Focus questions

- Should libraries provide access to what clients say they want, or to what librarians believe they need?
- When is a decision *not* to select, censorship?
- What are some distinctive features of the various library environments in which selection takes place?
- What are some common strategies that assist in the selection process?
- What are the standard selection criteria that apply in most situations?
- What factors should a library take into account in choosing the format in which to acquire an item? Are electronic formats different?
- Why is bibliographic checking essential?

Selection of resources is one of the critical professional tasks of the librarian – as important as cataloguing or information service, for of what value are these if there are not information sources available? Selection has long been a topic of professional discussion, enabling consideration of current issues associated with digital data and the internet to be placed in a well-understood framework.

The dilemma of selection – needs and wants

In the third edition of *Developing library and information center collections* and also at **http://lib.lmu.edu/dlc4** Edward Evans presents a detailed summary of what he terms the 'theory' of selection based on 11 major textbooks published between 1925 and 1985.[1] The principles in this extended analysis can be summarized in very few words:

either need versus want, or quality versus demand. From this dichotomy stem the key principles on which responsible and responsive selection is built.

The first principle is that the reader is the central focus of selection, the *raison d'être* on which collection development and information services are built. While one information professional may argue that the selection of library materials should aim at providing users with exactly what they want, another might maintain with equal conviction that the library should qualify this approach by selecting the best material available that meets the users' demands. A third librarian may go further, stating that the library should select simply the best there is without worrying about demand.

To state that libraries and information services exist to serve their clients and that selection is based on the principle of meeting users' needs and wants is simple enough, but several difficult questions arise from this straightforward principle:

- What precisely are these needs and wants?
- Who is responsible for articulating them?
- What is the correct balance between satisfying needs and wants?

There has long been discussion about whether libraries should provide access to what clients say they 'want', or to what professionally trained librarians believe clients should have – what they are thought to 'need'. A clear summary of the 'want versus need' debate was provided some years ago by Robert Broadus, who set out the case for selecting what clients say that they want under five basic arguments:

1 A librarian does not have the right to impose personal views about what is best for users.
2 People should be provided with what they will use, not with materials that will sit on shelves unread.
3 Collecting what people want does not automatically mean that only one level of quality will be the result, because users are different enough that their wants will result in a broad range of qualities.
4 If users financially support the library, they have a right to determine exactly what goes into the collection.
5 Giving people exactly what they want ensures that they will read, and this helps to build an important habit.[2]

The case for providing what users are thought to need, rather than what they say they want, was summarized by Broadus as:

1 The library has an obligation to meet user needs by supplying high-quality materials.
2 The library has a positive obligation to educate its users, and it does this by exerting constructive influence on thought and attitudes.
3 The library is not in competition with newsagents and bookshops, both of which supply what readers want very effectively.
4 The library ought to be improving the reading tastes of its users, and it can do this by providing information that otherwise might not be available or not be chosen.
5 Without motivation, public reading tastes on the whole are remarkably mundane and disinclined toward 'the best' in any field.

Both sides of the issue have been argued with equal conviction, and no one has yet proposed an argument from either perspective that is totally convincing. Each information professional must reach an independent decision and take a clear position in the need versus want debate; and this position will determine to a great extent what one selects for the collection. A flexible position attempting to incorporate the strengths of both arguments might draw on the following points:

- The library exists to serve its users and therefore must take account of what they say they want.
- But if the librarian selects only what users want, these people are not being given a chance to improve their knowledge and tastes.
- If presented with qualitatively superior materials along with exactly what they say they want, users may begin to appreciate and use the former.
- The library, to facilitate its recreational, informational and educational objectives, has an obligation to cater to all tastes, both high and low.
- The librarian as a professional selector should be trusted both to select high-quality materials in accordance with user needs and to supply their stated wants.

The dilemma can be resolved in part by going back to the purposes of the library or of the institution of which it is a part. Academic, research and special libraries try to provide access to good-quality materials only, whether suggested by their clients or by library staff, traditionally on the basis of objective recommendations. These libraries tend to provide the information their (expert) clients say they want. On the other hand, a school library needs to provide information resources which educate and inform, and which can contribute to the personal growth and development of its pupils. It will provide access to high-quality materials, but a wise teacher-librarian will also include some popular items (including, famously, Enid Blyton in the anglophone world) to encourage reluctant readers as well. The same applies to the public library – a balance must be found. Indeed, the resolution of this long-standing debate lies in finding a balance between these two viewpoints, which takes into account the purposes of the library and the institution it may serve.

Ideally selection should be:

- related to a collection development policy
- based upon a knowledge of the library, its present collection resources, and its clients
- where possible, based on subject knowledge, either through formal training in an area or through long acquaintance with it.

Basic requirements for effective selection

It is possible to subsume the 'need versus want' debate on selection into the famous Five Laws of librarianship propounded by the noted Indian librarian, S. R. Ranganathan (1892–1972). These laws, discussed in his work, *Library book selection*, are as follows:

- Books are for use.
- Every reader his book.
- Every book its reader.
- Save the reader's time.
- A library is a growing organism.[3]

The implications of these laws are clearly far-reaching, and everyone involved in selection needs to have a strong commitment to them as they relate to the selection process. In the end that commitment is more important than any number of procedures, allocations of responsibility, policy statements, complaint-handling systems or collections of selection tools.

Using Ranganathan's Five Laws, we can propose a number of general principles governing selection. These are presented here as starting points for developing one's own basic guidelines for effective selection.

1 The selection process is related to other professional activities and is dependent on them both for policy decisions and practical procedures. Selection is part

of the overall collection management process and must be viewed in this perspective.

2 One should update professional competence by regular reading in the library of literature concerning the principles and practices of collection management, selection, publishing, reviewing and acquisitions.

3 One must have an intimate knowledge of the library's purpose, its collections and its user groups. These are the key factors in effective, responsible selection of library materials.

4 A good selector will develop a sound understanding of how the publishing industry and the book trade operate; this includes how library materials of all types and in all formats are generated, distributed and sold.

5 One should become fully familiar with the publishing policies, advertising media, publicity outlets, names of senior editors and general reliability of those publishers whose lists are most directly relevant to the library's collection management requirements.

6 One should become fully familiar with the key reviewing media and should read reviews regularly in order to keep abreast of critical opinion on books and other library materials.

7 One should become fully familiar with trade and national bibliographies and their developing online equivalents, and should understand their strengths and weaknesses with regard to the library's requirements.

8 One should always be prepared to make well-informed, independent judgements regarding selection of materials for one's library, as the competent professional is in the best position to determine the right materials for the specific collection and its users.

Censorship

In the professional activity of selecting materials for collections, whether in print or electronic formats, the issue of selection versus censorship is a fundamental concern. The selection process is one in which the information professional makes informed decisions about what to bring into a collection, either by ownership or access. Selectors 'apply normative criteria as they compare materials and choose to include items'.[4] The philosophy underpinning this process is one of service to the community by providing free and open access to the widest possible range of information resources.

The 'philosophy' of the censor – if there is one – is entirely different, as Jenkinson has pointed out.[5] Rather than looking for what might be included, the censor looks for what might be excluded and seeks reasons to justify the removal of items from a collection, or their non-selection in the first place. Censors want collections to include only items that represent a particular, and preferred, point of view, while the selector seeks materials that represent a wide range of community views. The selector looks principally within the resources for criteria to justify their inclusion in a collection; the censor often looks outside the resources for reasons to exclude them – community views, the author's political affiliation, the reaction of powerful lobby groups, etc.

It is important to recognize that censorship is not an unchanging source of tension for the selector. As Higgins rightly opines,

> Like a chameleon, the issue of censorship in collection management policies has changed colour and shape not only because the contribution of domestic cultural capital is poorly understood, but also because electronic resources have alerted us to international cultures which are understood even less.[6]

She quite rightly indicates that both the internationalization of the resource base of libraries and the digitization of resources have caused censorship to evolve in quite unexpected ways. On the one hand, the internet has acted as a powerful force for freedom of expression – so much so, that general access to it is not permitted or is tightly controlled in several developing countries.

There are indeed practical difficulties with internet censorship:

- Access control programs (such as Net Nanny) work badly, and routinely deny access to innocent and useful materials. Pity the poor nursing student saddled with such a program, and who has to search for material on breast cancer.
- Most sites are in another national jurisdiction – especially if one is not working in the USA – and some appear out of any national jurisdiction; hence if problems arise any redress or control is either difficult or impossible.
- Legislative initiatives requiring restrictions on access to sites deemed offensive have been found ineffective (as in a recent court case in Germany, where America Online was held not to be responsible for material accessed through that network).

On the other hand, and despite the long-standing predilection of our profession, there *is* some case for limiting access to the information resources available through the internet:

- There is clearly a great deal of incorrect or potentially misleading information available, which is of genuine concern in areas such as health.
- While some access to pornography appears to require payment by credit card (or so we are informed by our students: we cheerfully claim no expertise in this area), many people have accidentally stumbled onto (or been sent) unwelcome material, and children especially appear at risk.
- Socially undesirable information (for example, on bomb making) is also available. Of course, what seems socially undesirable will vary from country to country, from culture to culture (and from government to government) – precisely the point being made by Higgins.

It is interesting to note that the possible solutions draw upon principles underlying traditional collection practice. They include training readers in the critical assessment of information – based very much on the 'criteria for selection' we suggest later in this chapter. In other words, information literacy has to encompass 'net literacy'. Every literate member of a global society has to have some skills in assessing the credibility of information.

Another strategy is known as the recommended sites approach, and looks very much like positive selection: instead of banning sites (such as with Net Nanny), libraries, librarians and educators should recommend useful sites. Such sites themselves will incorporate links to known, useful and credible sites. Children, students and indeed all readers with any specific information need will soon discover that these lead much more quickly and easily to usable information. The alternative is all too frequently the general search using a web browser which, as noted in Chapter 1, can yield hundreds, thousands or even millions of irrelevant hits.

One final strategy often suggested for the school or public library is to place the internet-enabled terminals in a public area of the library, so that their use is also publicly visible. It could be argued that this is the spacial equivalent of addressing censorship in a collection development policy: of making it a public and discussible issue. There is consensus in the profession that, whatever the difficulties, censorship itself must remain a public and discussible issue.

The selection environment

Whatever the library, and whatever the form in which the information comes, selection takes place within a common set of parameters. These include the library's existing collections, its present and anticipated readers, and its budget and staffing. Its collection development policy, if one exists, sits within these parameters and should specify, among other things, who should undertake selection and on what bases. The answers to these questions will vary from type of library to type of library, but common threads are frequently apparent. These include:

- standard, traditional selection criteria, including that resources should be up to date, available at a reasonable price, be of an appropriate academic or intellectual level, be authoritative and accurate, and relevant to the mission of the library
- criteria for different types of media
- professional oversight of selection recommendations, even where (as in universities) these are apparently delegated to clients who have significant subject expertise
- client input to selection decisions, even where (as in schools) professional staff appear to carry total responsibility for selection
- stated reliance on published reviews and other expert assessments.

How the mix varies can be seen in the following discussion of the selection environment in each type of library.

Public libraries

Ranging from major metropolitan library collections to a few hundred volumes in small village libraries, the collections of public libraries all share a common characteristic – diversity. Because user groups in the public library range across the entire social, cultural and economic spectrum, the selection of materials must reflect and cater to this diversity. The responsive public library will work to meet the educational, informational and recreational requirements of the full range of age groups, educational levels, cultures and interests represented in its service area. In practice this means that educational and informational needs are at least matched by recreational requirements, with this last category receiving more attention than in other types of libraries. Consequently, current titles produced by trade publishers receive the greatest emphasis in public library selection, as these materials are most suited to the general interests of the community.

Most selection in the public library is done by the librarian, and it is not unusual for the senior librarians to do virtually all of the selecting. It is more the norm, though, for the chief librarian to rely on input from other librarians, including those serving branches and mobile services. Occasionally this democratization of selection extends to the formation of a selection committee, but for a variety of reasons this approach has never been popular outside North America. It is an unwieldy system: consensus is difficult to achieve; regular meetings prove almost impossible to arrange; representation of all user interests creates too large a committee; and responsibility for selection is removed from the information professional, who after all is trained in this procedure. Still, in the literature (principally from North America) this method is often defended on the ground that it involves both local authority and community members, with positive ramifications in two areas:

- Justification of expenditure is easier if the local authority has been involved from the outset.
- Library materials are more easily defended against challenges if members of the community have been involved in their selection.

Indeed complaints about library materials tend to occur more in public libraries than in almost any other environment, and criticism is as likely to come from local government officials as from the general public. Therefore, selection in public libraries takes greater account of public sensitivity to issues and subjects than in most other types of libraries. In practice this means heavy reliance not only on positive reviews in trustworthy sources but also on careful examination of titles received on approval or by purchase. Although this may apply especially to children's materials, it should also be an important consideration in juvenile and adult materials involving race, gender, politics and religion.

Because speed of supply is essential in order to meet user demand generated by advertising and reviews in the popular press and other media, public libraries tend to make heavy use of approval plans, visits by publishers' representatives, trade literature promotions and timely reviews in the mass circulation magazines and newspapers. All of these permit rapid, often first-hand, evaluation, and this helps to ensure that materials are acquired before or while they are being sought by users. Other selection procedures such as standing orders, browsing in bookshops and use of the standard library selection tools more generally aid in selecting educational and informational materials.

School libraries

If public libraries have a particular concern for the community's recreational requirements, then school libraries have a special commitment to the educational needs of students and curriculum support for teachers. If public libraries are characterized by heterogeneous user populations, then school libraries may be said to serve relatively homogeneous user groups. These groups also form a captive audience, since students should read what is selected for the curriculum by teachers and librarians. Selecting educational materials for an identifiable range of students engaged in a specific set of curriculum activities may appear relatively simple, but there are once again a number of variables to be considered.

First, children have a range of educational needs and abilities, whether at primary or secondary level; all of these needs and abilities must receive attention if the library is to serve its developmental function in the educational process. In addition to the students, of course, teachers and administrators have some right to expect curriculum support and other professional materials in the school library, and this expectation adds yet another level to be considered.

Second, a wide range of subjects and disciplines must be covered in a school library, from such areas as literature and history to science and technical or practical subjects. Third, school libraries tend to have a greater variety of materials in their libraries because of the heavy reliance on audiovisual and multimedia materials in teaching. Therefore, the subject range, educational needs and levels and formats are all sufficiently broad to make selection a difficult and time-consuming activity in school libraries.

To this extent school and public libraries may be rather similar, but in selection procedures they differ significantly. Few school libraries rely as heavily on the librarian to do most of the selecting as is the case in public libraries. Instead the teaching staff provide substantial input in terms of both selecting and evaluating materials. In addition, in some schools the administrators and, to a limited extent, students are encouraged to become involved in the selection of materials. Occasionally (but again rarely outside North America) this range of selectors is formalized into a committee, but normally the teacher-librarian relies on a more informal arrangement and retains the final decision on selection. The additional variable here, of course, is the school head or deputy, who often exercises significant control over what is selected.

Obviously the problem of challenged materials can be difficult in school libraries because of the youth of the readers and the involvement of parents in their reading. This suggests that collection development policies and statements of selection procedures should have a major place in school libraries, as they should in public libraries. Many more teacher-librarians, therefore, should pay attention to developing formal policy statements and perhaps to establishing selection advisory committees to help defuse censorship before it becomes an issue.

Selectors in school libraries rely heavily on published reviews, and there are several reviewing journals catering specifically to materials for children and young adults. Teacher-librarians often find reviews a useful selection guide because they provide expert assessment of materials and also because teachers rarely have time to analyse materials themselves. In addition to published reviews, school librarians in Britain and elsewhere rely on recommendations and evaluations by teachers, on approval plans and other means of previewing materials. Previewing, in fact, plays a greater role in selection in this environment because of the amount of non-print material acquired for school libraries.

Academic libraries

When speaking of academic libraries, one encompasses a very broad range of collections. Some, such as those serving institutions largely devoted to teaching in specialist areas such as engineering or medicine, cover relatively few subjects; others, notably the main libraries of the older universities, cater to a very wide range of disciplines at levels ranging from first-year undergraduate to postdoctoral research. Levels of readership are also likely to vary considerably, from first-year undergraduates to the most advanced researchers. Nevertheless, the academic library sector embraces all of these variations, and this must be kept in mind when thinking about selection.

While the user community in an academic library may appear to be heterogeneous in terms of the range of subjects studied – even a smaller university is likely to offer hundreds of subjects in several degree programmes – it is in fact relatively homogeneous within itself and has definable boundaries of reading interests. That is, disciplines are being studied at specific levels, from basic undergraduate to advanced research, and both disciplines and levels can be determined with some accuracy from the institution's clearly defined teaching activities. There is generally substantial documentation upon which selectors can draw for information about user interests and needs: institutional handbooks, course syllabi, research reports, etc. Expert staff are also far more available for consultation than in, say, a national library context.

Selection in academic libraries has a number of characteristics that set it apart from other types of libraries. First, these libraries deal more intensively as a matter of course with the international book trade. While – at least for libraries in the English-speaking world – western Europe and North America are their primary foci, many also select widely from Asian, African, Latin American and Pacific sources. This means that the selection resources must be representative not only of all subject areas but also of various regions.

Second, languages tend not to be a limiting factor in academic libraries. Public libraries with multicultural user groups and special libraries in science and technology will have some foreign language materials, as of course will those in non-English-language-speaking countries, but it is the academic libraries that collect most heavily in foreign languages, either in support of specific language-linked programmes or because a reasonable percentage of users can read materials in other languages.

Third, academic libraries on the whole use a broader and more detailed range of selection tools. Trade publications, national bibliographies, reviewing journals, scholarly journals, indexing services – these and more are used in the normal course of events by selectors in academic libraries.

Fourth, selection is less the preserve of professional librarians in academic libraries than in any other type. In most instances it is the academic staff who are expected to have the greatest input in the selection process. The assumption is that academics, as experts in their disciplines, are also experts in the most suitable literature in these disciplines. While one may question this assumption and cite the example of subject or area studies librarians who act as selectors (or indeed cite academics who appear spectacularly out of touch with parts of their discipline), the norm is for selection to be largely out of professional hands. The librarians in academic libraries tend to select for non-circulating collections (reference works) and to monitor the selection by academic units.

This monitoring procedure can be formalized by the appointment of discipline or departmental liaison librarians. These individuals have responsibility for selecting material not specifically recommended by the academic staff and for ensuring that balance is maintained within their particular subject areas. They bring to the notice of the academic staff material considered of value and interest, in the hope that the academics will select appropriate materials for the collection.

While this helps to give the library a degree of control over selection, it is really through allocation of funds to departments, schools and faculties that most effective control is exercised. While the funds may be specifically for acquisitions, there are also implications for selection if librarians, when monitoring expenditure, can suggest that items are excessively costly or that a high percentage of the fund is being spent on only a small range of specific topics in a discipline.

Special libraries

In most countries special libraries form the largest, most disparate and least easily identified group of libraries. They range from small collections in a single room of a commercial firm or professional body to the multi-branch scientific and technical libraries of major industrial enterprises or government ministries. Also included in this group are a number of academic libraries which, because of the highly specialized nature of their collections, have the narrow subject focus more typical of special than academic libraries.

The narrow subject focus typical of such collections is matched in most cases by currency of holdings (except in special academic or research institute libraries). On the whole items in the working collection of a special library tend to be no older than 25–30 years, although some older materials may be held but relegated to closed-access storage. Also, a high proportion of the collection is devoted to serial titles – as much as 80% in libraries with a scientific or technical orientation. As in academic libraries, these collections can be characterized by a significant proportion of foreign-language materials.

These characteristics of special library collections, along with modest overall size in most instances, suggest a number of features common to selection for such libraries. In many cases the library will employ only one information professional, and even in larger institutions collection management is not likely to be in the hands of a professional appointed for that specific purpose. The librarian tends to be a subject specialist, either by training or through experience, as it is assumed that a professional with intimate knowledge of the field will be the best person to understand both reader needs and their information requests. These specialists, as in academic libraries, rely heavily on readers to suggest items for selection. Unlike colleagues elsewhere they are unable to rely much on standard selection tools, because they are either not specialized or not current enough. Information from publishers and suppliers and reliance on indexing and abstracting sources play a higher than usual role in selecting materials for such in-depth collections.

A final but most significant characteristic of selection in special libraries is the reliance on intimate, often relatively informal, knowledge of user information requirements. Because user profiles are so specialized, the information manager necessarily constructs a unique and detailed picture of each user's information needs much more readily than in other information settings. In libraries offering special dissemination services, including regular online searches and SDI (Selective Dissemination of Information), these profiles may be developed as part of a formal procedure; in other instances they may result from the librarian's daily contact with the users.

Selection strategies

Selection in most information settings is on an item-by-item basis, with selectors choosing specific titles from a variety of secondary bibliographic, previewing and reviewing sources. At the same time, though, a certain amount of selection can be 'automated' and delegated to various agencies in the book trade by a variety of means, most usually approval plans, blanket orders and standing orders. All of these have a selection function in that suppliers do the selecting in accordance with a specific profile, and thus give collection managers additional time for the business of item-by-item selection. They are, in effect, a type of outsourcing, and are considered next.

Approval plans

In this method of selecting and acquiring materials the library develops in association with a vendor a detailed profile of the library's requirements in specific areas plus budgetary limits, and depends on the supplier to select and regularly supply materials within the parameters indicated. The library then evaluates the materials supplied and returns those that it feels are unsuitable. Given the expense involved in administering approval plans, it is to the advantage of both library and supplier to have a profile that is extremely accurate and detailed, and for this reason a written collection development policy is often the basis of a suitable profile. When a plan is functioning effectively there will be few or no returns, although it is an advantage that the library does have the right to evaluate and return any item supplied. From the library's standpoint, then, an approval plan is a means of selecting on the basis of first-hand evaluation, which is often not possible in other purchase methods. From the vendor's viewpoint, it is a way of increasing sales by providing libraries with a package including materials that might otherwise be overlooked (and, of course, also of tying a customer to that vendor's service). Vendors have also claimed that per-item costs may be lower, but there seems no definite evidence of this.

However, in gaining these potential benefits, a library runs the risk that the vendor will supply what is convenient and to hand, rather than what may be of most value to the library. Experience with approval plans suggests that little is returned, probably not so much because what was supplied was appropriate as because the receiving library, not having the staff to supervise selection in the first place, also does not have the time to examine what is supplied. A further problem is that it is difficult to know whether any particular item will be included under the selection plan: should another copy of a wanted title be ordered, just in case?

At the very least, establishing an approval plan requires extensive consultation between library and vendor – should reprints be included? Will some items also be received on standing order? Some years ago the Canadian supplier, John Coutts, suggested that a worthwhile Canadian approval plan would involve the expenditure of at least C$20,000 per annum, so this strategy is unlikely to be of value to smaller or less-well-resourced libraries. Construction of a profile will hardly be possible outside the framework of a collection development policy.

New titles announcement services provide an alternative to the physical supply of titles that may or may not be especially relevant. The vendor sends a list of possible items to the library, which then selects – or arranges for its clients to select – those of interest. Many suppliers offer such a service, several combining it with a library profile so that only details of titles likely to be relevant are sent to the library.

In addition to the obvious advantage of allowing evaluation of an item before acquisition, approval plans save the library time and money that would be absorbed by the selection of a single item and the subsequent generation of an individual order. Theoretically they are also able to provide materials more quickly. However, this implies that the vendor is doing his job well, which may not always be the case. In every case the library must be prepared to monitor the approval plan, and this means having an effective monitoring programme rather than an ad hoc evaluation system. Monitoring, of course, costs time and money, and there is little information on the actual costs of this as compared with item-by-item selection.

When monitoring, one must be on the lookout for what the plan excludes as well as what it includes, remembering that the sense of security engendered by a market-oriented supplier may result in potentially wanted materials that are not supplied being out of print by the time they come to the library's attention. This raises the other major problem with approval plans: they may supply more than the library expects, or they may supply less. On the whole, however, the continuing popularity of this method suggests that, given an appropriate profile and adequate monitoring, it can function reasonably well.

Blanket orders

Both blanket orders and standing orders (the latter described in the next section) are less thoroughly defined than approval plans. The former tend to operate with the larger trade publishers, while the latter are usually limited to smaller specialist publishers; but there are other differences that distinguish these two types of services. In a blanket order agreement the library usually does not offer the supplier or publisher a profile. Rather, the collection manager instructs the vendor to supply every title in a specific subject area, within a specific price range, in a specific form or genre (all trade books, all fiction, etc.), in a certain language, from a specific geographical region or other variable of the library's choosing. The library sets these fairly broad parameters and relies on the supplier to provide titles accordingly. Traditionally blanket orders have not carried the right of return, and this tends to remain the case with publisher-operated plans. Other suppliers (agents, for example) permit a limited return privilege with some blanket order agreements.

There are two major advantages of blanket orders. First, they carry a very high discount for titles (typically no less than 30–35%), and this combined with the savings made compared with the cost of an item-by-item order makes such a selection method very attractive. Second, blanket orders on the whole operate efficiently in terms of getting titles to libraries soon after their publication. On the other hand a blanket order agreement, like an approval plan, requires monitoring, with the attendant costs and time involved. Also the general lack of return privileges and the trade publication focus of this method mean that it is not suitable for all types of libraries. In particular, blanket orders are less used by academic and special libraries, both of which rely more on standing orders.

Standing orders

Similar in intention to blanket orders, a standing order is used most often in two specific situations: where a continuation or a series in a specific field is likely to be of ongoing interest to the library, or secondly where a publisher has such a specific list that the library would probably select every item anyway. Such publishers are generally technical or professional, but can also include government agencies and international organizations. While such an arrangement may carry a limited right of return, on the whole this is not the case. Instead a unit price discount (often in the 30% range) may be offered if the library places a standing order with the publisher or supplier.

The assumption in the case of standing orders for continuations or series titles is that all items will be up to the standard of the title that generated the standing order – but of course this is not always the case. Today many libraries that traditionally have been important standing order buyers, particularly academic and special libraries, no longer use this selection method but prefer to order on an item-by-item basis. Recognizing this, some publishers and suppliers now operate standing orders with on-approval privileges. Here the library places an order for a series or continuation, and the supplier offers right of return. The disadvantage, of course, is that this arrangement may not carry the same discount as a straight standing order. It must be remembered, too, that standing orders must be monitored in the same way as serial subscriptions, and this adds to the cost. On the whole the second type of standing orders, to specialist publishers for all of their titles, seems to involve fewer problems as their subject focus is unlikely to change.

Approval plans, blanket orders and standing orders are effective selection devices as long as they provide materials within the library's collection profile in a timely and accurate manner. When monitoring indicates that any automatic selection procedure is functioning inefficiently, it is important that the library act to renegotiate or cancel the agreement. It is worth remembering that these procedures are not soft options but rather are meant to save time, and thus money, which can be spent elsewhere. When for any reason they begin costing more time or money than item-by-item selection, they no longer have a role as selection aids.

Criteria for selection

In developing sets of criteria to be used by selectors, there is a tendency for writers to be too thorough. They seem to forget that collection managers often do their selecting quickly and on the basis of limited evidence. Even David Spiller, in his standard text on book selection, suggests a rather large number of criteria and factors to be taken into consideration.[7] Some go much further, with the pinnacle achieved by Kenneth Whittaker, who devotes an entire (though now dated) textbook to the methods and sources for assessing books.[8] All of this detail he condenses into an appendix of seven broad criteria, but these are broken down into 50 subcategories. Whittaker's seven categories, rather different from Spiller's, are: people, plan, contents, organization, design, production and placing.

Experienced collection managers accept that this substantial list of categories is indicative rather than practical. While the beginner may wish to begin with such a detailed listing in order to develop a thorough understanding of selection practices, the reality is that such an approach obscures the goal of selection with a confusing plethora of criteria. Instead it may be productive to consider a much smaller set under six headings: authority of creators, scope, treatment and level, arrangement, format, special consideration or features.

Authority of creators

Here one is concerned with the qualifications and reputation of those who have created the material – authors, editors, publishers and, in the case of audiovisual materials, producers. To understand their suitability as producers of a given title one seeks answers to a range of questions:

- What are the author's qualifications, and has he or she written other works in the same area?
- What is the author's reputation as indicated in the reception of his or her other publications?
- How reputable is the publisher, and is it known as a producer of works in this particular field?

In these days of diminishing staff resources we doubt that everyone will have the luxury of seeking reviews for each individual item to be ordered. For some libraries without close and ongoing links with their clients – national libraries, perhaps public libraries – this is of course still appropriate. Others will only seek reviews for items about which there appears some doubt.

Instead, many experienced selectors look first of all at the publisher's name. All publishers build up reputations, good or bad: good publishers build up a reputation for publishing first-rate material in a particular area or areas. How do they do this? Their editors themselves have (or acquire) expertise in that area, and only accept material that will add to their reputation: they are building up a strong 'list' of publications in that area. Academic publishers – such as Academic Press – do this formally through 'refereeing': manuscripts are sent out to known experts in a field for confidential review and a recommendation on whether to publish, or if to publish, possible improvements the author may need to make. In effect, then, the top publishers in an area act as a filtering mechanism. Hence we associate Oxford University Press with quality reference titles, Phaidon with art, and so on. Lesser publishers – or publishers venturing into a new area – may also have a worthwhile title to offer. However, the chances are that an expert or attractive author will first try to have his or her work accepted by a major, recognized publisher in the area. New publishers and those with lesser reputations will get offered many titles rejected elsewhere (unfortunately, the laws of libel preclude us from suggesting the names of some publishers who seem to specialize in publishing such reject material).

From all this two simple recommendations flow, which are second nature to any expert collections manager:

- Never look at a work without also noticing its publisher. Soon, you will automatically associate publishers with both subject areas and with their general level of quality.

- Always examine, however briefly, the material your own library is purchasing
  – again, noting the publisher as well as the subject area and apparent quality.

As well as the publisher's name, the name and affiliations of an author can also provide an indication of his or her likely expertise. Publishers' advertising material will also provide an indication, of course, and may even include extracts from (favourable) reviews. As noted in the following chapter, almost all publishers now have internet home pages. These not only provide details of all their publications, as in their traditional printed catalogues, but are normally more up to date and often allow interactive search facilities. Certainly any note on the intended market for a title may indicate whether or not it could be suitable for your library.

Scope

Here one is concerned with the breadth and depth of coverage in the work, including both intended and actual coverage. What does the work set out to do, and does it achieve this? Is it meant to be a detailed analysis of the subject addressed, or is it meant to present a broad overview? Is it meant to be exhaustive or selective in its coverage? To determine this one examines the introduction and contents, comparing the work with titles of similar scope; or at least one relies on a surrogate, normally a review, which provides this information.

Treatment and level

One expects the scope to be treated in a way that is appropriate to the work's intended audience. Who, according to the author, is most likely to read the work? To see whether the audience intention is achieved, one looks for content that is pitched at the right level and that talks neither down to nor above the reader. This is best assessed by looking at the language, illustrations, reader aids and overall user friendliness of the work in terms of table of contents, bibliography, notes and index.

Arrangement

Treatment and level lead naturally to arrangement. Here one looks at the organization of content, paying special attention to both content and format. In particular how clearly set out is the development of ideas, and how logically does the author present a case? The material should be arranged in a way that facilitates the development of the text. Access to information should be facilitated by such features as a table of contents, bibliographic references and an index where appropriate. In other words is the arrangement (topical, chronological, biographical, etc.) suitable to the subject, and is access promoted by appropriate retrieval features?

Format

This component in the overall impression made by a work figures in several of the preceding categories, but it is also important enough to warrant consideration on its own, particularly when assessing non-book material. In particular one is concerned with technical and aesthetic considerations. Has the material been produced to a high standard physically, and is it likely to stand up to substantial use? Paper, print and binding in the case of book materials should be evaluated; one expects an item under consideration for a library collection to be physically durable yet presented in an aesthetically acceptable manner. Are the illustrations appropriate and produced to a high standard? Is the typeface clear and appropriate to the text? In the case of audiovisual materials, is the quality of sound and visual imagery clear and appropriately expressive?

How does a selector choose between the traditional print format, the multimedia, or the electronic version? In many cases, of course, there is no choice: the information is available only in a single format. In many other cases, alternatives to traditional formats are unrealistically priced. But what about the case where a real choice does exist? Noting that 'the information world is about content' not format, Demas has some straightforward words of advice on choice of an appropriate format:

- Identify information content that has value.
- Determine the nature of use it will receive, level of access required, and degree of longevity desired.
- Find the format(s) that best achieve these requirements.[9]

Take, for example, reference material. Directories that are superseded annually and then discarded will be better in electronic format, if available. Periodical indexing and abstracting services are so much more usable in electronic format (on CD-ROM, for example, with its searching options), that it may be appropriate to pay a premium to replace hard-copy versions. On the other hand, material that may be physically circulated outside the library, and most of all material for which long-term retention is desired, may sometimes be better in traditional formats. The library's collection development policy should give clear guidance on the relevant factors to take into account. A decision based on the particular needs of a particular library can then be made – but let that decision be an informed one, not one made in ignorance of the alternatives available.

In sum, the advantages of print-based media normally include:

- readability
- portability
- markupability
- affordability
- durability
- archivability.

In contrast the advantages of digital media normally include:

- accessibility
- immediacy
- currency
- searchability
- linkability
- interactivity.[10]

In choosing electronic resources, such as CD-ROMs or subscribed databases, one needs to take into account not only the traditional selection criteria (coverage, accuracy, timeliness, cost, etc.) but also such questions as:

- whether to provide non-networked, LAN, or internet access
- how many concurrent users or ports are required
- whether passwords or something like proxy server authorization is needed
- whether licensing agreements should or can be negotiated singly or by consortia
- whether to carry the print as well as an online version
- how user friendly the retrieval engine is
- choices of database features to be included
- means of archiving.[11]

Internet resources constitute one of the newer areas for collection management, but they, too, need to be carefully compared and evaluated, selected and presented in a coherent manner if they are to be accessible and useful to a library's readers. Three articles recommend criteria by which these resources may be evaluated.[12] These include:

- quality or value
- ease of use
- content or coverage
- cost
- hardware and software requirements
- currency, frequency of updates
- user knowledge required
- expertise of producers
- relation to other resources
- format
- copyright considerations
- stability and reliability.

In summary, most writers discussing not internet resources specifically but the larger area of electronic resources generally accept that many of the same criteria used to select traditional materials are appropriate for electronic resources.[13] However, 'selecting electronic information resources is inherently more complex than traditional print resources since they involve analyzing many other issues such as equipment, space, trade-offs with other resources, technical support, and vendor support'.[14]

Special considerations or special features

Finally, does the work have special features that set it apart from all similar works? If so, do these features mean that the item should be selected or rejected? Here there are so many possibilities related to the various forms and uses of documentation that generalization is difficult. Essentially, though, one looks for something special – 'star quality', in the jargon of talent quests – that will give an item some positive benefit to the users in the context of a particular collection. Does a particular children's encyclopedia contain more attractive colour illustrations than some other encyclopedia for the same audience? Does a new textbook cover a field so much more thoroughly than the competition that it can replace several titles already in the collection? These and similar issues, most of them of a comparative nature, should be considered in the final analysis.

While this set of criteria may be simpler than those proposed by Whittaker, one should not now imagine that selection is a simple task. For the collection manager who is up to date with the latest authors, intellectual trends and user demands in a field, selection may be a minor activity, but most collection managers have little time to remain *au fait* with developments across a range of disciplines or formats. For most professionals selection is a demanding task requiring the skilful balancing of funds, collection strengths and weaknesses, user needs and demands and other available materials. To wend one's way through this maze of demands, evaluation and selection according to ASTAFS (Authority, Scope, Treatment, Arrangement, Format and Special considerations) can be a useful formula.

Selection procedures

Moving from principles and criteria to procedures, the activity of selection needs to be clear, specific and accurate to ensure that costly errors are not made. To begin with, the procedure should ensure that no material is inadvertently ordered that the library already has. While this may seem obvious, experience suggests that up to 30% or more of all items a library is asked to purchase are, in fact, already held or on order. As Liz Chapman says, 'Never believe what anyone outside your service tells you about what is in stock. You must always check.'[15] Most clients who suggest items simply do not bother to check the existing collection first.

For the checking to be error-free, a complete and correct citation is needed. Without this, how can one be certain that an item is not already held? This is the first task undertaken by the library – frequently called bibliographic checking or verification, and usually carried out by clerical staff under the supervision of a professional. As part of verification, price and in-print status need to be confirmed. A straightforward purchase approval at £50 may not be so at £200, so price is usually considered a key factor in the selection decision.

In addition, the availability of an item in various formats needs to be established. As noted above reference material, in particular, may be both more useful and more used if obtained on CD-ROM. Finally, maintaining a satisfactory relationship with a supplier requires that a library order identifiable and available material – and only rarely, if ever, return items ordered by mistake.

The various procedures involved in selection have been, and are still being, transformed by access to the internet.[16] There are several sites developed primarily by librarians which are intended to assist with collection development and selection. Typically, these provide links not only to other libraries but also to acquisitions lists and collection development policies, along with publishers, vendors and discussion groups. Library sites almost invariably provide access to their online catalogues, which can be of obvious value in bibliographic checking, avoidance of unnecessary duplication of holdings, interlibrary loan, etc. There are also sites that index libraries themselves and sites that index their parent institutions such as universities.[17]

All of these internet-based information resources should be treated as essential first stops in the verification process. It must be added, of course, that probably no library at the time of writing can undertake full and complete bibliographic checking of all selected items using free, web-based selection aids alone. Therefore, the purchase of some selection aids is required; but how many should be purchased, and which ones? Here, there are two points of view:

- If one is selecting fewer items, then the purchase of only a limited number of selection aids is justified.
- If one is selecting fewer items, then it is desirable to be as well informed as possible about those few purchases – and so as wide a range of selection aids as possible should be available.

In our experience being parsimonious in the purchase of such working tools to complement those available free online is a false economy. The fewer such resources one can access, the longer the selection process is likely to take, resulting in inefficient use of time on a day-to-day basis.

Selection procedures statements

The various selection procedures are crucial yet complex, and for these reasons it is best to consider the need for a selection procedures statement that is used by everyone involved in the selection process. This should be a statement of specific practices about how materials are selected and by whom. A statement of selection procedures, then, is an administrative device designed to facilitate implementation of decisions about materials based on collection development policy guidelines. As in most administrative matters requiring consistency over time, it is helpful if procedures can be formalized in a written statement.

There are at least six reasons for advocating the adoption of a formal selection procedures statement, and many of these echo the rationale for having a written collection development policy. Such a statement

- sets standards for procedures to be followed
- reduces the likelihood of bias and personal influence
- provides continuity despite staff changes
- serves as an orientation and training device for new staff
- provides guidelines for complaint handling
- assists in weeding.

All of these reasons can be summarized as providing practical guidance in who should select and how selection is done. This practical guidance is most effectively contained in a detailed statement consisting of an outline of general procedures and a set of related attachments as indicated in Figure 5.1. (See Chapter 7 for the handling of gifts and donations, and Chapter 10 for weeding criteria.)

Essentially a written procedures statement must address two questions:

- Who will do the selecting?
- How will the procedure be organized?

With reference to the first question the best arrangement is a combination of library staff and users, ideally a balance between the two within the institutional constraints outlined above. Within the library selection may be done by the chief librarian (or only librarian); it may be done by division or department heads engaged specif-

I	Main procedures	
	1	Selection responsibilities
	2	How selection is to be organized
	3	General guidelines for selection
	4	Handling of gifts and donations
	5	Weeding criteria
II	Attachments	
	A	Sample purchase request form
	B	Sample evaluation form
	C	Statement on intellectual freedom
	D	Request for review of library materials

Fig. 5.1   *Outline of a selection procedures statement*

ically for this task (collection manager, acquisitions manager); it may be done by subject or area specialists; or it may be done by other professional staff as part of their general duties (reference librarians, technical services manager). Specific responsibility should be stated clearly in the written document. Outside the library selection should involve input from users of all types, and these should be specified clearly: administrators, institution staff, students, teachers, the general public, etc. The political importance of this is apparent.

Review of Chapter 5

This chapter started by discussing the balance that is needed between acquiring the material that clients say they want, and material that library staff believe their library should provide. Finding this balance requires taking the mission of the library into account.

Issues of censorship and intellectual freedom have been matters for debate in the library profession for many years. The availability of online resources, in particular through the world wide web, has sharpened the need for libraries to have both up-to-date policies and effective procedures to protect both clients and themselves.

The selection environment – whether libraries are public, school, academic or special – will make a critical difference to the selection criteria employed, the nature of client input and the degree to which reviewing sources are employed. Selection strategies will also vary, and may include use of approval plans, blanket orders and standing orders.

Whether used to assess traditional print, multimedia or digital information sources, the criteria employed are likely to draw upon the traditional ones of ASTAFS (Authority, Scope, Treatment, Arrangement, Format and Special considerations).

Bibliographic checking is necessary to ensure that a library's budget is allocated to best effect. This process has been transformed by the availability of information over the internet. Finally, we advocate the development of a formal selection procedures statement.

Where to now?

This chapter has covered a great deal of ground and, largely for that reason, it has not been possible to include as many examples of policies and current issues as we might have wished. Accordingly, after you have reviewed the focus questions we suggest that you seek examples yourself, on the internet if this is available to you. Below are some suggested issues to address.

- Has there been a recent censorship controversy in your area? Did it involve print or online media, and what were the issues raised?
- Not all libraries employ approval plans or blanket or standing orders. If yours does not, can you identify a library in your area that does? If you have contact with library suppliers, perhaps at a conference, do they offer these services?
- If you work in one particular type of library, see if you can find published material selection criteria appropriate to that type of library. Are these available online? Do they take electronic media into account? Online materials?
- Imagine you are setting up a virtual e-library in your area of expertise. What selection criteria would be appropriate for this?

Further reading

There is a plethora of material on the selection of library materials, both print and electronic. One of the most useful guides to selecting print materials in various categories, including fiction, is David Spiller's recent publication, *Providing materials for library users*, Library Association Publishing, 2000, which provides considerable detail on the selection of various categories of material for libraries. For electronic resources the best equivalent to Spiller is Alison Cooke, *A guide to finding quality information on the internet: selection and evaluation strategies*, Library Association Publishing, 1999.

Other guides to the selection and evaluation of electronic resources include an introductory, policy-oriented work: D. K. Kovacs, *Building electronic library collections: the essential guide to selection criteria and core subject collections*, Neal-Schuman, 2000, or, for a more practical discussion focused on web-based resources, D. K. Kovacs and A. Elkordy, 'Collection development in cyberspace: building an electronic library collection', *Library Hi Tech*, **18** (4), 2000, 335–61. Some other guides are mentioned in Note 12 below; see also the discussion in several items in a recent issue of *Library Trends* (**48** (4), Spring 2000.

There are numerous subject and area guides to selection, most notably those published by the American Library Association. Two classics are Patricia McClung (ed.), *Selection of library materials in the humanities, social sciences and sciences*, American Library Association, 1985; and Cecily Johns, *Selection of library materials for area studies*, 2 vols, American Library Association, 1991 and 1994.

Some publishers offer series devoted to reference materials in particular, with

Libraries Unlimited in the USA probably the leader in this area; one should look for this publisher's Reference Sources in the Humanities series, as well as its *American reference books annual.*

Notes

1 G. E. Evans, *Developing library and information center collections*, 3rd edn, Libraries Unlimited, 1995, Chapter 4. This chapter does not appear in the 4th edition published in 2000.

2 R. N. Broadus, *Selecting materials for libraries*, 2nd edn, H. W. Wilson Company, 1981, 30–51.

3 S. R. Ranganathan, *Library book selection*, Indian Library Association, 1952.

4 S. E. Higgins, 'Information, technology and diversity: censorship in the 21st century'. In G. E. Gorman (ed.), *International yearbook of library and information management 2000–2001: collection management*, Library Association Publishing, 2000, 102.

5 E. B. Jenkinson, *The Schoolbook protest movement: 40 questions and answers*, Phi Delta Kappa Educational Foundation, 1986.

6 Higgins, op. cit., 100.

7 D. Spiller, *Providing materials for library users*, 6th edn, Library Association Publishing, 2000. Latest edition of his *Book selection: principles and practice.*

8 K. Whittaker, *Systematic evaluation: methods and sources for assessing books*, Outlines of Modern Librarianship, Clive Bingley, 1982.

9 S. Demas, 'What will collection development do?', *Collection Management*, **22** (3/4), 1998, 151–9.

10 These lists are based in part on J. G. Neal (Eisenhower Library, Johns Hopkins University), 'The digital imperative: building the electronic library of the future', unpublished presentation at the 64th IFLA General Conference, Amsterdam, 16–21 August 1998.

11 D. Allison, B. McNeil and S. Swanson, 'Database selection: one size does not fit all', *College & Research Libraries*, **61**, 2000, 56–63. For an example of how this view is embodied in selection criteria, see the British Library of Political and Economic Science's *General statement of collection policy*, Appendix 1: Electronic sources: additional selection criteria at **www.blpes.lse.ac.uk/collections/ cdp/general.html#Appendix 1** [10 April 2001].

12 S. Piontek and K. Garlock, 'Creating a world wide web resource collection', *Internet Research: Electronic Networking Applications and Policy*, **4**, 1996, 20–6; G. F. Pratt, P. Flannery and C. L. D. Perkins, 'Guidelines for internet resource

selection', *College & Research Libraries News*, **57**, 1996, 134ff; P. J. Wolfe, 'Evaluating internet resources: criteria for evaluation as a collection development extension'. In J. W. Markham and A. L. Duda (eds), *Information across the waves: the world as a multimedia experience. Proceedings of the 21st Annual Conference of the International Association of Aquatic and Marine Science Libraries and Information Centres, Southampton, England, October 8–12, 1995*, International Association of Aquatic and Marine Science Libraries and Information Centres, 1996, 213–17.

13   P. Johnson, 'Collection development policies and electronic information resources'. In G.E. Gorman and R. H. Miller (eds), *Collection management for the 21st century*, Greenwood Press, 1997, 83–104; P. Johnson, 'Collection policies for electronic resources', *Technicalities*, **18**, 1998, 10–12; C. Holleman, 'Electronic resources: are basic criteria for the selection of material changing?', *Library Trends*, **48** (4), 2000, 694–710; P. Metz, 'Principles for selection for electronic resources', *Library Trends*, **48** (4), 2000, 711–28.

14   Johnson, 'Collection development policies and electronic information resources'.

15   L. Chapman, *Managing acquisitions in library and information services*, Library Association Publishing, 2001; Chapter 2, 'Pre-order checking', p. 5.

16   For more comprehensive coverage of this area, see A. Yochelson et al. (comps), *Collection development and the internet: a brief guide for recommending officers in the Humanities and Social Sciences Division at the Library of Congress* at **http://lcweb.loc.gov/acq/colldev/handbook.html** [25 April 2001]. Another useful overview is found at *AcqWeb* **www.library.vanderbilt.edu/law/ acqs/acqs.html** [25 April 2001], which describes itself as a 'gathering place for librarians and other professionals interested in acquisitions and collection development'.

17   Such as BUBL for the UK academic community at **http://bubl.ac.uk/** or the worldwide listing of college and university home pages at **www.mit.edu:8001/ people/cdemello/univ.html** [24 April 2001].

6
Selection resources

Focus questions

- How does one establish the existence, availability and price of resources?
- What is the role of reviews in selection?
- In what ways might publishers' and booksellers' advertising assist?

This chapter takes as its starting point the proposition that selectors are faced with a series of decisions, some relatively small and easy, others relatively difficult and costly. To increase the probability of being right more often than wrong, it is essential to be armed with as much up-to-date and accurate information as is conveniently available. This will not guarantee the selection of only the necessary and best resources, but it should increase the likelihood of being right more often. As in all practical endeavours, there comes a time when the decision must be made regardless of the completeness or otherwise of the available information – to go beyond this time is not good professional practice.

In this chapter the various kinds of selection tools are divided into classes, and characteristics of the classes described. There are many problems with this approach, including the initial problem of devising a classification scheme, deciding which are the characteristics that distinguish one group from another, and deciding how to recognize and measure these characteristics. But if the aim is to understand the nature of selection tools, then general guidance of this kind rises above the detail of which tools happen to be available today, and should allow some underlying principles to be understood.

Any selection tool should do either or both of two things; if it does neither, it is worthless, but if it does both it can be remarkably useful:

- It must identify the item, and provide the selector with enough information to allow him or her to decide what the item is; that is, it must act as an *alerting* device.
- It must evaluate the item, or tell the selector whether the item is any good for its stated purpose, and if it is not, in what particulars it fails; that is, it must act as an *evaluating* device.

There are several sets of general questions to be asked of any selection tool:

- Why does this exist at all? What can it do that is not already done elsewhere?
- How well does it perform in its coverage of current publishing?
- What types of material are intentionally included and excluded?
- What types of material are likely to be excluded because of their very nature, not because of deliberate choice?
- What subject areas are included and excluded?
- What kind of information is offered about the works mentioned, and how much of it is offered?
- For whom is the tool intended – librarians, general readers, subject specialists?
- What is the tool's physical format, and is it available in a number of different formats? How frequently does it appear? The format of the selection tool may bear no relationship at all to the formats of the works it covers.
- How current is it?
- If it cumulates in some way, what is the pattern of the cumulations? Does each cumulation supersede the earlier cumulations, or must some be kept for specified periods, for instance, pending the arrival of an annual cumulation?
- What is the form of the classification scheme used? If it differs from the customary Dewey Decimal Classification or Library of Congress Classification, what are the details of the differences?
- What are the rules for filing, and which subject headings are used?
- Is there any special methodology or approach that should be employed in order to make best use of it?

The ever-increasing world of resources offered for potential selection – monographs and periodical or serial literature, multimedia and electronic resources of all kinds – means that the relative importance of these questions, and even if they are worth asking at all, will vary from one situation to the next. All of this becomes a matter of informed judgement on the part of the selector.

Classification of selection resources

We have chosen to divide examples of the various types of selection resources into three main groups:

- bibliographies
- reviews
- advertising material.

Of these, clearly bibliographies can be both alerting and evaluating devices; that is, they can both identify and describe, and can also evaluate, sometimes if only by implication. Reviews, too, will ideally both evaluate and alert, but their main purpose must be to evaluate; and advertising material is wholly alerting – it does not evaluate, even if it purports to do so.

Bibliographies, or lists of works

There are several different meanings of the word 'bibliography', which can mean the study of the physical make-up of the book, sometimes called 'analytical bibliography', the study of the historical aspects of book production, called 'historical bibliography', or the preparation of lists of books or other works, called 'systematic bibliography'. This last group, which is of concern in this context, can be further subdivided into:

- lists of works based on some specific criteria, e.g. about one subject, written by one author, published in one country or published by a particular publisher
- lists of works cited as being used in the preparation of another work.

While it can be argued that library catalogues cannot properly be classified as bibliographies, no matter how well prepared they are, they are useful in stock selection and are probably best included under this heading.

There are several important questions to be asked of a bibliography when it is being used as a selection tool:

- What are the limitations of its subject coverage?
- Is it selective? If so, on what basis?
- What forms of material are included, and excluded?
- What are the technical aspects of its construction – form of entry, rules used and classification scheme used?

- Is it an alerting device, an evaluating device, or both, and in what degree?

Types of bibliographies include:

- subject bibliographies, both total and selective
- standard lists
- guides to the literature
- library catalogues (to a limited extent)
- national and trade bibliographies
- bibliographies of government publications
- bibliographies of periodicals.

To the extent that they are intended to be selective, many bibliographies are also evaluative. Such bibliographies often explicitly indicate that they are recommending only the 'best' books or other materials in their subject area, either for students or as a selection guide for libraries.

One of the best-known examples of a total coverage bibliography is the British Library's *Eighteenth century short title catalogue* (an immense work, republished by the Library in a microfiche edition in 1983). Of course, in most cases attempting to provide total coverage is more of an intention than the reality; antiquarian book-sellers take pride in asserting (sometimes incorrectly) that the occasional item is 'not in' some standard listing.

Subject bibliographies

Two examples of excellent selective coverage bibliographies are Mary-Paula Walsh, *Feminism and the Christian tradition: an annotated bibliography and critical introduction to the literature*, Bibliographies and Indexes in Religious Studies 51, Greenwood Press, 1999, which gives detailed, critical evaluations to nearly 1000 references in this specific field; and *Theological and religious reference materials*, by G. E. Gorman and Lyn Gorman and published in three volumes (Greenwood Press, 1984–86). With selective coverage bibliographies, as with any, it is important that the selector note the criteria for inclusions and exclusions, some implicit rather than explicit (one review of the Gorman and Gorman guide detected a bias against evangelical Protestantism, for example). Also important to note are the time period covered and the classification scheme employed.

Standard lists

There are numerous examples of current standard lists, a good one being H.W. Wilson's *Public library catalog* and the *Public library catalog electronic edition* (**www.hwwilson.com/databases/publibcat_e.htm**). The value of a list such as this depends entirely on the standards of the compilers, and as the *Public library catalog* is based on lists of books (8000 in the latest edition) selected for public libraries in the USA, it naturally has a US bias. In addition, the use of lists such as this will result in a form of circular selection pattern, as the list is compiled from the stocks of libraries that use it to select their stock, and also to measure the effectiveness of their stock selection programmes. There are many different standard lists for different purposes such as for schools, universities and children's libraries, and it is never difficult to find a list that seems designed for a particular type of library. However, care must be exercised to see that it meets the criteria set down for your own library's selection programme and collection management objectives, and that the standards of selection are suitable for your library.

There are also retrospective standard lists: many issues of *British Book News* and of *Choice*, and also some issues of *Library Journal*, include a select, evaluative list of the best books on a particular subject. They are also alerting in that they generally provide all the detail needed for acquisitions staff to order the books. Such lists can also be used for other collection management purposes, such as checking the library's holdings not only for what is missing and thus might be added, but also to confirm its strengths, evaluate the collection, establish a core collection, and as weeding aids (see Chapters 9 and 10).

Library catalogues

Depending entirely on the standards of selection for inclusion, some library catalogues can be evaluative. The catalogues of deposit libraries like the British Library are not evaluative (although invaluable for other purposes), but the carefully selected material in some special collections reflects selection rather than simple acquisition, and to that extent their catalogues are evaluative.

National and trade bibliographies

National and trade bibliographies are entirely *alerting* devices in that they tell the selector what is available without giving any indication of the value of the material they list.

Most developed countries have a national bibliography, and most of the major trade and national bibliographies have been available on microfiche for many years, are also available online through commercial databases, and usually on CD-ROM as well. Smaller, more specific, bibliographies are generally available in either print or online form, some being available *only* on the web.

As an example, the *British national bibliography* (available in a weekly printed version, a monthly CD-ROM and on BLAISE – **http://blaiseweb.bl.uk** – the British Library's automated information service), is based on materials lodged with the British Library under legal deposit legislation. It is important to note that it is 'based on', because it is a selective bibliography and selectors must note carefully the kinds of material not included else much time can be lost in fruitless searching. From a selection standpoint, the *BNB* is useful not only because of its largely comprehensive coverage but also because it lists all the information needed for ordering: author, title and subtitle, edition, publisher and place of publication, price, ISBN, subject headings and classification number. Of course, a national bibliography of this type is only one facet of a very complex bibliographic network that includes such services as co-operative cataloguing, the national database of monographs and serials, interlibrary loan support, etc.

Next come the trade bibliographies, and these too are best approached on a national basis. The general pattern is for a weekly trade journal to include, among its advertising and sales promotions, lists of forthcoming and recently published material derived from details provided directly by the publishers. This weekly listing is then cumulated in various ways, generally at least monthly, with other cumulations leading to annual and larger compilations which provide an almost complete listing of material reported as published. The standards of bibliographical description, while perhaps not reaching the levels demanded by bibliographers, are sufficiently high for ordering – which is of course the interest of the publishers reporting these data – and generally the descriptions provide much of the necessary information for the library selector. This form of listing is almost always accompanied by at least one form of subject approach, based on the same material, and the information is available online as well as in traditional print format.

The American book-trade journal, *Publishers Weekly*, published by R.R. Bowker, aims to list most of the works published in the USA, and supplies the information in a form that is designed for use by the trade in ordering. It is cumulated in a monthly, *American Book Publishing Record*, issued by the same publisher. A similar publication issued by H.W. Wilson is the monthly *Cumulative Book Index*. This claims to list all books published in English in the USA and in Canada, and a selection of those published elsewhere. Like *Publishers Weekly*, it is based on information supplied by the publishers, and thus depends on those descriptions for its accuracy and coverage. Like most H.W. Wilson publications, it is in dictionary catalogue form and is extremely logical in layout and easy to use.

A related form of bibliographic tool is provided by the collation of publishers' catalogues themselves, as distinct from the listing of information taken from those catalogues. *Publisher's trade list annual* (*PTLA*), published by R.R. Bowker, is the oldest example. It comprises a collection of publishers' catalogues, but not all publishers contribute; in fact, comparatively few are now included which makes it of little value to most libraries. Furthermore, to be of much use *PTLA* needs to be combined with some form of index, such as *Books in print* (*BIP*), also published by Bowker. Originally an author–title index to the *PTLA*, *BIP* now includes material not in that publication. Also needed is a form of subject index to these various compilations, and Bowker's *Subject guide to books in print*, issued since 1957, is precisely what the title says it is.

Of more value as a bibliographic tool in the electronic age is the Title Information Preview Service (TIPS) offered by the American company, Brodart. Available on the web at **www.brodart.com/books/colldev/tips.htm**, TIPS actually includes reviews of new and forthcoming titles which are tailored to the profile of the individual subscribing library. Information on services such as these, and on the US book trade scene generally, is found in relevant chapters of G. E. Evans, *Developing library and information center collections*, 4th edn, Libraries Unlimited, 2000.

Similar publications, of course, exist for the UK. *The Bookseller* is published weekly by Whitaker and is available on the web at **www.thebookseller.co.uk**. *The Bookseller* supplies the information for the listings of forthcoming and newly published books that subsequently form *Whitaker's books in print* **www.whitaker.co.uk/wpublish.htm#wbip**, which in the 2000 edition consisted of nearly 14,000 pages in five volumes. According to the work's own online promotion,

> *Whitaker's Books in Print 2000* is the definitive source of bibliographic data in hardcopy and it contains details of English language titles published in the UK, Ireland and in Europe including publisher and distributor details, plus a separate alphabetical listing of series. The titles are in alphabetical author, and alphabetical title sequence.

In fact Whitaker Information Services offer a range of additional materials similar to *Books in print*. Available at **www.whitaker.co.uk/bkbank.htm**, these include *Whitaker BookBank* and *Whitaker BookBank Global*. The former, available on CD-ROM, is devoted to anglophone publishing in Britain and Europe and is issued monthly, bi-monthly and annually. The latter, issued monthly on two CD-ROMs (or on a single CD in the compact version), covers publications from most of the anglophone publishing world (Britain, Europe, USA, Australia, New Zealand, Southern Africa). Whitaker Information Services is a good example of how one company is making good use of electronic delivery to provide up-to-date and comprehensive information to libraries. More information on this company and others is found in Chapman's excellent work, *Managing acquisitions in library and information services*, Library Association Publishing, 2001.

Bibliographies of government publications

The term 'trade publishers' must include the world's biggest publishers, the United States Government Printer and Her Majesty's Stationery Office. It is well known among reference librarians that even the most interested member of the general public is likely to hear about a new government publication first through a mention in a daily paper. The reasons for this are not difficult to see when one considers the topical nature of some government publications, their sometimes limited appeal, and the bibliographical problems of listing such an enormous output.

It is necessary to have a guide of some kind, preferably a fairly detailed one, in order to chart a path through the maze of government publications. In addition to the normal problems associated with identifying material, problems may be encountered simply because of the sheer volume of the publications and the daily or weekly nature of some. To find one's way around government publications it is essential for the librarian to make extensive use of guides published for each specific country. In the UK, David Butcher, *Official publications in Britain*, 2nd edn, Library Association Publishing, 1991, provides an appropriate starting point; for the USA, see Joe Morehead, *Introduction to United States government information sources*, 5th edn, Libraries Unlimited, 1996. Unfortunately, countries whose government publications output is less well organized than that of the USA or UK are less likely to have up-to-date published guidance available. For countries such as Indonesia or India, major libraries such as the Library of Congress have set up local offices in order to track down these and other fugitive publications.

Bibliographies of periodicals

Periodicals (serials, magazines, journals) have a similar pattern of useful guides. The major international directory is *Ulrich's international periodicals directory including irregular serials and annuals*, published in New York by Bowker, which lists all the necessary information for ordering and is similar to a trade bibliography. Some library serials vendors publish similar guides, based upon their own databases. The question of the bibliographical details of periodicals is quite different from the problems of the suitability of those same titles for selection in the library. There is a need for specifically evaluative services, and a good example is that provided by William A. Katz and Linda Sternberg Katz with their *Magazines for libraries* (published by R.R. Bowker, first issued in 1969 and in a 9th edition in 1997), which is very much an evaluative work, classified and annotated, and is useful for all libraries except perhaps the specialist.

Reviews

Reviews comprise the second of the three major groups of selection resources. Reviews should be evaluative and in fact most are, in one sense or another, even though the standards of the evaluation may be suspect. Because it is physically impossible to see and evaluate every resource, librarians must learn to evaluate their sources of information on the worth of a item. Reviews must be treated with caution, of course, but there are few real alternatives. Although many librarians make considerable use of book and other reviews in the processes of selection, most are intended for individual readers and serve many roles of which selection is but one.

Some of the points that must be taken into account in the evaluation of sources of reviews are:

- For what audience are they designed?
- How accurate and objective are the reviews themselves?
- Do the reviews compare the items reviewed with other titles?
- What is the scope of the journal in which they appear?
- How many reviews are published over a given period?
- How relevant are the subjects covered to this library's collections?
- What kinds of reviews are not included?
- Are various kinds of non-print and electronic materials included?
- How international is the coverage?
- How timely are the reviews?
- Are the reviews signed, or if they are not, is the reputation of the journal such that this is not important?
- Can the librarian be assured that the reviewers have the competence to review the kinds of books they attempt?

- Do the reviews conclude with specific recommendations? What is the balance between favourable and unfavourable?
- Is the format of the item assessed?

Guides to reviews

If book selectors should undertake selection on the basis of reviews – thus substituting the presumed subject knowledge of the reviewers for their own presumed lack of it – it is necessary for them to have access to book reviews. Apart from the straightforward but rather haphazard method of perusing the journals, one must use book review indexing and abstracting services. These fall into two groups: the digests and the indexes. *Book review digest*, published in New York by the H.W. Wilson Company since 1905 and now also as a database **www.hwwilson.com/NewDDs/wn.htm**, is one of the best known of the first type, and displays all its faults: understandably it has a US bias, and covers relatively few journals (109 in 2001). The entries are short, but do give some idea of the flavour of the reviews.

The indexing services certainly cover more journals and more reviews, but by their very nature are able to provide little more information about a review than where to find it. *Book review index*, published by the Gale Group **www.galegroup.com/** since 1965, is a good example of this kind of location service. It is available as either a three-issue subscription for the current year or an annual cumulation for the past year, and lists reviews appearing in some 600 sources. This obviously offers greater coverage than that of digests such as *Book review digest*.

In the past, there were also several specialist book review indexes (such as *Index to book reviews in the humanities* and *Technical book review index*), but many of these have now ceased publication, as databases and the internet have taken over as the principal means of identifying book reviews. In our own profession, for example, LISA indexes book reviews appearing in the professional literature; in geology and the earth sciences, GeoRefS indexes book reviews.

Review journals

The coverage in subject specialist journals like *English Historical Review* is substantial, with about 50% of that journal used for book reviews. While it may be an invaluable book selection tool in its discipline area, there are always the problems of assessing the reviewers themselves, and in areas of greater specialization the dangers associated with bias in reviewers become more pronounced. Whether one starts with subject specialist knowledge or not, it becomes necessary to build it up if you are to work successfully in such an area.

Library periodicals can be subdivided into 'official' and 'commercial'. The official journals of library associations, such as *The Library Association Record* and *American Libraries*, often carry reviews, generally written by librarians. The reviews tend to be short, evaluative and useful, and one can expect the editorial policy to be less responsive to publisher and advertiser pressure than that of the 'commercial' periodicals like *Library Journal*, the American journal published by Bowker. *Library Journal*'s reviews are very short but generally most useful, and as the journal also carries the occasional review article it is a very helpful publication for the book selector.

Almost every newspaper carries a book section, but in general the reviews are not a great deal of use to the serious library selector. Perhaps the principal value of the weekend papers is to allow the public librarian to be reasonably certain of what readers are likely to be asking for on Monday morning. The editorial policy of the book page is likely to be much influenced by advertising, despite editors' protestations to the contrary, and book reviews have to be judged with that in mind. *The Times Literary Supplement* (**www.the-tls.co.uk**) and *The New York Review of Books* (**www.nybooks.com/nyrev/**), both of which might well be classed as periodicals, have long been among the best general book selection sources, even though the scope of the books reviewed may be narrower than that of the stock of the average library, and the usual caveats about potential for bias in reviewers must be made.

Finally we consider specialist selection journals designed for the library book selector. Perhaps the best-known example is *Choice*, published by the Association of College and Research Libraries in the USA. This is an excellent tool for all but the smallest public library, because of the great variety of the American colleges for which it was designed. Reviews are short and authoritative, and each issue has a long article on the best books on a particular topic. Several thousand titles are reviewed each year, and this journal must be regarded as essential for any serious library collection. *British Book News* is almost a British equivalent, certainly in standard if not in coverage or size. It is restricted to British publications, now includes around 200 reviews per issue, and also includes a regular article on the best books on a particular topic.

Online reviews

Online reviews are now readily available on the web – and here it is the online bookseller, Amazon (**www.amazon.com**), which is probably best known. However, the reviews on this site are all very brief and, although some are excerpted from reputable sources, many appear to be based on publishers' advertising. On the other hand the equally short reviews from customers are often interesting and appear quite genuine. This website is very user-friendly and, as well as providing access to these reviews, it sometimes includes contents listings and suggests other titles a reader may be interested in, which may be helpful if you are seeking to build up the collection in a specific area. Ordering material is also very straightforward – provided you are prepared to send a credit card number over the internet. Many of the items are simply not available outside North America, and our own experience has been that they are dispatched promptly and arrive in good condition. It is not surprising that the range and pricing offer serious competition, not only to other online bookshops but also to bookshops in the High Streets of small towns throughout the world – and to many traditional library suppliers as well.

As well as Amazon, there are many other sources of online reviews.[1] These include such well-known sources as *Booklist* and the *New York Review of Books*, as well as purely electronic sites such as *Electronic Book Review* ('ebr') at **www.altx.com/ebr/**. However, it is fair to say that some of these have to be treated with caution: one of us asked a group of students to find online reviews of several reference tools, including Microsoft's *Encarta* encyclopedia. The students had no difficulty at all in finding reviews of this – but many of these were on Microsoft's own home page! Needless to say, all of these were very positive. With world wide web information sources we need to ask these questions:

- Is this credible?
- Is it independent?
- What are the author's qualifications for reviewing this item?
- How easy is the website to use?

In short, while the medium may be new, and access to online reviews can certainly be far quicker, exactly the same questions must be asked of what is found as would be asked of a print source.

Advertising material

Before dismissing publisher's advertising as an information source, consider that:

- It can be far more up to date than any secondary sources, listing material scheduled to appear in the months and years ahead.

- The formal alerting sources themselves rely on material provided by publishers.
- While the claims of publishers must always be viewed with some scepticism, factual details about such matters as an author's qualifications and affiliations are presumably accurate.
- Many publishers regard their reputation as one of their greatest assets, and will be unwilling to jeopardize it.

Advertising may come in several forms, and from booksellers as well as publishers:

- *Display advertising*, which comprises all the printed and graphic media intended for mass consumption, and would also include television and painted signs on the sides of racing cars if books were at the same level of profitability as are tobacco and alcohol. Such advertising is very likely to influence demand in a public library.
- *Publishers' blurbs* – sheets promoting a particular title, often with quotations from favourable opinions – which, although printed, are used for direct mailing and so cannot be classed as 'mass'.
- *Advance notices* from publishers, bookshops and library suppliers, which are perhaps the most contentious form of advertising in that they are designed to look as though they are some form of 'official' notification. It is not that 'advance notices' are in any way deceptive, but rather that they must always be seen for what they are, a form of advertising, regardless of the manner in which they are presented.
- *Publishers' catalogues*, which can be very helpful to circulate around a library or indeed to library readers.
- *Publishers' websites*, which should provide the most up-to-date information available about any particular title, including availability and price.[2]

Of course, publishers and booksellers are in business to make money, and their advertising is designed to help them do just that. Marketing and distribution are among the most difficult areas of any business operation, and if very active steps are not taken by publishers and booksellers to let librarians and other potential purchasers know what is available, then there is little point in authors writing books (or producing material in other media) at all. The 'best' book is of no use until someone reads it. If books and other resources are not actively and aggressively distributed, then it is unlikely that many will find their way into libraries. This need to sell is of course the sole *raison d'être* of the advertising, and no matter what form this advertising takes, it is still advertising. One must also beware of the effect that the likely revenue from advertising might have on the editorial standards of the journals involved, reflected in the kind of conclusions reached in the reviews, as it has been suggested that pressure can be brought to bear on review editors if the reviews are not generally favourable. It would be possible to make some kind of check on this by comparing the amount of advertising by a publisher in any particular journal with the number of reviews of that publisher's products that the journal carries, but as yet this appears not to have been done.

There is constant argument about whether advertising does or does not add to the cost of an item. Of course it does; but as it should also increase sales, fixed costs can be spread over the greater number of units and thus unit costs reduced.

We mentioned publishers' catalogues, which come in an amazing variety of forms and styles, and have as their purpose to make it easier for potential purchasers to buy the books. It is common knowledge that using publishers' advertising is a very widespread practice in selection. Depending on the librarian's acceptance of the value of the expertise available to publishers, one might dismiss it all as not worthy of the attention of the selector, or alternatively accept the proposition that a considerable amount of quality selection has already taken place in the editorial offices of the publishers, in the sales offices of the distributors, and in the purchasing offices of the agents or retailers. What is certain is that all advertising, no matter what its form and no matter how much it seems to look like evaluative material, is essentially alerting material. It will tell the librarian what there is, but it will not necessarily tell anything at all about the quality of the material or its suitability for a library.

This point needs to be stressed because some advertising material is designed to look official or professional, when in fact it is still just a form of advertising. Included in the information are author, title, imprint, collation, series notes, ISBN, DC or LC class numbers, pagination, date, price. Most suppliers also include a series of codes representing information they have seen as useful to librarians, such as country of origin, author's approach, intended readership, language, and sometimes an annotation. In essence, these services provide a form of advertising that is remarkably well directed at its potential markets.

Review of Chapter 6

This chapter has discussed some of the tools selectors have available to them. These can either identify items, evaluate them, or both. A series of questions that might be asked about any tool include what it covers and does not cover, for whom it is intended, how up to date it is, and so on.

Selection tools were divided into three groups: bibliographies, reviews and advertising material. Bibliographies can attempt to provide total coverage or be limited by subject matter or area, and may be evaluative or merely alerting tools. Many are now available in electronic form, and this trend can be expected to continue.

Reviews themselves need to be evaluated in order to assess their credibility and authority. The traditional indexes and abstracts of book reviews – such as *Book review index* and *Book review digest* – are now being complemented by subject-specific databases as well as internet review sources. While some reviews are published in newspapers, for most selectors those published in professional journals and specialist review titles (such as *Choice*) will be of greater value. Online versions of traditional review journals, such as *The Times Literary Supplement*, and indeed online review journals, are becoming increasingly common.

Finally, publishers' advertising material can be extremely valuable in an alerting role, provided that it is not accepted as evaluative, however much it may appear to be so.

Where to now?

Once again, we suggest that you review the focus questions at the beginning of this chapter. Following the lead of several recent authors,[3] you might then identify some traditional print-based selection resources, and:

- Attempt to find some substitutes, not only as free, searchable web-based tools, but also in non-print media. What are the advantages of the online and new media alternatives? What are their disadvantages?
- Locate some reviews available online. How well do these measure up to the criteria we suggested at the start of the section on reviews?

Further reading

Some of the most comprehensive work on selection resources appears in textbooks on collection management, collection development, selection and acquisitions. Accordingly, we refer interested readers to two of these, one from the USA and one from the publisher of the present work: G. E. Evans, *Developing library and information center collections*, 4th edn, Libraries Unlimited, 2000, especially 'Selection aids' in Chapter 4; and L. Chapman, *Managing acquisitions in library and informa-*

tion services, Library Association Publishing, 2001. The latter is especially up to date in terms of the web addresses of most standard selection tools used in the UK.

On the business of reviews and reviewing, we are again well served by some excellent literature. Two of the older but still useful books on this subject reflect both British perspectives: A. J. Walford (ed.), *Reviews and reviewing: a guide*, Mansell Publishing, 1986; and American: B. Katz and R. Kinder (eds), *The publishing and review of reference sources*, Haworth Press, 1987.

As will be apparent from the notes to this chapter, the *AcqWeb* site at **http://acqweb.library.vanderbilt.edu/** provides the obvious starting point for collection managers when searching for selection resources available over the internet.

Notes

1   The *AcqWeb* site lists several at **http://acqweb.library.vanderbilt.edu/acqweb/ bookrev.html**. These include review sites for libraries, the popular press, scholarly sites and electronic reviews, as well as review sites listed by subject. It also provides links to other directories of review sites, such as *Yahoo!*'s listing of literary reviews at **http://dir.yahoo.com/Arts/Humanities/Literature/Reviews/** [both sites verified 30 April 2001].

2   Publishers' websites are also listed on *AcqWeb*: **http://acqweb.library.vanderbilt.edu/acqweb/pubr.html**. In Britain, the Book Industry Communication site at **www.bic.org.uk/** and in the US the Bookwire site at **www.bookwire.com/** provide an industry approach [all sites verified 30 April 2001].

3   J. Horner and N. Michaud-Oystryk, 'The efficiency and success rates of print ready reference vs. online ready reference searches in Canadian university libraries', *Journal of Academic Librarianship*, **21** (2), 1995, 97–102; M. L. Saxton, 'Reference service evaluation and meta-analysis: findings and methodological issues', *Library Quarterly*, **67** (3), 1997, 267–89; S. S. Lazinger, 'Updating reference 101: free searchable bibliographic tools on the web', paper presented at 64th IFLA General Conference, Amsterdam, August 1998: code 018-123-E, division VII (copy accessed on *IFLAnet Unplugged 1998* CD-ROM); J. Janes and C. R. McClure, 'The web as a reference tool: comparisons with traditional sources', *Public Libraries*, **38** (1), 1999, 30–9.

7

Acquisitions processes and procedures

Focus questions

- Why do most larger libraries acquire material from library suppliers rather than bookshops or publishers?
- How should a library choose and evaluate suppliers?
- What are some of the difficulties in acquiring serials?
- What are the particular difficulties associated with electronic media and licensing?
- How should a library go about processing gift and exchange material?
- How can a library acquire material that is out of print?

In the preface to this volume, we defined acquisitions as the employment of a range of methods to provide access to the information required by readers. The basic principles of acquisitions are straightforward enough: a library needs to set up procedures to obtain this information as economically and as quickly as possible. Once established, these procedures are usually executed by support staff, under only the general direction of professionals. However, the establishment and ongoing modification of these procedures, and the choices and decisions they embody, are high level professional tasks that merit consideration here.

Choice of supplier

For many years, almost all larger libraries have effectively outsourced much of the work of acquiring information resources for their collections to library supply firms, or vendors (called 'jobbers' in the USA). There are in fact many ways of acquiring material, and in some circumstances each one of them may be most appropriate.

Bookshops or travelling salespeople can be the most convenient, having the advantage (especially important for school and children's libraries) that you can examine a title before deciding whether to buy it – and, of course, every title you see is available, and with a known price. In addition, there are sometimes good political reasons for a library, such as a public library, to purchase at least some material locally. Against these advantages, buying from local bookshops or visiting booksellers is undoubtedly more expensive, and the range of stock is inevitably quite limited.

Online booksellers, such as Amazon.com, can be equally if not more convenient than high-street bookshops. Their databases often provide a range of 'value-added' information, such as publishers' blurbs, published reviews and even reviews contributed by customers; can be kept very up to date; and ordering is certainly easy. These days, many libraries have access to corporate credit cards which can facilitate online purchases, although keeping track of payments may not be easy.[1] On the downside, shipping charges can offset the attractive prices, especially if ordering from overseas and if material is required urgently. Many such businesses are truly 'virtual' bookshops, too, and will not necessarily have the materials sought in stock (despite the claims on the website).

Publishers should have available a full range of their own in-print stock, and can usually supply very promptly. However, most are set up to deal with larger orders from bookshops and library suppliers, rather than often very small orders from individual libraries, and will usually charge full price (if only to avoid the appearance of competing unfairly with their usual customers). The library that chooses to purchase direct from publishers will also end up with a large number of small-value invoices from many different publishers, and it (or its organization) will have the expense of processing all these separately. In addition, libraries purchasing English language materials outside the UK or North America will also find that, in many cases, local stock is not available and orders have to be indented – and some publishers are very poor at providing reports on what is happening with orders that they cannot supply immediately.

For all that, in some cases there may be good reason to buy direct from the publisher (and these orders are usually referred to as 'direct' orders):

- It may be quicker, especially with smaller, non-commercial publishers.
- Some publishers specialize in mail order sales, and have developed excellent customer-oriented sales processes.
- Libraries whose parent organizations belong to professional associations may be able to secure member discounts (for example, the Association for Computing

Machinery in the USA offers substantial discounts on its extensive publications programme).

- In the case of orders for very large amounts of money, it may be preferable to deal direct with the publisher.
- It is often easiest to purchase electronic media requiring licensing by negotiating directly with the publisher.
- Some publishers may either refuse to deal with library suppliers, or be so difficult for any intermediary to deal with that it is simply easier to contact them direct. Some government departments and agencies fall into the latter category.

However, in most cases libraries find it easiest to deal with a *library supplier*, as:

- These firms are set up to undertake precisely this job. Their reputation and hence their continuing commercial viability depends on them doing it to the satisfaction of their library customers alone.
- For monographs, library suppliers are usually able to secure discounts from commercial publishers, which cover all or most of their own costs. In the case of material published in another country, sale to a library at 'published price converted' (the original recommended retail price, converted at the current rate of exchange) is usually cheaper – sometimes far cheaper – than a bookshop price for an imported item.
- Most library suppliers now offer various online search and ordering options (such as the Blackwells Collection Manager service).
- Suppliers provide good follow-up and reports on order status – which can usually be tailored to the particular needs of a library.
- Library suppliers consolidate invoices for multiple items, saving considerable invoice processing costs. In addition, invoices can usually be paid in a library's own currency (obtaining foreign currency drafts can be difficult in some institutions).

Many suppliers now also offer various 'value-added' services: end-processing such as putting on library ownership stamps, security tags, barcodes or book loan stationery, and covering books with plastic if required. Other services commonly provided by vendors include cataloguing, and with serials, 'consolidation': receipt and entry of individual issues into an automated system, end-processing, and supply in batches ready for immediate shelving. Of course, these services cost additional money – but possibly less than a library would have to pay its own staff to undertake them. The UK National Acquisitions Group has attempted to develop a model to assess whether overall cost savings are, in fact, possible.[2] Perhaps of greater importance, the costs of end-processing will show up in the budget as expenditure on materials rather than on staff, which may be politically advantageous.

By now, it should be obvious why larger libraries make such extensive use of library supply firms, usually only resorting to bookshops for urgently required items known to be available, or to publishers for some of the reasons noted earlier. But if most libraries would use a supplier, which one or ones? And on what basis should the decision be made?

We have no intention of recommending particular suppliers in a book such as this. For one thing, recommendations can change as the service of individual firms waxes or wanes; for another, not every library has identical or even similar needs. Instead, we suggest that you meet and talk about suppliers with your colleagues: in your city, in your country, and in your type of library, and see what their recommendations are.[3] However, what we *can* discuss here are the bases on which you might make such choices – and, perhaps, suggest some of the range of choices now available.

Should your supplier be local or in the country in which the material is published?

Using a local supplier will ensure that your library's money stays in the local region (or in your own country), and of course your supplier will be easy to contact, easy to follow up, and accept payment in your own currency. If stocks are held locally, then this supplier may be fastest in supply as well. However, a supplier in the country of origin of the material you are ordering will probably be able to offer the better price, be faster with supply of many less popular items, and have better access to smaller or more difficult to contact publishers. Usually, the balance of advantage seems to be that, if you are buying a substantial amount of material from a country, it is better to have a supplier in it.

Should your supplier be a subject specialist?

Some suppliers specialize in particular areas – E. J. Brill in Leiden, for example, specializes in Orientalia. Such a supplier may be of great assistance in building up a collection, especially of older materials of which they may have substantial holdings in stock. You should, however, expect to pay something for this special expertise.

Should you opt for one or several suppliers?

If you direct all your business to a single supplier, you would expect to build up a special relationship with that supplier and its staff, which might include preferential pricing and service. You will also be in the best position to take advantage of any value-added services your supplier offers – and, of course, you and your staff will not have to decide to which supplier to send any particular order.

Against these advantages, no one supplier will be best at everything; individual suppliers certainly do fluctuate in service standards, as staff and management change over time; and lastly, there is an argument against 'putting all your eggs in one basket'. Suppliers have been known to go out of business, or be taken over by another with whom you would not have considered working.

In choosing a supplier or suppliers, the best advice appears to take into account the size and type of your own library. In our opinion, a small library is best advised to choose a well-regarded, general library supplier and place the great majority of its business with that firm – and make sure that the firm knows that it is getting all this business. Even a small library is then a reasonably important customer. Very large libraries are better advised to choose a small number of suppliers in the major countries from which they purchase material, and alter the balance of spending between them as service standards fluctuate.

Can you purchase material through your membership of a consortium?

Consortia were discussed in detail in Chapter 4; D. Ball and J. Pye have recently considered the issues involved in consortium purchasing.[4] Purchasing this way can share some of the workload among members, and as a bigger customer you may be able to get a better deal – if at the cost of some independence.

Are there legal constraints on your choice of supplier?

Some government libraries are required to purchase material through a tender process. This is almost always inappropriate – it is, after all, a process designed to enable the cost-effective purchase of single, very expensive items such as building construction. With library materials, price is more difficult to judge (is a 15% discount off the local bookshop price better or not as good as published price converted?), and poor supplier service (inadequate reports, poor follow-up of items currently unavailable) can cost far more in terms of library staff time than any promised price savings. In any case, as noted, no one supplier will be best at everything. In the Australian federal public service, special libraries have managed to have the concept of a panel of vendors accepted (rather than a single vendor); orders can then be directed to any member of this panel. In fact, if you are obliged to tender for supply, arranging it through a consortium is probably the least painful way of doing it. However, the ideal is still open choice.

Evaluating suppliers

If you are to choose a supplier or suppliers wisely, change suppliers or change the balance between suppliers, then this should be on the basis of their performance. How you might evaluate a supplier? The obvious criteria to take into account are all apparently quantitative:

* price
* speed
* percentage of items received
* number of problems encountered.

The difficulty with all of these criteria is that they are not under the control of the supplier alone. The price is set by the publisher, and may have been increased between the time of your decision to purchase and your supplier's order to the publisher; alternatively, if purchasing from overseas, the foreign exchange rate may – indeed, probably will – have changed. Equally, a supplier cannot be blamed for delays at the publisher's end (or for a dock or postal strike). It is clearly not the supplier's fault if you order a high proportion of items that are either no longer or not yet available. Finally, some publishers are notoriously difficult to deal with – not so much the commercial ones, but the town council that publishes a local history, or the community organization that is run by volunteers. Of course, *how* a supplier handles the inevitable problems that arise is most important – but hardly easy to quantify. Having said all that, though, suppliers do vary on how well they perform in all these areas.

The least desirable way of assessing supplier performance is on price alone. Quotations can be manipulated: just as supermarkets have 'loss leader' specials to entice the shopper in, a supplier asked to put in a competitive tender can tender low in order to gain the business, then raise margins in subsequent years. To continue with the supermarket analogy, low-priced stores sometimes have so few staff it is impossible to get assistance. With a supplier, too few, too new, too low-paid staff similarly spell trouble for their unfortunate customers. However, a lower quotation is hard to argue against to an institutional accountant. Reputable suppliers will resist the temptation to quote too low, risking losing customers in the short run, and then hoping to regain them when the library discovers how little and how poor is the service it is paying less for.

Another, newer criterion for suppliers is electronic access: do the suppliers provide online access to their databases, and permit online ordering if this is required? If it is, how well do the suppliers' systems integrate with the library's? Here, the establishment of international standards for publication data – Electronic Data Interchange, or EDI – has helped greatly.[5] Clearly, the automated systems as well as the staff operating them need to be able to communicate with each other.

Communication of all kinds is, in fact, another key criterion. Unless you live and work in a very remote locality, you should consider choosing from the suppliers whom you see regularly, either because they take the trouble to visit your library, or regularly have a stand at the conferences you attend, or have an office in your region. Indeed, the cynics would say that some kind of inverse square rule operates here: the suppliers a collection manager sees regularly will almost certainly be those with whom there are very rarely any problems, and those few quickly sorted out. Suppliers seen less regularly may well be greeted with a host of issues saved up for them. Finally, the suppliers you would *really* like to see never come near you – perhaps because they know what their reception would be like. Of course, e-mail, the telephone and, as a last resort, even letters will supplement face-to-face contact, but it is better and easier to work with someone you know personally.

One way to assess supplier performance fairly is to place simultaneous, parallel orders with different suppliers for multiple copies of the same titles. This is possible for a university that requires multiple copies for its short loan or reserve area. One of us has in the past undertaken such an exercise, but it requires a great deal of effort, careful tracking and analysis, and is not possible for a full range of material, or indeed for many libraries. Even when it is possible, caution is still needed in assessing the results, bearing in mind that one library's order profile will differ from another's, that substantial numbers are required to overcome sampling errors, and that supplier staffing and procedures do change. For obvious reasons, such studies are never published. Only through personal contact with colleagues will you get to hear of them.

An unscientific alternative is to direct parallel streams of essentially similar orders to, say, a pair of competing suppliers over a long term. If your order volume is sufficiently large, and if you keep full records and analyse these, you will be able to reach some general conclusions about relative performance. This is, in fact, how most collections managers make judgements about suppliers. What worries us is that many do so without full record-keeping and analysis, possibly on the basis of inadequate sample sizes, and perhaps being unduly influenced by any recent or major problems encountered.

Evaluation of serial suppliers is even more difficult, as fewer libraries order multiple copies of serials (and even fewer would be willing to forego any second subscription discounts). Furthermore, if you have decided to change supplier, this can all too easily result in interruptions in supply and general confusion. Waiting until the end of the current subscription period will be essential.

Because of its importance, supplier evaluation is both much discussed in the profession and also the subject of some useful literature.[6] If one is responsible for the expenditure of well over a million pounds or dollars, then common sense as well as professional ethics require such business decisions be based on reliable data. If possible, then, you should gather your own such data – and then cross-check it with professional colleagues in other libraries.

Having carried out some form of evaluation of your suppliers, then, what will you do next? Of course, you may decide to alter the balance of your purchasing in order to favour those who are currently performing better – but you should also tell your suppliers what your findings were. They are in the business of meeting your needs: if there are areas where their performance needs to be improved, how can they do this unless they know there is a problem? Just as in libraries, in library supply firms more junior staff do much of the work but do not decide on the policies or procedures. If you are a library user and have experienced a loan problem on several occasions, telling the librarian may be more productive than complaining to the loans staff. Likewise, telling the supplier's representative gives the supplier the opportunity to revise their policies and procedures. If you have chosen carefully in the first place, not all the news will be bad and this feedback will be more in the nature of fine-tuning the relationship.

Choosing and working with a supplier is an important task for any library, as the aim is to build up a harmonious and mutually beneficial partnership. Libraries have not, on the whole, seen themselves as in the same business as their vendors, nor have they attempted to work in close collaboration with them. Yet in areas such as library supply and in the provision of tailored value-added services, such close collaboration may provide real benefits.[7]

Such close relationships, and supplier choice generally, can also introduce real ethical issues, too frequently ignored. In Case Study 7.1 we raise some of these.

Case Study 7.1

Out to lunch

Joan was a very proper person. Her friends used to laugh at her, saying she was too close to the stereotype of the librarian for comfort. She took her job as Acquisitions Librarian at the County Library very seriously, almost always working extra hours, and was feared by many of the junior clerical staff under her supervision, who did not wish to be caught gossiping while at work.

For many years the County Library had dealt with a long-established, local supplier. However, at a recent conference Joan had attended a party put on by a rival supplier offering a new (but very expensive) consolidation service; seeing her interest, a representative subsequently took her out to dinner to discuss this. Two months later, the representative called at the library and made a presentation to the senior staff, including Joan and the County Librarian, who both went out to lunch with him at an expensive local restaurant. Afterwards, he sent Joan an attractive book just published by their parent company, thanking her for her time.

Before the start of the new financial year, the library decided to change suppliers and adopt this new supplier's consolidation scheme. To check that it is working satisfactorily, every two or three months the representative calls at the library, always taking Joan out to lunch. Last Christmas, she received another book from the firm.

- What are the ethical issues raised by Joan's acceptance of these, relatively minor, expenditures on her?
- How would you reply if invited out to lunch by a supplier?
- Would it influence your behaviour – and if the answer to this is no, how would you persuade the chief librarian of this?
- How might the service of the new supplier be evaluated? (Presumably, not by the quality of the restaurants.)

Order processes

Ordering current, commercial monographs is straightforward: you simply decide what you want, choose a supplier and ask them to purchase the titles for you. Usually the credit of a library is good (although many are far too dilatory in paying their suppliers), so that you would expect to be invoiced only when and if the items are provided.

Serials are different. Publishers almost invariably require payment in advance; hence library suppliers also need to be paid in advance. This has several consequences:

- If the publisher goes out of business, you lose both your journal and your money.
- If your library supplier goes out of business, you lose *all* the subscriptions you have placed with that supplier *and* your money for them; accordingly, you may well need to establish the business credit of an intended supplier.
- If your library or your supplier is late paying for a serial title, you may miss out on issues already published, because these are already out of print; instead, your subscription is likely to be extended to compensate (always a poor and inconvenient alternative: your records need to be adjusted to the new subscription deadline, and you will need to acquire the back issues).
- Finally, you have to arrange your budget to cover substantial expenditure at the period of serial renewal (usually towards the end of the calendar year). The impact of this is discussed in the following chapter.

If in general it is good business practice to place library orders with a supplier, it is even more desirable to obtain serials through a supplier. It is, after all, the business of a serial supplier to know the current address, price and frequency for all the titles to which all their customers subscribe, anywhere in the world. Ordering, paying and claiming are all not only very time-consuming in themselves, but much of this activity occurs at the one time of the year. Checking a computer-generated list from a supplier is much more straightforward – and if a mistake is made, or not picked up, a supplier can usually correct it. Publishers are rarely so forgiving.

On the other hand, serial suppliers usually have to charge the library for their services. This is because serial publishers give lesser or no discounts to suppliers. Most libraries regard this as money well spent.

As well as orders for monographs and serials – traditional, straightforward commercial material – a library also needs to arrange for standing orders, continuations, blanket orders, electronic media and licensing, gifts and exchanges, deposit collections, and obtaining out-of-print (OP) materials. Approval plans, blanket orders and standing orders were introduced in Chapter 5, Selection, because these are both the way in which items are chosen and the means by which they are acquired. Here we note only that payment for standing orders is usually on receipt (so a standing order may be cancelled at any time, except for items already dispatched), and the order continues until cancellation or the series ceases publication.

This is in contrast to *continuations*, which are items also published irregularly but for which an eventual end is envisaged. A common example of a continuation is an order for a multi-volume encyclopedia, which will cease when the last volume is received. In fact, there are many variations on the ordering, publication and payment for items published in multiple parts, with which a good vendor should be able to cope relatively easily.

Even with a vendor, though, some common sense rules apply to all orders – for monographs, serials, audiovisual or electronic media:

- Order the correct item. As noted in Chapter 5, a complete and correct citation should be supplied – including ISBN and/or ISSN if available.
- Make your requirements clear. How it to be sent to you – by airmail if from overseas? If it is a serial, from when do you want it to start? If you want a duplicate, make sure 'second copy' or some such is quite clear on the order.
- Make sure your address is clear, short and consistent. This is particularly important for items, such as serials, to be sent to you by the publisher. Many publishers have automated labelling systems which can mutilate longer addresses. Subsequent correspondence and claims can become hopelessly confused if a variety of addresses is used. In fact, when a library is obliged to change its name or address – something which frequently afflicts the libraries of government departments – some confusion is almost guaranteed. Quote both names and/or addresses in all correspondence, and with serials, try to change over from the time of subscription renewal.
- Do you have any particular invoicing requirements, perhaps imposed by your parent organization, which must be met?
- Check items on receipt.[8] If an incorrect item is supplied, you can return it for credit. If, however, someone has put a library stamp on it, you've bought it – even if you didn't want it. Note that this does not apply to faulty items (for example, with pages missing, repeated or bound upside-down). These can normally be returned for replacement at any time.
- Leave easy-to-follow records for others. Records which are 'in your head' make life impossible for your colleagues, your staff, any possible successor – and unless you have a perfect memory, for yourself, too.

With serials in particular, without good record-keeping and efficient housekeeping complementing ordering procedures it will not be possible for the collection to meet readers' needs, nor for maximum value to be obtained from the not inconsiderable investment made.[9] Hence, there is a need to:

- Record dates received. This will make following up subsequent possible missing issues easier.
- Check newly ordered titles *do* start.

- Claim missing issues promptly. Even though this is easier said than done, most publishers have policies which require you to claim missing issues within a set period, such as six months, or they will charge you for replacements. This is usually only an issue with titles from overseas, especially if sent by surface mail. The publishers' perspective is that libraries are only a small part of their business, yet make the most claims.
- Don't claim a second time until a reasonable period of time has passed.
- Ensure binding procedures do not remove serial issues from the shelves just when their usage is likely to be greatest – when they have just been received. (Indeed, not all serials need binding at all.)

Note that serial *cancellations* will usually only take effect from the end of the current subscription period.

Case Study 7.2

Biomathematics and Dr Schmidt

Many journal publishers quote multiple prices: for individual subscribers, for individual subscribers who belong to the professional association that publishes the title, for libraries (always more expensive) and for libraries in other countries (more again).

The special library serving the biology research group had recently suffered a major funding cut and Jonathan, the librarian, had been forced to announce a major cut in the number of serial subscriptions. Lists of all current titles had been drawn up, with their current prices, and the research staff were asked to indicate which items they considered essential to their work (A), which desirable (B), and which might be considered for cancellation (C).

The initial reaction to this was not positive. Dr Schmidt, a leading researcher and heavy library user, initially returned the list with all of the biomathematics titles marked 'A'. Subsequent discussion with her was both heated and inconclusive.

Dr Schmidt has now returned to Jonathan with an intriguing proposal: for a greater saving than the amount he was requesting she make, the library could cancel its institutional subscriptions to almost all the biomathematics titles. Dr Schmidt, who is a personal member of most of the major biomathematical associations worldwide, would then subscribe to these titles personally. The invoices and the issues would be addressed to her, but at her work address, and she would merely pass all of these on to the library. The result would be maintenance of all their current biomathematical subscriptions at greatly reduced cost.

- Is this proposed arrangement feasible?
- What are the ethical issues that might be raised by it?

- Can you see any practical problems if Jonathan agrees to go along with Dr Schmidt?

Electronic media and licensing

If serials are more complex to acquire than monographs, the terms on which many electronic products are offered to libraries are sometimes little short of a nightmare. Some of these concerns were covered in Chapter 5: inadequate bibliographic details, information about the formats in which the item is available, system requirements and so on. From the point of view of ordering, we may add that:

- Many CD-ROM products are not sold to the libraries that pay for them, merely licensed – and must be returned if a library cancels its subscription. Instead of building up a reference collection, one hires it.[10]
- Although the technology permits off-site use, most licensing agreements prohibit this unless substantial additional payment is made.
- Electronic versions of journal publications from major publishers – such as Academic Press – may *only* be available to those who also subscribe to the paper version, and *only* at additional cost.

Libraries in the USA, the UK, Australia and elsewhere have taken collective action to address some of these problems. Groups of institutions approach publishers and attempt to negotiate special pricing on a whole country basis.[11] This works with many items because the size of the market – and the size of the payments – is large enough to tempt publishers. But it is no solution for smaller libraries or in developing libraries where the collective buying power is simply not great enough.

It has often been observed that the brave new world of the internet and the world wide web is just as likely to deepen the gap between the information rich and the information poor as it is to bridge it – in fact, both these trends appear to be at work simultaneously. Here is another, unwanted example.

Gifts

Gifts are another way in which a library may acquire material – in many developing countries, an extremely important way. Indeed, some libraries *only* obtain material for their collections through gift. Gifts may be unsolicited (unasked for) or solicited, or come through an exchange agreement.

Unsolicited gifts

Unsolicited gifts (unless of cash) usually bring with them a cluster of related concerns:

- Is the item appropriate to the library collection? The costs of processing, storage and, perhaps, of eventual weeding can greatly outweigh those saved in initial purchase – there is no such thing as a 'free' book. The general rule should be that a gift is only accepted if it is an item the library would have wished to purchase, had purchase been possible. In particular, much material offered through donation is out of date. Something unwanted by a individual or another library because of its age is unlikely to be of real value anywhere else either.
- Is it an item that will need future updating (such as much legal and statistical material), and if so, will the continuations or updates also be donated, or will they be at the cost of the library?
- If it is a formed collection of items, can the library retain only those components it actually wants and dispose of the remainder? How is it to discard unwanted material? Circulation of duplicate lists is very labour-intensive and uncertain (many items will not be requested by others).
- Can the library meet any special requirements imposed by the donor? For a collection, these frequently involve that the collection be kept together, usually unhelpful to potential readers. Other requirements may include that a catalogue of the collection be published (labour-intensive and expensive yet unlikely to be much used), or that access be restricted (something that should be covered in a written collection development policy). On the other hand, arranging a formal ceremony to mark the handover of a significant collection, or the insertion of special 'Donation' book plates inside volumes accepted, may well be appropriate.
- Is the donor seeking some kind of tax relief because of his or her donation to a public institution? This can be a very time-consuming burden to the library, and also involve guarantees that all material will be kept permanently.[12]
- Is the relationship with the proposed donor such that the gift should (or must) be accepted for political, rather than collection development reasons? This is considered in Case Study 7.3.

Overall, the problems potentially associated with gifts to a library, and the staffing implications and political considerations associated with gifts, make it imperative, in our view, that a library develop formal policies in this area and document these in its collection development policy.

Case Study 7.3

The Vice-Chancellor's collection

The foundation Vice-Chancellor of the University was a very strong, if idiosyncratic character. As was apparent, he didn't believe in ordinary politeness, and he almost always got what he wanted.

A few months before his retirement he approached the University Librarian with the offer to donate to the library most of his personal academic collection, together with a large amount of material relating to the foundation and early development of the institution. The Librarian accepted this offer almost instantly – no other option was really possible, and there was one final (and important) budget round to go before the VC left. Besides, much of the material might be of interest.

Some months later, several truckloads of what a junior staff member succinctly described as 'junk' arrived in the library delivery bay. Many of the books were out-of-date textbooks, of the kind a library working party had been weeding from the open shelves. Several of them were in poor condition, and quite a few had inked annotations (in the VC's usual pugnacious style). The material on the foundation and development of the institution consisted of:

- barely legible carbon copies of correspondence
- dinner and other invitations
- some personal correspondence, apparently unrelated to the University
- some personnel files, including a couple of scathing handwritten comments on promotion applications.

None of this material was in chronological, or indeed in any other apparent order. All of it has been placed at the back of a storage room in the basement of the library, along with a collection of broken furniture, old typewriters, and piles of computer printout from the previous integrated library management system.

The former VC has now asked the Librarian when his collection will be processed, and suggested that a function be arranged to mark its donation to the library. That request has been passed on to you, as Collections Manager, for advice. What would you recommend to the Librarian?

Solicited gifts

Solicited gifts are much more straightforward. These may be items a library wants, but which are either not available for purchase or which the library believes it may be able to obtain as a gift. In either case the approach is the same: a letter is written requesting the items as a gift (a well-organized librarian will have a standard form letter drafted), while internally an adaptation of the normal acquisitions routines is used to ensure that items are not requested twice, that they are processed appropriately on receipt, etc. All gifts should, of course, be acknowledged when received, perhaps using another standard form letter.

Libraries with very limited budgets will not need to be advised to seek as much by donation as possible. In government publications circles, it is well known that many government agencies will supply libraries with their publications on request – even if they are also available as priced items from the official government publisher. Others whom it may be worth approaching for gifts include associations and societies. Only commercial publishers are fairly certain to be resistant.

Of course, the most valuable donation to any library is money. While fundraising as such is outside the scope of this volume (see Chapter 8, note 2 for some recommended literature on this topic), one variant often useful in developing countries is an offer of materials from the donor country, to be selected by the staff of the recipient library. This at least ensures that the material will meet relevant selection criteria.

Deposit arrangements can be considered a special category of solicited gifts. A publisher – often but not always a government or international agency – who wishes to ensure availability of its information arranges to deposit a set of its publications in selected libraries. This is sometimes on condition that it be made available to members of the general public, or that all material supplied is made available, or that some or all is retained indefinitely. The effect is similar to receiving a cost-free blanket order for that publisher's material. Of course, it is also sometimes possible to purchase a deposit collection of an agency's (or a publisher's) materials.

Exchange arrangements

Exchange is another method of acquisition. It is an approach particularly well suited to the needs of libraries belonging to organizations that produce publications documenting their work. Geological survey organizations, for example, publish the results of their own national surveys – and geological survey organization libraries have a well developed international exchange network. This is particularly well suited to the needs of geological survey organization libraries in developing countries, who are often short of the hard currency needed to purchase overseas material. Wealthy first-world geological survey organizations publish a large amount of expensive material, third-world geological survey organizations rather less, so an 'all-for-all' exchange arrangement has the incidental benefit of advantaging the third world partner. Other exchange agreements may be on an 'item-for-item', 'page-for-page' or a 'cost-for-cost' basis, particularly if not all of one partner's publications are of interest, but inevitably have the disadvantage that more record-keeping is involved than with 'all-for-all' agreements.

Exchange arrangements can be of special value in obtaining material from international partner organizations, from countries that do not have a developed book trade, and for items, such as official or semi-official publications, not well covered by the commercial market. Items that may be offered in return could include monographs, serials including annual reports and technical reports, and duplicates. A final advantage of exchange agreements is that the library is usually not required to fund the material it dispatches overseas. (The parent organization does this – sometimes unknowingly.)

However, all exchange agreements seem to break down from time to time. Agreements need to be properly documented, the dispatch and receipt of material monitored, and contact maintained with exchange partners (ideally including at least some personal visits) – all of which takes time and effort. Some countries have established foreign exchange centres in an attempt to minimize these costs while maximizing the mutual value of the exchange.

Out-of-print material

It has often been observed that the most difficult item for any library to acquire is the one that has just gone out of print (OP). Unless a reprint is planned, the publisher has presumably by then satisfied all the volume demand for it. Items that have been out of print for some time may frequently be acquired through secondhand or antiquarian bookshops, as those who purchased them finally discard them (or die). Older, classic or research items may be reprinted by specialist publishers, such as University Microfilms International (UMI).[13] Such reprints may come as print on paper, microform, CD-ROM, as online databases or, most recently, as e-books. For such titles, it is also worth checking whether they may available in electronic form on the internet, thanks to such undertakings as Project Gutenberg. Many libraries circulate lists of duplicate or unwanted materials, but again, these are mostly of older material. Of course, OP items will also be received through gifts to a library but these will rarely, if ever, be of the items one was actually seeking.

If an item is recommended by a library reader and then found to be out of print, it is always worth checking that it really is worth the effort of attempting to obtain it. Assuming that it is, and that it has only recently become OP, an alternative is to borrow it on interlibrary loan to photocopy and bind the copies. This is permitted under the copyright acts of several countries if the item is genuinely OP, but such bound photocopies are both clumsy and expensive to produce. Another alternative is microfilming, if only low research-oriented usage is anticipated. Readers do not like microfilm, and the medium is not suited to heavy usage.

A library's approach to retrospective collection building may be either passive or active. A passive approach involves waiting for appropriate items to be offered to you: scanning numerous secondhand catalogues and duplicates lists, a task that is not only labour intensive but involves experienced professionals (who can recognize what may be of interest) and is also time critical, as usually only single copies are available of items listed. To be successful an immediate fax, e-mail or telephone call should be made when a wanted item is found.

In many respects an active approach seems preferable. Here, the library develops a list of items that it is seeking, known as a 'desiderata' list. This is then sent to the library's regular vendors, most of whom offer OP services, or to secondhand and antiquarian bookshops, or – if appropriate – to other libraries. More recently a number of firms have set up 'book-finding' services, most of them available over the internet, and these offer an attractive alternative.[14] Larger bookshops also sometimes offer OP services. Of course, any one list should only be sent to one firm at a time, and as many firms specialize in particular subject areas it is also sensible to arrange desiderata lists by broad subject category. One disadvantage of using desiderata lists is that the dealers know what items the library is seeking, and may charge accordingly – but in our view the savings in staff time still outweigh this. In any case, the library can always decline if the price seems unreasonable. When one of us worked in this area, a well-known antiquarian dealer appeared to have a similar approach to items requested from his published catalogues. When we attempted to order these by return of post, they had almost always 'already been sold'. A few weeks later, we would be offered the same items again, as 'an additional copy' of each had 'now been located' – but always at a substantially increased price.

Building up a significant retrospective collection in a subject area in which a library had not previously collected is a major undertaking. Typically, it will be undertaken in collaboration with the subject experts for whom it is intended, and be supported by the provision of special funding. Here, too, close co-operation with one's suppliers is essential.

Review of Chapter 7

This chapter started by considering why most larger libraries use library suppliers rather than attempting to purchase material directly themselves, but noting that there sometimes can be good reasons for buying from a local bookshop, online bookseller or direct from the publisher. Some of the factors you might take into account in choosing a supplier or suppliers were then indicated. Evaluation of supplier performance is far from easy, and many libraries do not have the volume of orders and other resources necessary to do this properly. Instead – and in addition – most rely on sharing information about suppliers with their professional colleagues.

If obtaining monographs is usually straightforward, obtaining serials can be more difficult and there is a correspondingly stronger case for employing a supplier. There are even greater problems in obtaining access to electronic media, including through licensing, with negotiation through consortia a preferred approach for many.

Gifts can be either unsolicited or solicited, or perhaps obtained through deposit or an exchange arrangement. In all cases the rule should be that a gift is only accepted if it is an item the library would have wished to purchase, had that been possible. Out-of-print (OP) materials can be very difficult, expensive and time consuming to acquire; sometimes photocopying of material obtained on interlibrary loan may be an alternative.

This chapter introduced a major area of contact between the library as an information agency and the business world which provides most of that information. In the next chapter, Budget management, we also consider the financial links between the library and its own organization. Both sets of relationships must be satisfactorily managed if the library is to achieve its mission.

Where to now?

Once again, we suggest you review the focus questions at the beginning of this chapter to ensure you have noted its principal content. You might then wish to consider how your own library currently undertakes some of the tasks that we have covered here:

- On what bases have its library suppliers been chosen? On what bases – if any – are they regularly evaluated? What material is not obtained through a supplier, and why?
- Are serials obtained from the same suppliers? Are some serials obtained direct

from the publisher, and if so, why?

- How well is gift material covered in your library's collection development policy? Having read this chapter, do you now think that this section may need revision?
- Has your library any exchange agreements? How long is it since these have been reviewed?
- What arrangements does your library make to obtain OP material? Are these satisfactory?
- What co-operative arrangements are there in your country for obtaining access to electronic media? Does your library participate in any of these – and if not, could it?

Perhaps the single most useful advice we can provide is that you join your professional association, if you have not already done so, and make contact with your colleagues working in the collection development area. Immediately above we suggested that you consider the suppliers your own library currently employs:

- Do any of your colleagues use the same suppliers?
- Have their experiences, good and bad, been similar to yours?
- Are there other suppliers you might consider?

Further reading

This has been a very practically oriented chapter, and consequently there is less published material to which we can refer you. However, our first recommendation is quite clear: L. Chapman, in *Managing acquisitions in library and information services*, Library Association Publishing, 2001, a completely revised version of her earlier *Buying books for libraries*, Clive Bingley, 1989, provides clear, sensible and practical advice for the newcomer to this area.

For further discussion of vendor selection and evaluation, in addition to the articles cited in note 6 you may also wish to look at the ALA Collection Development and Management Committee's *Guide to performance evaluation of library materials vendors*, Acquisitions Guidelines 5, ALA, 1993, and H. S. Miller, *Managing acquisitions and vendor relations*, Neal-Schuman, 1992.

For a recent overview of serials librarianship, see H. Woodward, 'Management of printed and electronic serials'. In C. Jenkins and M. Morley (eds), *Collection management in academic libraries*, 2nd edn, Gower Publishing, 1999, 161–81.

In our discussion of alternatives to the purchase of secondhand copies of OP material, we noted that in many countries it is permissible under the copyright act for a library to make photocopies of material otherwise unavailable. What is the situation in your country? There will probably be some guide to copyright law that you could consult. In the UK, for example, see G. P. Cornish, *Copyright: interpreting the law for libraries, archives and information services*, 3rd rev. edn, Library Association Publishing, 2001; or in the USA, K. D. Crews, *Copyright essentials for librarians and educators*, American Library Association, 2000.

Considerable published guidance is now available on negotiating licences for electronic products. As well as the ARL guidelines, *Licensing electronic resources* (see note 10), several papers in *Economics of digital information: collection, storage and delivery*, Haworth, 1997, more readily available as *Journal of Library Administration*, **24** (4), 1997, will be of interest.

One area not covered in this chapter, yet of concern to many libraries, is government publications. Here, both the structure of government publishing and the likely problems vary from country to country – and it is unfortunate (if hardly surprising) that it is the better-organized countries, such as the UK and the USA, which are more likely to have published guides to government publishing. For the UK, you may wish to start with D. Butcher, *Official publications in Britain*, 2nd edn, Library Association Publishing, 1991; and for the USA, J. Morehead, *Introduction to United States government information sources*, 5th edn, Libraries Unlimited, 1996.

Notes

1   J. Flowers, 'A status report on credit card use by acquisitions departments', *Against the Grain*, **10** (5), 1998, 19, 27; S. K. Allen and H. S. Miller, 'Libraries on the book buying merry-go-round: internet booksellers vs. library book vendor', *Against the Grain*, **12** (2), 2000, 1, 16, 18, 20, 22. See also L. Chapman, *Managing acquisitions in library and information services*, Library Association Publishing, 2001, 122–4.

2   National Acquisitions Group, *The value to libraries of special services provided by library suppliers: developing a costing model*, National Acquisitions Group, 1996.

3   Chapman, op. cit., suggests some of the questions you may wish to ask on pp. 52–7.

4   D. Ball and J. Pye, 'Library purchasing consortia: their activity and effect on the marketplace'. In G. E. Gorman (ed.), *International yearbook of library and information management 2000–2001: collection management*, Library Association Publishing, 2000, 199–219. See also I. Snowley, 'Tendering for periodicals supply: how librarians can manage the process', *Serials*, **8** (3), 1995, 227–30.

5 J. Luther, 'Innovations affecting us: second generation online systems from book vendors', *Against the Grain*, **9** (5), 1997, 88–91; R. Withers, 'Biz of acq: online vendor services', *Against the Grain*, **10** (4), 1998, 74–6; L. Muir, 'Why should public libraries use EDI?', *Library Computing*, **19** (3/4), 2000, 192–7.

6 K. E. Cargille, 'Vendor evaluation'. In K. A. Schmidt (ed.), *Understanding the business of library acquisitions*, 2nd edn, ALA, 1999, Chapter 7; L. A. Brown, 'Approval vendor selection: what's the best practice?', *Library Acquisitions*, **21** (3), 1998, 341–51; and J. Walther, 'Assessing library vendor relations: a focus on evaluation and communication', *The Bottom Line*, **11** (4), 1998, 149–57.

7 This is also the conclusion of J. R. Secor and G. M. Shirk, 'The coming restructuring of library book vending', *Libri*, **50** (2), 2000, 104–8.

8 Chapman, op. cit., has a thoroughly practical chapter on the need for care in opening parcels, invoices, what to consider if there appears to be an error, and claims: Chapter 8, 'When the orders arrive', pp. 99–112.

9 There are, of course, not only books and articles but even whole journals devoted to serials librarianship, such as *The Serials Librarian* and *Serials*. We take serials librarianship, as such, to be outside the scope of this book.

10 For advice on signing licences see P. Brennan, K. Hersey and G. Harper, *Licensing electronic resources*: **www.arl.org/scomm/licensing/licbooklet.html** [24 April 2001].

11 Ball and Pye, op. cit.

12 The US situation is summarized by two articles in an issue of *The Acquisitions Librarian*: C. Marsh, 'The library perspective on non-cash charitable contributions', **3**, 1990, 37–52; and T. C. White, M. J. Michael and G. A. Gordon, 'Gifts: the answer to a problem', **3**, 1990, 53–61. In Australia, such donations are covered by the Federal Government's Cultural Gifts Program. See Department of Communications Technology and the Arts, *Taxation incentives for cultural donations* (folder of materials), and P. Clayton, 'The taxation incentives for the arts scheme', *Australian Library Journal*, **37** (1), 1988, 5-13.

13 UMI is now officially Bell & Howell Information and Learning. *AcqWeb* has a directory of reprint and on-demand publishers: **http://acqweb.library.-vanderbilt.edu/acqweb/pubr/reprint.html** [24 April 2001].

14 D. Black, 'In search of out-of-print books: the past, the present and the future', *Georgia Library Quarterly*, **35** (1), 1998, 11–17.

8
Budget management

Focus questions

- How are most library budgets formulated?
- What are some of the advantages of outsourcing in materials supply?
- What are some of the problems associated with the prepayment of serials subscriptions, and what may be done to address these?
- What is the difference between commitment and expenditure, and why is this distinction important?
- Why do most larger libraries use some type of formula in the internal allocation of their materials budgets?
- What are some of the hidden cost implications of licensing of electronic media?
- What is the underlying purpose behind the audit of library systems and procedures?

The classic definition of a budget is that it is a plan expressed in financial terms. This book is not the place for an extensive discussion of the various approaches to budgeting, nor indeed to planning generally.[1] Instead, in this chapter we will cover only those aspects of budgeting of particular relevance to collection management.

This chapter focuses on budget *management*, not on obtaining a budget in the first place. We are only too well aware that, for many libraries in developing countries, and for some in the developed world, fundraising is of much more immediate importance. Fundraising ('library development' in the USA) is a topic that deserves greater treatment than we can provide in the present volume. Readers are instead referred to the by now considerable literature on it.[2] Another issue of concern to many libraries is budget cuts (or at least, failure to increase materials and other funding in line with increases in costs and usage). Again, there is a very large literature on this – in fact, at times it seems that every current professional journal issue makes some reference to the need for more realistic funding provision. This, too, is really outside the scope of the chapter.

It is worth noting that in many organizations, the whole budget process can be an intensely political area. Unless this is an sphere in which you are both skilled and comfortable, it is usually best to leave the question of an overall budget allocation for the library to others who are – perhaps the chief librarian, or powerful supporters elsewhere within your organization. On the other hand, those who find they do have these skills should also find both they and their library have an assured future.

Drafting the budget

The conventional approach to budgeting is to take last year's budget, add something to cover expected inflation in the coming year (making separate provision for monographs, serials, multimedia and electronic materials, as the rates of increase in costs varies greatly across media), add an estimate for proposed new activities and, in most countries, factor in another estimate to allow for exchange rate fluctuations in the currencies in which the library purchases materials. The problems with this approach are apparent: not only may these various estimates be inaccurate, but last year's budget itself may not have been an appropriate benchmark. However, unless your organization has adopted a different budget mechanism, this will at least provide a starting point.

Other approaches to budget formulation include the use of a formula, programme budgeting and zero base budgeting. *Formulae* are usually specific to an organization.[3] They provide an appearance of objectivity and equity (and so are frequently hard to argue against), but do this by basing allocations on only a select group of relevant factors and ignoring others that may be equally relevant, and at the potential cost of inflexibility. *Programme budgeting* seeks to tie resources to areas of organizational objectives and activities and is often associated with a longer-term approach to planning. Unfortunately, its emphasis on the measurable and costable can disadvantage libraries – it is not easy to provide cost justification for better service; it seems to require a great deal of paperwork and statistics; and the final outcomes often seem at least as political as they are objective or scientific.

These objections apply to an even greater extent to *zero base budgeting*. This requires justification of budget allocations without reference to past allocations, in order to overcome the inevitable organizational bias towards continuing as always, whether or not this is appropriate. However, the general experience seems to be that zero base budgeting does not, in fact, result in significant reallocation of resources, and for libraries, the possibility of stop/go funding poses particular problems with serial commitments. If your organization has adopted any of these budget strategies, you would be well advised to read up on their claimed benefits and practical disadvantages in some detail.

It is usually easier to obtain a budget increase (or argue against a budget cut) to cover material costs than it is to gain any additional staff needed to process these materials. A common response to this has been to outsource as much as possible of the processing costs; whether or not outsourcing actually saves money (and at least one recent article suggests it may not),[4] it does at least transfer the costs from the staffing to the materials line. As noted in the previous chapter, for many years almost all larger libraries have effectively outsourced much of the work of acquiring materials for their collections to library supply firms. These firms are now offering an even wider range of 'value-added' services, including the provision of book stamps and security tags and plastic covers if requested (or 'end-processing'). For serials, the options are even wider, as shown in Case Study 8.1.

Case Study 8.1

Serials consolidation in a special library

Parliaments that are interested in libraries usually have good ones, for they can allocate sufficient resources to make this happen. However, one particular parliamentary library suffered from crucial space constraints (as the politicians and their numerous staffs were obviously of greater importance than library staff, processing or storage space). This library decided to investigate outsourcing its serials. In considering this, factors it took into account included:

- cost
- speed of supply
- vendor record-keeping (the supplier checking issues were received on time and missing or late issues chased up)
- end-processing services offered (spine labels and so on)
- batch airfreight shipping of processed serial issues to the library.

Several serial supply firms were contacted, and asked about their terms of supply, prices, etc. At the same time, known library customers of these suppliers were contacted informally, and asked for comment on their general levels of service, and in particular on any experience with their serials consolidation services.

A relatively junior staff member undertook this task, and compiled a report comparing the services offered and making the recommendation that the library trial one vendor's service with a batch of serial titles in a couple of subject areas. The library's senior management accepted the recommendation and a trial began.

The junior staff member was asked to set benchmarks to determine whether, and to what extent, the trial could be considered a success.

- As an exercise, what would you suggest might be appropriate criteria for success?

The advantage for suppliers of providing end-processing and serials consolidation services is not simply one of more business. These services work best for a library if it deals with a single supplier, which for a supplier means the prospect of gaining *all* of a library's orders. For the library, in turn, it means that a supplier must be able to meet all of its requirements – and be a business with whom you would want to establish a long-term partnership.

If one is to factor estimates for inflation and currency fluctuations into a budget, these need to be seen to be based on credible evidence. For material inflation estimates, consult the trade journals, such as *Publishers Weekly* which publishes an annual price survey, or your library's suppliers, who may be able to give a more informed estimate. Join an appropriate electronic discussion group, and seek the advice of your colleagues. For longer-term currency estimates, consult the financial press or, if your organization is one that has significant foreign currency dealings, use the organization's own official estimates.

The budget cycle

As noted in Chapter 1, collection management staff need strong links to the staff responsible for budgeting and accounts, not only within the library but also in the wider organization of which the library is part. This is of particular importance, because accounts staff are usually unaware of the special nature of library purchasing requirements: they are typically set up to process and account for small numbers of relatively expensive orders (such as for equipment, or large quantities of identical items such as boxes of stationery), and not large numbers of inexpensive but unique items (such as books).

The budget in any large organization goes through a well-marked cycle, as illustrated by Case Study 8.2. The library of the organization has to fit into its parent's budget cycle. This is relatively easy for monograph, multimedia and electronic media purchases, as:

- These can be spread relatively evenly throughout the budget year.
- Suppliers can, if necessary, be asked to wait for payment until the next financial period.

However, the overall pattern of library resources budget planning, commitment and expenditure is markedly seasonal.

Case Study 8.2

Department of the Environment Library

At the beginning of every month the Department of the Environment Library checks its expenditure on resources and its commitment from the previous month, and plans its financial expenditure for the month ahead. Throughout the year, it attempts to place a steady flow of monograph orders. However, like most libraries, the Library has to fit in with the budget cycle of its parent organization, in this case the Department of Environment and the government public service as a whole. Here, the Department works on a July to June financial year. Thus the Library's annual budget cycle is as follows:

July

For the first five months of the new financial year the Library works on 5/12ths of the previous year's budget, and must keep overall expenditure within this amount. Amounts based on last year's budget are allocated to the library's various budget codes (monographs, serials, etc.).

August

The book fund is part of the Departmental budget, and in turn of the government budget as a whole. As soon as the budget is presented, the actual amount likely to be available for the current financial year is known, and the Library's budget allocations can be calculated. However, actual expenditure has to remain within last year's figures.

November

In this month the government's budget should be passed, and the full amount of the Library's funds is now available to it. Forward estimates for the coming financial year are required. Serials renewals start to arrive.

December

During the period of December and January most of the serial renewal invoices should arrive. International invoices, in particular, will need prompt processing. This is the heaviest period of expenditure, as the Library spends more on serials than any other information resources.

Because the staff are so busy, only urgent monograph orders are dealt with. There are always problems with staff wishing to take leave during the Christmas period.

March

From now until May the Library has to ensure that all of its resources funds are expended. Suppliers are asked to invoice the Library for anything that will be due before June. Monograph orders that are more than six months old are chased up. If it seems possible there may be some money left, desiderata files are looked at and departmental officers asked if there is any material they require. All orders of this kind placed at this stage of the financial year go to the supplier with the proviso that unless they can be supplied by 1 June, the order will be cancelled, as the Library does not want a large carry-over into the new financial year.

May

All foreign currency invoices are finalized and sent to the Accounts Section, as they will cease processing invoices in the middle of June and foreign currency payments are more complex and time-consuming.

June

Final invoices for the year go to the Accounts Section. Occasionally, some last minute processing of invoices will be possible if the Department seems likely to end the year with any unspent allocation.

As is apparent from Case Study 8.2, serials present a quite different set of problems to those of other library resources. Most payments are due at the one time – typically around the end of the calendar year, for the following year's subscriptions. Unfortunately:

- Most organizations prefer to spread payments throughout a year, rather than make large payments at a single time. Government organizations – not only government departments, but also universities, schools and scientific research institutes – usually receive their money in equal instalments, spread throughout the year, so this is not unreasonable. Hence, large payments for serials can require juggling of payment of other accounts, and thus understanding and co-operation from the organization's accounts area staff.
- Problems will occur if the organization's internal financial year begins relatively close to the period of serial renewal, as most accounts centres cease processing at the end of their financial year in order to finalize their annual accounts and statements.

- A large amount of staff checking work has to take place within a relatively short time.
- In countries where annual holidays are usually taken over the Christmas/New Year period, both accounts and library staff will wish to take holidays at the period of peak workload.
- Finally, as serials are almost invariably prepaid, any delays in payment can result in missing issues.

The impact of these factors is shown graphically in Figure 8.1. For this, we assume we are dealing with a library spending approximately £120,000 each year on its serial subscriptions. The gross disparity between expected expenditure – the regular pattern of expenditure associated with most cost centres, such as salaries – and actual serial expenditure is apparent. M. S. Martin offers an alternative illustration of the same type of pattern, but based on a July-June financial year, and displayed as cumulative expenditure.[5]

While vendors will sometimes offer to accept payment throughout the year, often this amounts to payment even further in advance. The only real answer for the collection manager is to be aware of these potential problems, plan to spread the annual renewal cycle workload out over as long a period as possible, and keep in constant touch with the library's vendors and the organization's accounts section.

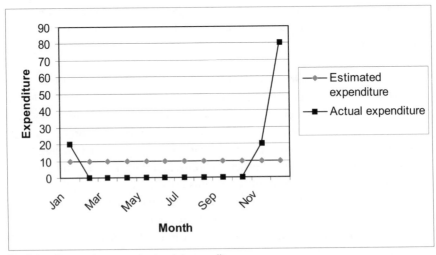

Fig. 8.1 *Expected versus actual serial expenditure*

There is one event in the wider organization's budget cycle that deserves more comment here: the end-of-financial-year rush in many organizations to ensure that all monies have been expended. Public sector organizations, in particular, often have a well-founded belief that if money allocated in one year is not fully spent, less will be allocated in the following – whatever the real reasons for the under-expenditure may be. Many of us have heard about foolish expenditure decisions made by desperate accountants in the closing days of the financial year. Small businesses sometimes even advertise in newspapers in an attempt to capture some of this last-minute largesse.

Here is both a potential problem and an opportunity for a well-organized librarian. The problem is simple: you should arrange your own expenditure so that there is never any doubt that all the budgets for which you are responsible are fully expended by year's end. This almost certainly means you need to over-order to a calculated extent, because it is probable that not all the invoices you require will arrive on time. The opportunity, however, lies in being in a position to benefit should some other area(s) in the organization not be able to do the same. To do this, you will need:

- a set or sets of invoices needing to be paid, all of which are fully processed and merely require the money – ideally, these will be for a range of possible amounts
- approval from the suppliers whose invoices are involved to carry them over to the new financial year should no additional money be available
- good personal relationships with the staff in the accounts area of the organization, so that you will be one of the first people they think of if there is money over in some other accounts (in fact, you will probably have been in their offices only days before, lamenting your inability to pay those very invoices); and lastly,
- a good political reputation for the library in the organization as a whole, so that last-minute diversion of unused funds to the library will be seen as appropriate and useful.

Is this too cynical an approach? All large organizations waste resources on some areas of dubious value. Unless collection management is quite the wrong area for you, you should not need to be convinced of the value and need for the resources you are seeking to obtain. In any organization, the sections that tend to do well are those that are well managed: make sure that your area *is* well managed, not least financially well managed – and then simply ensure that you are in the right place at the right time.

Budget control

When a library orders an item, and hence will incur a financial expenditure on receiving it (or when invoiced in advance, as with serials), then it is committed to that purchase. In order to know how much money remains available, it needs to keep a record of what is known as its *commitment*. When the invoice for that item is received, then that money is actually spent: this is *expenditure*. Commitment and expenditure are not the same thing, for several reasons:

- Some items may never be received.
- When invoiced, they may well turn out to cost more or, occasionally, less than originally estimated.
- Shipping or other fees may have been added.
- If the item was priced in another currency, the rate of exchange will almost certainly have varied by the time payment is required.

Commitment, then, is merely a 'best guess' estimate of what the library may be required to pay. Only very small libraries will not need to keep records of their commitment – indeed, unless all orders have to go through an external purchasing section, only the library will be in a position to maintain this record.

Larger libraries will seek sophisticated automated systems which track commitment automatically. If a significant amount of material is purchased in foreign currencies, then it makes sense to keep the records of that commitment in the original currencies. This applies to currencies that comprise a significant proportion of purchasing – for example, the US dollar for British libraries. If there is a major movement in exchange rates, the probable commitment can readily be recalculated.

For expenditure, on the other hand, even the smallest library will need to keep records. Here, however, since even many large libraries have their payments processed through the wider organization's accounts section, there is a choice to be made about recording expenditure: should this be done by the accounts section or by the library, or both?

There are strong arguments for records of expenditure to be kept by an accounts section, as not only will this save library staff additional work but also that section will of course accept its own records as correct. Most accounts sections will keep their own records in any case, even if the library also maintains its records. However, one of us has worked in an organization where the official accounts were never less than a month behind, sometimes several months. The delay was such that the official expenditure records were of no current management value. Other factors that may lead a library to keep its own expenditure records may relate to additional information that may be of value: in monitoring vendors, or in tracking allocations to various internal funds (a topic considered immediately below). However, the general principle should be to avoid duplication of effort if at all possible.

We cannot conclude a section on budget control without noting two other issues, one all too frequently apparent, the other all too frequently ignored. By their very nature, contingencies cannot be planned for, yet most who have worked in this area for any length of time can recall last-minute budget cut crises; some may also recall unexpected budget additions. M. S. Martin devotes a whole chapter to such budget adjustments.[6] Needless to say, being up to date with routine work, and knowing exactly what one's current financial position is, provides the basis for a successful response. Reserving a portion of the overall vote as a 'contingency' fund, and the preparation of desiderata lists (discussed in the previous chapter), are strongly recommended if variations in funding seem possible.

Lastly, we note that routine monitoring of the budget is often ignored by inexperienced managers. Not sure of what everything means they are reluctant to show their ignorance, and besides, everything seems to be all right. When a problem does subsequently become apparent, unfortunately by then it is often a major one – and one that should have been apparent months ago, if only the regular budget reports had been examined as a matter of course. Once one has become accustomed to the format and usual activity, the time involved is usually small as one is only looking for exceptions to the regular patterns. As for any difficulty in asking one's superiors to interpret budget statements, why not ask the experts in the accounts section? Throughout this book we stress the importance of establishing and maintaining good contacts throughout the organization. Staff in accounts are likely to be very willing to help, for they know from experience that when budget problems are discovered, too late, these invariably involve a great deal of extra work for them too.

Internal budget allocation

Within any large organization, there will always be competing demands for resources. This is the very essence of internal politics within most organizations, and no decisions about resource allocation are likely to be apolitical. This is certainly true of a library's materials budget: should more resources be expended to support one group of clients rather than another? Arguments in favour or against such a proposition will always be political in intention and effect, even if, as in many organizations, organizational culture requires they be couched in apparently rational or objective terms. We assume that the library's collection development policy will cover related issues such as the desired balance between print, multimedia and electronic media, though even here the interpretation of that policy will be open to question: as always, the devil will be in the details.

Having acquired our budget, then, should it be allocated:

- By the librarian? These decisions will be subjective, and hard to defend.
- By the clients? In practice this will mean by the vocal or powerful or active clients, perhaps to the detriment of others.
- In accordance with past practice? This may not, or may no longer, be appropriate, and may well be seen as inequitable (especially by those in new areas).
- In accordance with a formula? We have already noted the inflexibility and other disadvantages of formula-based budget allocation.
- Or should there be no allocation at all? The result of this is that the library simply spends until all the budget has been committed. The assumption is that all requests are equally valid.

In the past, smaller libraries have tended to have the librarian allocate, or simply spend until the budget has all been committed; larger libraries have tended to employ client committees, or simply follow past practice. However, formula-based allocation has become increasingly popular – as is now evidenced by a large literature on the topic.[7]

There is increasing pressure to be seen to adopt an approach that demonstrates rationality, accountability, the relationship of expenditure to organizational objectives, and equity between competing interest groups. All of these factors help explain the increasing popularity of formulae: development of a formula can open up the budget allocation process and force assumptions to be formalized and defended. The discussion, then, should no longer about whether to adopt a formula, but about the development and implementation of a formula-based approach which realizes these benefits, but minimizes the inflexibilities and other problems noted at the beginning of this chapter.

Accordingly, a formula should:

- be developed for a specific organization and its library, so that it can take into account local factors that are important
- be developed co-operatively by both library staff and clients, and publicized, at least in the non-public library sector, to the client community – to do otherwise would be to take an unjustifiable political gamble in many organizations

- include as many relevant factors as possible, so as to minimize inequity
- include separate provision for general or multidisciplinary areas
- provide for some expenditure to be under the control of library staff, such as for reference material
- consciously adapt and build upon the many formulae already described in the professional literature
- allow for the reallocation of uncommitted allocations towards the end of the budget cycle (we have seen too many organizations where some areas cannot order needed materials, while others sit on money they will never require)
- provide for regular and meaningful review.

To this, we would add some further elements of flexibility: an additional, 'reserve' or contingency fund under the control of the librarian, perhaps. If a library is introducing a formula for the first time, or making major revisions to an existing formula, it would make sense to phase in the new formula over a period of years, so that those who will lose under the new arrangements have an opportunity to adjust.

Having developed a formula and had it accepted, it will be necessary to provide timely and meaningful reports to the clients who collaborate in collection development.

Intellectual property and charging issues

Many collection management librarians have become responsible for negotiating site licences for electronic media. Such decisions rely in part on credible comparative costing, and may at times also involve decisions about pricing; these matters are beyond the scope of this volume. They are well and clearly covered in Herbert Snyder and Elisabeth Davenport, *Costing and pricing in the digital age: a practical guide for information services*, Library Association Publishing, 1997. As the authors of this work rightly note, 'There is a general need for more sophisticated accounting skills in all aspects of librarianship, as librarians are called upon to justify in financial terms the continuing provision of service in the face both of increased costs and decreased funding support.' This is certainly true in the area of collection management.

Let us move on to another area of electronic access of special concern to academic libraries: securing access to material originally made available in traditional formats. Some of the problems of dealing with publishers have been most apparent in the development of 'electronic reserve' systems in university libraries. There are many reasons to replace multiple paper copies of high-demand items with an electronic equivalent:

- Traditional systems are essentially designed to ration access, to the disadvantage of individual students.
- There are problems of theft and mutilation.
- There are high staff as well as material costs.

Since many items placed on 'reserve' or in a high-use collection are of journal article length, many libraries are now creating (or purchasing) digitized copies. Students can then browse online, or print their own copies for retention. This permits simultaneous access by as many students as need it, preserves the originals, and caters for remote or off-campus students. Instead of paying for the photocopies, students could pay for the laser printing – and a proportion of that cost could even go to the publishers as royalties. The problem in most countries is the restrictive current copyright law. To overcome this, a library has to contact every publisher whose works it seeks to include in its electronic reserve.[8] In Australia, Monash University tried such a system – but found that, although over 40% of publishers gave approval for their material to be included without seeking royalties, over 50% did not respond at all. 'Almost certainly, in the majority of cases the letter ended up in the "too hard" basket.'[9] Electronic reserves will eventually become commonplace – but at some, perhaps considerable, budget cost.

Audit and stocktake

Audits

An audit is an independent examination of the financial affairs of an organization, in order to ensure that acceptable accounting policies have been followed, and that any relevant regulations and statutory requirements have been met. The latter are of particular importance in many public sector special libraries, such as those of government departments, where the regulations rarely take into account the special nature of library purchasing.

In the budget management of information resources, the crucial elements are most likely to involve delegation of authority, limitation of possible fraud and full records of accountable items.

Delegation of authority, in relation to who may authorize orders and payments

The general rule here is that delegations need to be written, and that they must specify amounts.

Limitation of the possibility of fraud

Here, accepted practice is that one person should be responsible for 'raising' (authorizing making) an order but another for 'acquitting' (authorizing payment for) it.

Imagine what might happen if such a rule did not exist. Suppose that a manager has a relative who runs a small business. The manager could accept an over-priced quotation from the relative, then authorize payment for this excessive amount, and finally (perhaps) share in the proceeds with the relative. If, however, a second person had been responsible for acquitting the invoice, then the corrupt manager would have to involve them in the deal as well – not impossible, but very much less likely (and more risky).

We are not aware of any corrupt librarians who have managed to gain from such practices. (There may possibly have been some, but if so they have not advertised the fact.) However, for a small library the impact of this rule is that it may be difficult to find two separate and appropriate people to authorize orders and payments – and impossible in a one-person library. Some special arrangements will need to be reached with the organization's accounting section.

Full records of 'accountable' items

'Accountable' items, or assets, are those an organization needs to be able to produce or account for on demand – typically, cars, computers and major pieces of furniture. Many public sector organizations have little stickers with numbers on them, attached to such items.

If a library treats its books as accountable items, then in a stocktake it will need to be able to produce either the item itself, or a current loan record for that item, or a record which shows that it has been officially written off. All of this involves tedious (and expensive) record-keeping.

Better, if possible, to treat library material as 'consumable'. 'Consumable' material does not need to be accounted for; typical examples include stationery and other items whose purchase cost is trivial in relation to the costs of record-keeping. Pens and paper are 'consumed' in most organizations. If library materials are also treated as consumables, then records need not be kept. Some libraries have adopted this general approach, but still treat some very expensive items (such as rare books) as assets and maintain full records of these – a compromise that may be acceptable to the organization's auditors.

Stocktaking

This leads us directly to the topic of stocktaking. One of us had the unfortunate experience of working for a university library where the university auditors were changed on more than one occasion. Every time a new set of auditors was appointed, they would find their most junior and inexperienced member of staff, and suggest that he or she start with something thought to be really straightforward: a stocktake of the library.

In practice, few large libraries undertake full stocktakes – it is simply too expensive. To check that every item in the catalogues is in its right place, or officially on loan, may have the incidental benefits of locating catalogue errors, tidying up the shelving and sorting out loan problems, but it takes staff away from their day-to-day duties and leaves them with a huge and unwanted pile of arrears to be dealt with. The undoubted gains for readers are outweighed by the inconvenience to these readers, let alone the costs in terms of staff time.

There are, of course, circumstances when a full stocktake is likely to be desirable: very small libraries can undoubtedly benefit from such an exercise (so long as staff time is available), and even in large libraries, high-risk collections (such as university library short-loan or reserve collections) and high-value collections should probably be checked regularly. But for the collections as a whole, the alternative most libraries adopt, if they are obliged to undertake some form of stocktake, is the *sample stocktake*. A sample of, say, 500 items is randomly selected from the shelf list,[10] and only these items are followed through onto the shelves and in the loan records. This has several advantages:

- It is obviously very much faster and easier than a full stocktake.
- Most auditors appear to accept this approach.
- If there are any major problems in the cataloguing, shelving or loans areas, then these should show up in the sample, and the library can devote its resources to investigating and solving a real problem.

The other approach to the identification of problems in the cataloguing, shelving or loans areas – in the provision of information to readers – is to undertake some kind of materials availability survey. Typically, this will start with the items a group of readers are actually seeking, and examine their success and the reasons for any failures.[11] This is likely to be a much more productive and worthwhile exercise than a sample stocktake: frequently, problems are also identified in areas such as client use of the catalogues, signage, OPAC and computer access. While description of such a project is largely beyond the scope of this volume, such a holistic

approach to client problems in information access is likely to be much more useful and enlightening than the results of a simple sample stocktake. This is discussed
in more detail in 'User-oriented measures' in the following chapter.

Overall, however, the audit requirements most libraries must meet are intended
to ensure not only that their systems and procedures meet acceptable accounting
policies and any relevant regulations and statutory requirements, but also that the
resources they receive are being properly and effectively employed. A well-man-
aged library should be able to demonstrate that this is indeed the case.

Review of Chapter 8

This chapter started with the formulation of a library's materials budget, and how
this can and should fit in with the wider organization's budget cycle. Prepayment
for serials subscriptions is likely to be one of the major problems, and the importance of good communication with an organization's accounts section has been
stressed. Every larger library will need to maintain records of its commitment, but
many will be able to rely on the organization's figures for actual expenditure.

Within a library's material budget, the allocation of resources to particular client
groups is likely to be at least as much a political as a professional issue. If a formula is developed, this should be as the result of a careful process and allow for
flexibility, for review and, if necessary, for phasing in.

Acquisition of electronic media presents some special challenges. Finally,
libraries need to establish procedures that meet accepted accounting requirements
and demonstrate that the resources they receive are being properly and effectively
employed.

Where to now?

Given the practical focus of this chapter, our suggestions are practical rather than
academic. If you are currently working in the materials acquisitions area in a library,
and have not already done so, we suggest you establish personal contact with the
staff of your accounts area. Many librarians make the mistake of communicating
by memo or e-mail and the occasional telephone call. As any text on interpersonal
skills will attest, this is not the way to build or maintain personal relationships. By
visiting the staff who work with the library on its accounts, ideally on their own
ground, you will not only create the opportunity to inform them of the library's
unique needs but also learn of the constraints under which they (and so you) must
operate. If these are the constraints under which your organization operates, are

there also opportunities that together you can seize?

Much the same applies to a library's clients. Library staff, and you as a staff member with particular responsibility in the area of collection management, need to build ongoing relationships with your clients, in your mutual interest – and this too cannot be done by mail or e-mail alone.

Further reading

For the librarian who has a close working relationship with accounts staff, it makes sense to have at least a basic grasp of the principles of organizational accounting. Many introductory accounting texts provide this; one possible starting point might be 'Strategic planning and budgeting', Chapter 24 in R. N. Anthony, D. Hawkins and K. Merchant, *Accounting: text and cases*, 10th edn, McGraw-Hill, 1999, 755–75. Resource management in libraries is covered in greater detail and by a variety of contributors in D. Baker (ed.), *Resource management in academic libraries*, Library Association Publishing, 1997. The second of Baker's chapters, 'Resource management – the context', provides a useful overview, while other chapters cover issues (such as space planning) not included in the present volume. As noted earlier in this chapter, costing and pricing issues – along with an introduction to some of the central concepts of accounting, and the principles of decisions about capital investment – are also covered by H. Snyder and E. Davenport in *Costing and pricing in the digital age: a practical guide for information services*, Library Association Publishing, 1997.

Another relatively recent work which covers the overall content of this chapter in greater detail is M. S. Martin, *Collection development and finance: a guide to strategic library-materials budgeting*, American Library Association, 1995. This covers preparing the budget, the traditional budget process, access and ownership issues, internal budget allocation and monitoring, and all of this from a practical and flexible point of view. R. S. Rounds, in *Basic budgeting practices for librarians*, 2nd edn, American Library Association, 1994, is very good on the different types of budgeting, and has good ideas on needs assessment, budget presentations and budget management. Slightly older but still useful is E. Shreeves (ed.), *Guide to budget allocation for information resources*, Collection Management and Development Guides 4, American Library Association, 1991.

Those seeking the wider context may care to look at B. R. Kingma, *The economics of information: a guide to cost-benefit analysis for information professionals*, Libraries Unlimited, 1996, which gives a good introduction to the economic issues behind budgeting. (A second, 2001, edition of this had been announced, but was not yet available at the time of writing.) Wider again, even philosophical in its approach, is S. A. Roberts 'Economics and collection management'. In G.E Gorman (ed.), *International yearbook of library and information management 2000–2001: collection management*, Library Association Publishing, 2000, 59–98.

As indicated in our discussion of book fund allocation formulae, those considering development or revision of their own formula are well advised not to start without scanning the by now extensive literature on this topic. J. M. Budd's 'Allocation formulas in the literature: a review', *Library Acquisitions: Practice and Theory*, **15**, 1991, 95–107, provides a good entry point to this literature, although much has been published since (see also the references in note 7 in this chapter). The annotated bibliography at the end of this volume suggests some additional readings.

Although we described materials availability surveys as outside the scope of this volume, it is clearly not outside the responsibilities of a collection manager. You need perhaps to assess and certainly to be able to demonstrate the library's commitment to making information available to its clients – and undertaking a stocktake would have to be one of the least useful, most ineffective ways of doing that. Accordingly, we suggest you start by reading F. W. Lancaster *If you want to evaluate your library . . .* , 2nd edn, Library Association Publishing, 1993. This standard work provides practical and rigorous advice on a wide range of evaluation methodologies, including document delivery services of the kind relevant in the present context, and also in reference, resource sharing, cost-benefit and quality control. You could then consider the possible applicability of some of the approaches described to a project in your own library.

Notes

1   For a discussion of budgeting in libraries, see the further reading suggested at the end of this chapter. Planning more generally is covered in most library management texts, such as R. D. Stueart and B. B. Moran, *Library and information center management*, 5th edn, Libraries Unlimited, 1998.

2   See, for example, V. Steele and S. D. Elder, *Becoming a fundraiser: the principles and practice of library development*, 2nd edn, American Library Association, 2000; and D. Farrell, 'Fundraising for collection development librarians'. In *Collection management and development: issues in an electronic era. Proceedings of the Advanced Collection Management and Development Institute, Chicago, Illinois, March 26–28, 1993*, edited by Peggy Johnson and Bonnie MacEwan, American Library Association, 1994.

3   In the past there have been attempts to derive formulae for specific types of library, in particular university libraries, in an attempt to persuade reluctant organizations to increase their library materials allocations. V. W. Clapp and R. T. Jordan, 'Quantitative criteria for adequacy of academic library collections', *College & Research Libraries*, **50** (2), 1989, 154–63, a reprint of a *College & Research Libraries* article originally published in 1965, is probably the best known of these. See also G. A. Crawford and G. W White, 'Liberal arts colleges and "standards for college libraries": a quantitative analysis', *Journal of Academic Librarianship*, **25** (6), 1999, 439–44; and T. Graham, 'Funding arrangements for UK universities and their libraries', *New Review of Academic Librarianship*, **2**, 1996, 27–40.

4   R. Wade and V. Williamson, 'Cataloguing costed and restructured at Curtin University of Technology', *Australian Academic & Research Libraries*, **29** (4), 1998, 177–89.

5   M. S. Martin, *Collection development and finance: a guide to strategic library materials budgeting*, American Library Association, 1995, 87.

6   Ibid., Chapter 10.

7   See, for example, D. Packer, 'Acquisitions, allocations: equity, politics, and formulas', *Journal of Academic Librarianship*, **14**, 1988, 276–86; J. M. Budd, 'Allocation formulas in the literature: a review', *Library Acquisitions: Practice and Theory*, **15**, 1991, 95–107; C. Cubberly, 'Allocating the materials fund using total cost of materials', *Journal of Academic Librarianship*, **19**, 1993, 16–21; M. Evans, 'Library acquisitions formulae: the Monash experience', *Australian Academic & Research Libraries*, **27** (1), 1996, 47–57; S. Lafferty, P. Warning and B. Vlies, 'Foundation resources: formula-based allocation of an acquisitions budget in a university library', *Australian Academic & Research Libraries*, **27** (4), 1996, 289–94; J. Hutchins, 'Developing a formula for library resource planning'. In D. Baker (ed.), *Resource management in academic libraries*, Library Association Publishing, 1997, 119–36; G. Ford, 'Finance and budgeting'. In C. Jenkins and M. Morley (eds), *Collection management in academic libraries*, 2nd edn, Gower Publishing, 1999, 39–69; and many others.

8   D. L. Bosseau, 'Anatomy of a small step forward: the Electronic Reserve Book Room at San Diego State University', *Journal of Academic Librarianship*, **18** (5), 1993, 366–8.

9   H. W. Groenewegen, 'Electronic reserves: key issues and innovations', *Australian Academic & Research Libraries*, **29** (1), 1998, 1–12.

10   A random sample is one where every item in the set (in this case, in the collection) has an exactly equal chance of being selected. One methodologically correct method of selecting such a sample is to use a table of random num-

bers – found in the appendixes of almost every statistics text – and use this to identify accession or automated system numbers, discarding those random number groupings that do not relate to accession or system numbers. For fuller details, see such works as I. S. Simpson, *Basis statistics for librarians*, 3rd edn, Clive Bingley, 1988, or P. Hernon, 'Determination of sample size and selection of the sample: concepts, general sources, and software', *College & Research Libraries*, **55** (2), 1994, 171–9. Selecting an appropriate sample size is another matter dealt with by almost all statistics texts. The library staff – or perhaps the auditors – determine how accurate the results should be or, to use the statistical jargon, what 'level of confidence' is required. Simpson covers this on pp. 44–8.

11 The basic approach was described by T. Saracevic, W. M. Shaw and P. B. Kantor in 'Causes and dynamics of user frustration in an academic library', *College & Research Libraries*, **38** (1), 1977, 7–18. Librarians who reported using this approach include R. H. Smith and W. Granade, 'User and library failures in an undergraduate library', *College & Research Libraries*, **39** (6), 1978, 467–73; N. A. Radford, 'Failure in the library: a case study', *Library Quarterly*, **53** (3), 1983, 328–39; J. Hagerlid, 'The availability study as a tool for collection evaluation in a closed stacks library', *Tidskrift for Dokumentation*, **40** (4), 1984, 127–35; A. C. Ciliberti et al., 'Material availability: a study of academic library performance', *College & Research Libraries*, **48** (6), 1987, 513–27. Other published work in this area includes P. B. Kantor, *Objective performance measurement for academic and research libraries*, ARL, 1984; J. Mansbridge, 'Availability studies in libraries', *Library and Information Science Research*, **8** (4), 1986, 299–314; D. Revill, 'Availability as a performance measure', *Journal of Librarianship*, **19** (1), 1987, 16–30; D. Revill, 'An availability study in co-operation with a school of librarianship and information studies', *Library Review*, **37** (1), 1988, 17–34; N. A. Van House, *Measuring academic library performance: a practical approach*, American Library Association, 1990; and N. A. Jacobs, 'Book availability surveys'. In D. Spiller (ed.), *Academic library surveys and statistics in practice*, Library and Information Statistics Unit, 1998, 43–6.

9

Collection evaluation and review

Focus questions

- What are the reasons for collection evaluation?
- What procedures are involved in collection evaluation?
- What are the principal user-centred methods of collection evaluation?
- What are the principal collection-centred methods of collection evaluation?

Accountability, especially among public sector organizations, has become a driving force behind the growing emphasis on and interest in performance indicators. At one time collection managers were content to regard the size of a collection as the measure of its worth, but we have moved beyond this simplistic approach. As Magrill and East warned more than two decades ago,

> . . . there are those who distrust the seemingly precise results obtained from manipulation of basic figures subjectively assigned. In some of the operations research applications, models are based on assumptions which cannot be verified by librarians in their day-to-day experiences with library users.[1]

Today we are more inclined to use performance indicators to 'prove' that our funds are being expended in return for improved services that benefit the widest possible range of users. In terms of collection management, collection evaluation and review is essentially a means of gathering and assessing performance indicators about the use and strength of collections of information resources. Therefore, it is an essential component in the accountability process. The growing emphasis on accountability has been accompanied by significant advances in the ability of auto-mated library systems to provide tailored management information reports that can be used for data collection and analysis, and this has facilitated the conduct and use of collection evaluation studies. Combine the current management ethos with technological capabilities, and we have the potential for revived interest in collection evaluation as part of collection management after a period of relative neglect.

In most countries developments along these lines have been relatively haphazard, or have focused on one specific aspect – for example, in the USA (and much less in Britain) these has been emphasis on Conspectus as the most appropriate approach to evaluation (see Chapter 3). In the UK a series of discrete reports, when combined, provide an excellent set of performance evaluation guidelines – most notably the compilation by Bohme and Spiller; these are discussed at some length by David Spiller.[2]

The rationale for collection evaluation

Evaluation of a collection of information resources is the process of getting to know its strengths and weaknesses using techniques that are likely to yield valid and reli-able results (in other words, techniques that measure what they set out to measure and provide results that can be replicated if necessary). Collection evaluation is defined as the process of measuring the degree to which a library acquires the materials it intends to acquire in accordance with stated parameters (usually in a collection development policy). In the words of Magrill and Corbin (1989), 'Col-lection evaluation is concerned with how good a collection is in terms of the kinds of materials in it and the value of each item in relation to items not in the collection, to the community being served, and to the library's potential users.'[3]

A properly conducted collection evaluation exercise is a demanding and time-consuming process, and it will usually be undertaken with a view to understanding the strengths and weaknesses of the collection, with the aim of producing some-thing better by retaining and enhancing the strengths, and reducing or eliminating the weaknesses. In other words evaluation of a collection should lead to a more objective understanding of the scope and depth of the collection, and provide a guide for collection planning, budgeting and decision making.

The aims of collection evaluation

As professionals, collection managers want to know how well a collection is meet-

ing the demands and needs of its users and potential users. As administrators spending other people's money, and under increasing pressure to justify why and how
they are doing so, they may well need the fullest possible understanding of the
way the funds are being expended, and a basis for timely action to make improvements or economies. These are the broad professional aims of collection evaluation,
which is a function of collection development and is related to the planning, selection and pruning of collections. Regarded in this light collection evaluation has
a number of aims:

- To search for more accurate understanding of the scope, depth and utility of
  collections.
- To prepare a guide and a basis for collection development.
- To aid in the preparation of a collection development policy.
- To measure the effectiveness of a collection development policy.
- To determine collection adequacy or quality.
- To help rectify inadequacies in library holdings and to improve them.
- To focus human and financial resources on areas most needing attention.
- To provide justification for book budget increases.
- To demonstrate to administrators that something is being done about the
  demands for 'more money'.
- To establish the existence of special strengths, as well as weaknesses, in the col-
  lection.
- To check the need for weeding and collection control, and to establish areas
  of priority for these operations.

These are listed broadly in a descending order of importance, given that the primary concern is to aid the library in achieving the objective of satisfying its users.
Thus the first five aims listed require the most attention. The need to understand
the present state of the collection – the first aim – underpins all the others, as on
that understanding are built the subsequent tasks of preparing guides and policies for collection development (second and third aims), and of measuring the
effectiveness of those policies (fourth aim). One develops measurements of the adequacy of the collection so that attention can be further focused on the areas in
which the collection is less than adequate (fifth aim), and on the practical measures that must be developed to rectify these shortcomings (sixth and seventh aims).
The political nature of all operations such as this is highlighted in the eighth and
ninth aims, in which one takes steps to ensure not only that the library is moving
towards a better service for its clientele, but also that those who control the

purse-strings are made aware of this. The last two aims listed are the necessary operations that follow from the previous steps.

The starting point must be the goals and mission of the institution. From these come a clear idea of the purpose of the collection, including any co-ordinated collection arrangements with other libraries. Only on this basis is it possible to set objectives for any evaluation. If a collection manager is uncertain about the objectives of the institution or those of the evaluation, then the outcome is likely to be unfocused at best. What steps are being recommended as a result of the findings? What are the likely results of action or lack of action? Such outcomes relate to objectives. Equally, one must recognize that many collection managers taking part in evaluation exercises see little reward for themselves personally, and some may even suspect that knowledge of actual costs and performance could well lead to questioning of the viability of some operations, with consequent changes in the status quo.

Acknowledgement of this reality, however, does not remove the need for the compilation of convincing reports, based on sound evaluative methods, designed to determine the scope, quality, accessibility and usefulness of existing collections with a view to ensuring that development can proceed in line with current needs and institutional goals.

Caveats about collection evaluation

In Chapter 5 we noted the tension between supplying what readers need, rather than what they want, or say they want. There is a difference between these three concepts of need, actual demand, and expressed demand and, while published work seems not to concern itself with 'subconscious needs', there is little doubt that we must be concerned with 'yet unexpressed demand'. The collection of a library must be managed in such a way that readers' needs can be anticipated as much as possible and material is made available at the earliest expression of any demand.

It is probably true that user perceptions of how good a library is have very little to do with the collection's size and scope, or any other objective measures of quality, and a great deal to do with how well it provides what each individual user is looking for. While it might be the collection manager's professional duty to supply what he or she thinks people need, it may also be a political and economic necessity to meet their expressed demands – there is a great deal of evidence to suggest that the budget decision-making process is very much influenced by user satisfaction. Whether a library service is really any good is less important than whether the users and decision makers think it so.

There is also evidence that studies that focus on the activities and procedures of information professionals (how good are we at doing our job?) are much less useful than are those based on information users, and that user studies in general consider factors that are beyond the control of managers. The range of variations in individual use patterns is so great, and so far out of the control of the collection manager, that it may be better to concentrate on organizational variables, which are both less variable and more controllable.

It is important to remember that the information-gathering methods used by people in different fields vary enormously. Ease of access seems to be the most important single criterion, with relevance, pertinence, accuracy and currency of information being relatively less important. A researcher prefers to ask an accessible colleague rather than go to a library, and overall there is little doubt that to many people a library means little as a source of information. The truth seems to be that, although librarians can identify some factors such as education, family life patterns and environment that allow the prediction of library use, there are other demographic factors that appear to have no effect, and those factors that do have an effect seem to account for only a small part of library use.

The various findings that lead one to these conclusions may be closely related to another serious problem in use studies. An assumption is made that if a researcher or librarian wants to know something about people, the simplest way to find out is to mount a survey to ask them. However, studies have shown that a considerable amount of the variation reported in library use may be no more than variation in interpretation of the meaning of the word 'use'. The question of different interpretations of meaning is dealt with most notably in the classic study by Bookstein, who found that much work is required before studies of library use have any practical significance.[4] It is difficult to demonstrate with any degree of certainty that the use of libraries has any definite influence on anything else, because the question of the causes behind library use is still unanswered. Use studies provide very little help when it comes to collection management, because, despite the fact that librarians and other researchers have been studying library users for many years, we still do not have a satisfactory understanding of why people do, or do not, use libraries.

In the last 50 years, in other words, evaluation has become both more sophisticated and more specialized, although not necessarily any more definitive in its results. We have come to recognize that collections can be assessed by focusing either on the materials themselves or, alternatively, on the use of these materials. In the first group of methods, collection-centred, we have access to a variety of well-tested approaches, including list checking, use of collection standards, expert review, and comparative use statistics. In the second group, focusing on usage, we can undertake circulation studies, in-house use studies, user surveys, shelf availability tests, analysis of interlibrary loan figures, citation studies, and document delivery tests. Each of these methods has particular strengths and weaknesses, and today they are often used in combination in order to compensate for the latter – this is a key factor to keep in mind as one reads about the evaluation methods in this chapter, which are treated as discrete approaches for descriptive purposes here. There is no single correct way to carry out such a task. Using a number of complementary methods to compensate for the weaknesses of each is often described as 'triangulation' in research. It is also worth emphasizing that information professionals have a sound corpus of literature on which to draw in conducting their own studies, including useful 'how-to-do-it' manuals by Lockett and Hall and the extensive bibliography by Nisonger, which is partially updated in serial format.[5]

Steps in conducting an evaluation

The essential steps in conducting collection evaluations do not differ from those in any piece of quantitative research. Accordingly, in this section we merely summarize the principal steps, and refer readers to a number of useful works on quantitative research methods, such as Busha and Harter, Powell, Leedy, Babbie and others.[6] These steps are relevant to both the user-centred and the collection-centred approaches to collection evaluation (discussed later in this chapter).

Set purpose and objectives

Define the purposes of the study and the specific objectives to be met; ask if the information being sought is really needed, and precisely how it will be used when it is gathered. For instance, if one is interested in the subject areas of a reference collection that are being most heavily utilized, it is generally not worth collecting detailed information about the age, gender and social background of users. The next step is to ask what would be done with the information once it is gathered. It is imperative to ensure that a causal relationship can be shown to exist between two factors before they are measured, as it is possibly the most elementary error in survey design at this level to assume that an observable action that precedes a second observable action is necessarily the cause of that second action.

Review previous research

The next step is to survey previous studies. There is much to be learned from an evaluation of the objectives and methods used in other surveys – at the very least some insights could arise, and at best a plan or an instrument might be suitable for replication. While one needs to take into account any unique or different circumstances between the institutions, it is nevertheless always worth considering whether someone else's evaluation can be adapted for present needs – this is simply a common sense approach to being a critical consumer of research.

Select data to be collected and methodology

Determining the methodology to be followed and the precise data to be gathered are necessary in order for the collection manager to be certain of what answers are needed, *before* the questions are developed to elicit those answers. Here, we suggest a methodical approach: set out your objectives in a table as a series of questions. Then, alongside each, list how you propose to answer that question. Finally, in a third column list the data that will answer that question.

To provide a hypothetical example, let us assume we are evaluating a library's collection of CD-ROM databases (see Table 9.1) as part of a wider evaluation.

Table 9.1   *Data collection table*

Objectives phrased as questions to be answered	Method to be used	Data required
Which databases are most used?	System log analysis	Connect time
Which databases are most useful?	Reader survey	Question 6 of draft survey

By adopting such an approach you can ensure that every question you need to answer in your collection evaluation will, in fact, be answered. The last entry in the right-hand column in Table 9.1 suggests another issue: frequently, we have seen surveys that are longer than they need to be (and so less likely to be answered). By going backwards from the final questions to be included in a survey to its objectives, it is often possible to identify questions that need not be asked at all. For example, questions about the age and gender of database users, while of some interest, would be irrelevant in answering this question and could be omitted.

It is worth bearing in mind that some of the data needed may already be available in some form – for instance, in the example in the table, the system logs were presumably already available. Automated systems collect a great deal of data about their operations which are not routinely analysed.

Select population sample

Having determined what data are to be gathered and which methodology is to be employed, the manager then selects the sample of the population to be studied (note that here a 'population' can consist of *things*, such as all the books, as well as a population of people, such as all library users). This will certainly mean the careful study of a reputable textbook on survey design and the understanding of the simplest facets of sampling technique. The basic premise is this: if the sample is accurately taken, then the characteristics of the sample approximate those of the group from which it was taken (the population). There are four key factors to be taken into account in sampling:

- The sample must be such that every member of the stratum or sub-group being sampled (not necessarily the total population) has an equal chance of being selected.
- Generally a large sample will produce more accurate results, but a trade-off must be made between sample size, sample accuracy and total cost.
- The sample must be of that part of the population being studied, and must be taken under conditions that avoid the introduction of bias. For example, surveying items on the shelves only would exclude those on loan, which are likely to be of greater value.
- Because any sample will produce figures that merely approximate the total population, a decision must be made at the time the survey is being planned on the level of precision (accuracy) and the level of confidence (that is, how confident can the surveyor be that a true answer would have fallen within the range indicated by the sample?).

Each of these factors will be affected by sample design and by cost. To put it simply, a trade-off is always necessary between cost, accuracy and reliability. However, a bad sample, no matter what the cost, will still be a bad sample, and a good sample can be a remarkably accurate and useful method of estimating the characteristics of a total population. These and other points are made clearly and in considerable detail by Alreck and Settle, whose work on survey research is as good as the earlier, library-specific guide by Maurice Line, and now more widely available.[7]

Carry out a pilot study

Unless you are merely replicating someone's else's study, or perhaps repeating an evaluation carried out some time earlier in your own library, it is very unlikely you will have been able to determine all of the necessary details in your first attempt. Questions that seem quite clear and unambiguous to the person asking them can prove very far from so to others; something an experienced professional can do easily may be challenging to the junior staff who are asked to do it in practice; it can prove unexpectedly difficult to transfer data accurately from a form to a computer spreadsheet; and so on. Much time will almost always be saved and the quality of the results greatly improved by carrying out a trial run with a small sample before undertaking the full survey.

Edit and analyse the data

Determining the methods of analysis of the data, or of the observations, is much less of a chore in these days of computer-based data management, but the basic problems remain. It is necessary first to edit the data that have been returned from the survey, to make certain that what is entered into the computer database or spreadsheet is as accurate as possible. Sometimes this is because forms are completed in a hurry, or because of the different meanings attached to the same words by different people. Coding will almost always involve some subjective decisions about what was meant by the person filling out the form or completing the survey, or whatever data collection instrument has been employed. These interpretations need to be decided on a consistent basis, and for this a table of coding decisions is employed. Then, every piece of potentially ambiguous data will be treated in exactly the same way – even if the decision is that a particular question must be regarded as unanswered.

The second part of the analysis is the decision on the form of presentation of the results, which must be such that it describes the overall pattern accurately and simply. While sometimes tables of figures can provide useful detail, in most cases graphic presentation will tell the story at a glance. Either way, the test is always that the presentation method should be clear, simple and accurate, and should reflect the characteristics of the population studied.

Facilitate replication

Finally, it is crucial to chart the passage taken through the particular exercise for the benefit of others who may want to try the same kind of exercise, and to make it possible for the whole exercise to be repeated under similar conditions simply so that the results can be verified. In other cases a library will wish to be able to repeat the analysis at some future time in order to measure any changes that may have taken place.

In sum, it is imperative that collection analysis be linked to the aims and objectives of the institution and thus of its library. With this in mind, the evaluation should identify the specific questions to be asked, starting always by asking what kind of information is needed, which will suggest what answers are required and hence what questions should be asked, and also by questioning whether that information may be available from other sources. In addition it is important that the subjectivity of the various measures of the quality of collections be reduced as much as possible. This can be done by the use of quantitative techniques which count not only items of stock and the numbers of times they are used in some way or another, but also measure interactions between users and the library's services. It is also important that the chosen processes measure and evaluate those aspects that actually have an effect on use. That is, we need to rely less on descriptive factors and more on causal factors.

Methods of collection evaluation

Collection evaluation consists principally of two types of approaches. The first is user-centred, meaning that concentration is on the individual user as the unit of analysis, with 'user' being defined as the person using the materials in the collection. The second is collection-centred, meaning that the evaluation techniques focus on examination of the collection in terms of its size, scope, depth and significance. There was a time when books of this sort insisted that each was equally valid and equally useful. While their validity remains unchallenged, the reality is that their usefulness has changed somewhat over the years.

In relation to collection evaluation the important results of, among other documents, the Follett Report and *Academic library effectiveness* have been to establish a set of key indicators generally deemed most relevant for collection evaluation.[8] These are listed by Spiller as:

- number of loans per capita
- items on loan per capita
- loans per item per annum, or 'stock turnover'
- percentage of items borrowed/not borrowed
- proportion of interlibrary loans to total loans
- ratio of ILLs received to ILLs lent

- a 'needs-fill' measure on whether users find what they seek
- user satisfaction with stock.[9]

These all boil down to measures of use (or user studies), which we have advocated as the principal means of collection evaluation for nearly two decades and which, despite their 'ancient pedigree', remain the most broadly useful means of evaluating a collection.

By definition collection-centred evaluation involves the evaluation of a collection. Yet in the digital age, libraries will no longer have 'a' collection. Instead they will consist of a hybrid collection: a physical collection of print, multimedia and digital objects complemented by access to the emerging worldwide virtual library. Clients should not need to know whether an item is 'held' locally or merely available on demand: if they want a particular piece of information, their library can access it for them. Distinctions between the held and the available on demand will increasingly be unimportant – indeed, the two will increasingly be seen by clients as part of a seamless whole.

The result of this is that use- and user-centred evaluation methods are increasingly the assessment methods of choice. Accordingly, evaluation now tends to focus on techniques of user or client evaluation: usage studies, client surveys, document delivery studies, and availability studies (but information availability studies, *not* 'shelf' availability as in the past). Only in exceptional circumstances – the assessment of an historical collection, for example – will there be much place for collection-oriented evaluation. Note, however, that if there is a reason to undertake a collection-centred evaluation, online bibliographies and online catalogues provide additional tools for such an assessment.

In the remainder of this chapter the question of how collections can be evaluated is discussed, and to do this effectively it is necessary to make some basic assumptions:

- Use of a book is a measure of its value.
- Past use of books is a valid indicator of likely future use.
- Circulation figures are an indication of the actual use of an item.
- Measurements of use inside and outside the library are closely related.

Against this approach is the argument that measures of past use show what was done, whereas what ought to have been done is perhaps more important. Underlying methods of analysis of use or user statistics there is a basic assumption that value is directly proportionate to use. However, it could be suggested that availability of material, rather than ideas of perceived value, is the most significant factor affecting material use. Thus measurement of use is a doubtful method of measuring value, even though it may well be a good measure of availability; and that to calculate in terms of use is almost certain to guarantee the status quo. There is also an implied assumption that knowing what people need can be translated into a service that people will use to satisfy their needs.

Considerations as basic as 'what are the institution's missions and goals?' need definition, and the precise purposes of the study must be spelled out. It is essential that the study be designed with an overall view of its usefulness and applicability. As a starting point, the following questions need to be asked and answered:

- What is the goal of the study?
- What are the parameters of the study?
- Which aspects of collection use are to be analysed?
- Can the necessary information or significant data be gathered?
- Is the method appropriate for the purpose?
- What is the possible range of findings that might result from the surveys?
- What are the practical benefits that might result from any findings?
- What are the implications of the process itself in terms of likely impact on services, operations and the political environment in which the library operates?

Once these have been addressed satisfactorily, it is then possible to determine which type of measure is the most suitable for the specific evaluation exercise – but bear in mind the above statement about likely primacy of use- and user-centred methods.

User-oriented measures

Use and user studies

Use and user studies measure actual use by readers, and assume that heavy use of a collection means it is a 'good collection'. An implicit assumption in this approach is that a measure of the use of a book is a measure of its value to the library. This assumption is the basis of the work on collection weeding by Slote, in which he argues that in weeding one is aiming to reduce the stock to a core collection that will satisfy 95–99% of present use as measured by loan statistics.[10] While it is not difficult to collate figures that indicate classes of books that have not been used in the past, and thus are likely not to be used in the future, it may not be possible to do the same for individual items in the collection. Nevertheless, there is little doubt that the best method of establishing likely future use of any individual work is its shelf-time period, that is, the time the work has remained on the shelf since last issued, or since its accession. Most writers have now accepted that past use is the most reliable indicator of likely future use in large research libraries, although they stress that there are great variations in different subject areas and that the method needs to be applied with caution.

There are at least eight problems inherent in the use and user studies approach.

1 It is necessary that some statistics have already been gathered for at least a reasonable period.
2 Statistics gathered on the use of certain parts of any collection do not necessarily reflect the use of other parts, or of different uses of the same parts.
3 There are problems in measuring in-house use, as most of the methods either rely on user co-operation or on staff who are involved in other work at the time, or are used in uncontrolled areas of the library.
4 The method measures demands rather than needs, and thereby raises the important question of whether measures of what has actually been required in the past should be taken as reliable indicators of what ought to be needed in the future.
5 Any surveys of actual users must of necessity ignore potential users, unless it is to be assumed that the potential users will have the same needs and make the same demands as do existing users.
6 What is the real meaning of 'use' as it is understood by the readers being surveyed? As Bookstein has shown, there is considerable variation in what readers understand by the words 'use' and 'read', and that the term 'use' seemed generally to be linked in the minds of respondents with some measure of 'usefulness', rather than with the simple act of 'making some use of'.
7 Familiarity with the collection will influence the advice and recommendations given by staff to readers. It is almost inevitable that where professional advice is offered, there will be a tendency to recommend material that is familiar or has recently come to notice, thus influencing the results of any use study.
8 Finally, and by definition, studies of use and users ignore non-users. It is at least possible that some present non-users could become users if the library were to offer a different or expanded range of resources (and the non-users were advised of this). Over 20 years ago, Lancaster drew attention to an inherent problem with basing library management decisions solely on usage:

There is a strong tendency for the managers of information services to do more of the things that their present users are asking them to do. Perhaps the most obvious example is buying more books or periodicals of the type that present users are asking for. Doing this, however, tends to move information services closer to the needs of present users and further away from the needs of present non-users . . . The decisions of managers of information services tend to be most influenced by those demands of present users that occur most frequently. This leads to a self-reinforcing situation . . . The services thus become increasingly exclusive, ever favoring present users over present non-users, ever favoring the heavy users at the expense of the light ones.[11]

Document delivery tests

Document delivery tests are used to assess the capability of the library to provide users with materials at the time they need them. These tests must measure the following features:

- the extent to which the collection is able to provide the material needed in specific subject areas
- the speed with which the material is provided
- the effort the user is required to expend in order to get results
- the level of precision of the system expressed by its ability to provide what is needed and to filter out what is not needed.

It is important to design the study so that it does not interfere with normal work routines. This introduces a difficult problem: a time and method that best suit staff requirements may not be the best in terms of objective measurement. Indeed, almost the reverse is true; for instance, a time that suits work patterns could well be a 'slack period' and would measure a 'non-typical' delivery pattern. An effective approach would be to design an instrument that lists a number of documents (or references to them) thought to be those most likely to be needed by the users, and then to determine how many of the items are owned by the library, how many are available at the time, and how long it takes to make them available.

Although the technique is said to simulate the processes employed by a user who walks into the library and searches for a document, it may be difficult not to introduce unconscious variations. The best way, of course, would be to make use of real-time situations, but this would almost certainly result in some unnecessary complications; it could not only lower the quality of the service being offered at the time but also introduce an unmeasurable bias.

Among the advantages of document delivery tests are these: they provide objective information on the ability of the system to satisfy specified user needs; the data can be compared among different libraries; they are not difficult to design, to understand, or to install. However, these advantages are counterbalanced by several disadvantages: it is difficult to compile a list of representative citations for use in checking actual delivery procedures; they require repeated comparable tests; and since staff who perform the tests are familiar with library procedures, the results can underestimate the problems faced by users, who are less familiar with using libraries.

A variant on this approach is to analyse interlibrary loan requests, which of course reflect material users have actually asked for but which is not held. This can be especially useful in identifying serial titles frequently requested, perhaps in a special library. Against that, ILL records ignore direct or reciprocal access to other collections and, if the ILL service is poor, all ILL use will be discouraged no matter how much some items may have been wanted.

Shelf availability tests

In a sense shelf availability tests are a subset of document delivery tests used to determine whether items presumed to be in the collection are actually available to users. The importance of shelf availability per se is open to question, because simple measures of what is, or is not, available when asked for may have little to do with any measures of value. This is certainly called into question by the classic work of Trueswell, who calculated that 99% of the circulation requirements in two American universities could have been met by 25 and 40% respectively of the two collections.[12]

These tests have several advantages: they do report failures of real users, and are thus more likely to reflect what is actually happening, rather than what is thought to be happening; they can be used to identify reasons for user failure outside the scope of collection development policies, and thus can be useful for other purposes (such as improving reshelving procedures); and they can be repeated readily. Among their disadvantages are that: they depend on the co-operation of users; the design and operation of each study is difficult and time consuming; and they do not identify the needs of non-users.

Circulation studies

These studies are used to identify the less-used parts of a collection for weeding, to identify a core collection, perhaps for duplication or special treatment, or to identify use patterns of selected subject areas for adjustment of funding and collection development practices, and also to identify user populations. While this approach may reflect current circulation patterns, this not necessarily a measure of what the pattern ought to have been, or of what is likely to be done in the future. Also, the data must be relatively sophisticated, showing loans by different classes of borrowers, by different classes of materials, by different loan periods. Some method of comparison of the figures with those of acquisitions in the relevant subject areas should also be included.

The principal value of circulation studies is that they enable a library to focus on developing what Day and Revill call the 'active collection'.[13] More specific advantages of circulation studies include the following: with computerization of circulation procedures the data are easily collected and easily arranged for analysis; the duration of a study is flexible; sample sizes can easily be adjusted to suit changing circumstances; the units are easily counted; the information is objective. Among the disadvantages, one may mention that they exclude in-house consultation and thus are almost certain to under-represent actual use. They may indeed misrepresent it, for although some research shows a high correlation between volumes used in the library and volumes taken out on loan, other work throws some doubt on this.[14] Circulation studies reflect only successes, and do not record user failures; they may be biased through the inaccessibility of heavily used material; they could fail to identify low use through obsolescence or low-quality material.

In-house use studies

These studies can be used to record the use of material consulted in the library. In-house user studies give more complete pictures of in-house use than other methods, and they can be used in conjunction with circulation studies for more accurate information on specific parts of the collection. On the other hand, they rely on user co-operation, so they are difficult to use in uncontrolled areas. Also, certain aspects of timing and of the non-recording of materials in circulation may bias results, and they also reflect only successes and do not report failures.

It is necessary to define precisely what is meant by 'in-house'. For that purpose some kind of marking of material is used so that it can be seen if it has been disturbed, and use may be more narrowly defined by taking into account only material taken from the shelves and left on tables for re-shelving. Because there is also a considerable amount of variation in use of different parts of a collection, it is unwise to make any decision on the basis of in-house studies that could not be verified and supported by other kinds of measures. As Altmann and Gorman have shown, in-house use on its own, or more properly the variation known as 'density of use', 'may favour the retention of low-use titles possessing a high density of use compared with a high-use title occupying a large amount of shelf space'.[15] This, of course, would defeat the purpose of a use study employed to determine items for withdrawal or discard.

Qualitative measures of use

At the beginning of this discussion of use and user studies it was stated that they measure actual use by users, but this is not the full picture. In fact there are also some qualitative measures, generally non-quantifiable, which rely on opinions rather than counting. These generally consist of surveys of user opinions and have as their primary goal the determination of how well a collections meets user needs. Because 'use' can only be measured when it is a recordable transaction, even the most sophisticated use study cannot disclose whether the material was in fact what was needed, or indeed whether any result other than the mere transaction itself was achieved. Thus it is necessary to survey not only the users to ask questions about their degree of satisfaction, but also experts in order to gain critical assessments of the quality of the material. The normal pattern for studies of this kind includes either specific structured questions plied through interviews or questionnaires, or rather more general open-ended queries, using the same kinds of method.

These user studies have the following advantages: they can be used to evaluate qualitatively the effectiveness of the collections and services in meeting user needs; they provide information to help solve specific problems, to modify particular programmes and to assess needs for new services; they define the make-up of the community of library users, identify groups that need to be better served, provide feedback on successes as well as on deficiencies, and improve public relations; they assist in the education of user communities and in identifying changing trends and interests; they are not limited to existing data; they permit direct feedback from users; they can be as simple or as complex as is desired (or can be afforded).

Their disadvantages are almost as numerous: they measure demands rather than needs; it is difficult to design a sophisticated survey; data analysis is difficult; the passivity of some users can make surveying difficult. As well as these disadvantages, some users simply may not co-operate, thus skewing results; the method may focus on user interests more than on collection development policies; and (unless a special effort is made to obtain responses from those who do not visit the library) the surveys consider only actual users, not potential ones. Problems arise also from the propensity of users to provide information that may well reflect their intentions or their memories rather than provide a more accurate portrayal of the past or of future needs.

However, and as noted earlier in this chapter, in the end libraries are funded not because of what they do and how well they do it, but as a result of the *perceptions* of these things held by funders and by the community that a library serves. Measuring and reporting on such perceptions is arguably as effective a way of securing continuing funding as providing more 'objective' data about such things as collection quality and usage.

Collection-oriented measures

The second group of evaluation methodologies comprises collection-oriented measures. The principal methodological approaches include the application of standards, the use of checklists and verification studies, and the use of citation analysis. In general they work on an assumption that the collection should be moulded to a 'stimulus-response' pattern based on the needs of those who use libraries most frequently.

They are best thought of as a group of statistical descriptions of collections, concentrating on size, subject areas, usage, expenditures and other factors. The principal methodological techniques are those dealing with size and patterns of growth. They comprise the investigation of the question of minimum size in relation to level and size of specific areas, such as teaching programmes, also taking into account the budget in relation to the same kinds of areas. Statistics on size are easily available, easily understood and are easy to compare, but are of questionable use when measuring how good a collection is.

Verification studies

One of the most important methodologies is verification studies, measurements of the adequacy of the collection to supply materials in demand, requiring the checking of standard lists and bibliographies. They are easy to summarize and to compare and can be used to measure 'quality' of the collection; but they need to be matched with the library's specific objectives and require appraisals by library users and experts.

The lists used to check the collections may be standard checklists – for example, those on nursing and health studies by Brandon and Hill.[16] These comprise listings put together for quite specific purposes such as to allow a teaching institution to supply material necessary for the preparation of essays and project papers, and for independent background reading, or composite lists such as the various guides to reference books which are often used as checklists for establishing core collections.

The weaknesses of this kind of checking are: the various lists must of necessity be out of date as soon as they are published; they are often designed with American conditions in mind; they tend to induce conformity by encouraging librarians to collect what is already held by other similar libraries; and carrying out such studies can be very boring for staff (and so lead to errors). It is essential that such lists be assessed for their suitability for a particular library. Indeed, in some situations specially designed lists may be the only answer.[17] The checking may also cover only a small part of the library's holdings in any specific subject area, and could well overlook many important works held by the library but not listed in the checklist.

One variation is to evaluate the library against listings of sources used by scholars in the preparation of well-known works, and in effect to ask whether such books could have been written using only the resources available in that library. This method has the attraction that not only will it check the collection at a practical as well as a theoretical level, but also it will check the holdings in many peripheral subject areas that might have been covered by the works in question. Another variation is to make up the initial list from several reviewing and selection tools, assuming that the appearance of any specific title on a multiplicity of lists is an indication of its acceptance as a worthwhile acquisition.

Citation analysis

One seemingly more accurate quantitative measurement of use is citation analysis, another form of checklist approach. It involves a study of the footnotes, bibliographies and reference lists in published scholarly works with a view to discovering what books and journals are cited most often (and so are presumably the key works in their area).

This can be useful in fields in which no standard lists exist; however, it under-represents material which is important but which is otherwise under-cited, such as review articles and annual summaries in particular discipline areas. There is also the danger of a 'closed circle':

reference ➤ citation ➤ reference

Also, the method relies on the assumption that more heavily cited material is more likely to be used than is less heavily cited material. Enough has been said about the dangers of equating 'use' with 'value' for the usual caveat to be understood here. Studies have shown that a small core of works contains a substantial part of the relevant literature in any subject area; indeed, the study of this effect, in reality no more than a 'local' application of the normal distribution in statistics, has become almost a minor 'growth industry' in collection management in recent decades, with the generous application of Bradford's law.[18]

It is worth noting that citation studies have been vigorously criticized in recent years, with an emphasis on the need for re-evaluation of the Cited by Leading Journal (CBLJ) approach so often used in selection decisions. Altmann and Gorman, for instance, have argued that CBLJ introduces a bias that may be entirely inappropriate for many specialized or geographically unique collections. Altmann and Gorman also maintain that local use studies must be employed as a complement to any impact factors that are divorced from a specific institutional context.[19]

The advantages of citation analysis are: data are easily arranged; the method is simple and thus studies can be replicated with comparative ease; it can help to identify trends in published literature; the lists can be compiled easily using online databases. On the other hand, disadvantages include the following: it can be difficult to select source items to reflect specific needs; certain sub-areas in any one discipline may have use and citation patterns different from those of the general literature; research patterns in some subjects do not lend themselves to citation study; the inherent time lag may not reflect changes in disciplines or in publishing patterns; and when used in isolation, for all its apparent arithmetical respectability, it can be a questionable measurement for collection management decisions.

In fact, there are many good reasons why it is dangerous to accept that citation analysis and citation use studies provide much useful information at all. One problem is that there is a variety of reasons for citing references; the author may not cite all the papers he used; works that were cited may not have been used very much at all; some ideas may be incorporated without reference to their source; papers that oppose an argument may not be cited, or may be cited simply to be refuted; and references may be included simply in order to dress up a paper. In addition, citation of a friend or a superior, or simply the seminal and prestigious works in the field, is not unknown. There are several papers that cover this weakness of the citation analysis method, and it is recommended that they be given some attention. Two quotes from a paper by Herner and Herner, for instance, give an idea of the flavour of this kind of problem: 'How people get information and what they cite are frequently quite different . . . The second fallacy is the extreme subjectivity involved in trying to divine why an author cited a publication.'[20] Nevertheless, and despite the evidence that can be amassed against the efficacy of citation analysis for measuring use, it is still seen as one useful tool – as Michael Koenig says, 'what is important tends to be what is cited'.[21]

Case study 9.1

Upgrading the law collection

William Shakespeare University had taught law for many years, but only in 'service' subjects: an introduction to the legal system and to legal materials, together with subjects on administrative law, on intellectual property and so on; all for students studying other courses, such as management. However, recently it had been decided to offer a degree course in law. Two law professors have been appointed, substantial funding from a major donor has enabled the foundations to be laid for a new law building (to be named after the donor), and the University Library has been asked to build up its legal collection. This is of particular importance, as the legal profession accredits university law courses based in part on the adequacy of their holdings.

The University Librarian has asked you, as collection manager, to evaluate the present law collection as the basis of a funding submission:

- Would you adopt one collection assessment method or several?
- Of how much value would a user survey be, given that there are as yet no students completing law degrees at the university?
- Which collection assessment methods are likely to be most persuasive to a visiting accreditation panel?

The next generation

As we have suggested, it is increasingly unlikely that any collection manager today undertakes a collection evaluation exercise simply to determine the 'goodness' of a collection. Rather, libraries are driven by the need to determine the adequacy of their collections (in terms of quantity, type, currency, location) in relation to intended service priorities, for accreditation reports and in defence of budget requests. That is, collection evaluation now is linked to client and stakeholder satisfaction above all else, and this requires greater flexibility than in the past. When evaluation was viewed as either collection-centred or use- centred, there was a certain rigidity in approach.

The emerging emphasis is not on collection building but on collection management, which means that we are expected to understand how a collection under review is intended to be used, and by whom. Once the service priorities of a library have been determined collection managers will want to ensure that it is capable of meeting these priorities.

If we view collections as a means of meeting service priorities, then it becomes irrelevant whether we are using collection-centred or user-centred methods, and in fact a combination of methods often gives the most adequate picture of the health and value of a collection. As a consequence, there is emerging a consensus that evaluation should focus on five elements which are not typology-specific but outcomes based:

- size
- utilization
- access
- age
- condition.

If these are seen as neither collection- nor user-centred but simply as a menu of evaluation techniques, then they can be mixed and matched to suit a particular context. For example, one might look at utilization indicators such as circulation and in-library use in combination with size and access indicators in order to achieve a clear understanding of how circulation might be increased. The modern collection manager must be willing to mix the methods described in this chapter to create a blend most suitable for evaluating a specific collection.

Review of Chapter 9

The current stress on accountability in public sector organizations has made collection evaluation of increasing importance. It involves identifying the strengths and weaknesses of a collection in relation to its aims, ideally as set out in a collection development policy.

The essential steps in a collection evaluation are to set the purpose and objectives of the study, review any relevant previous research, decide upon what data are to be collected, and how, select a sample, carry out a pilot, edit and analyse the data, and finally make it possible for the study to be repeated or replicated.

We then introduced the two types of collection evaluation: user-centred, focusing on the needs of the users of a collection; and collection-centred, focusing on the items in the collection itself. In a digital age, the importance of user-centred collection evaluation has increased, as it is no longer the case that readers are limited to accessing what is in any one physical collection. Much collection assessment is based on the assumptions that use is a valid measure of value; that past use indicates likely future use; circulation measures use; and that use inside and outside a library are similar.

Use-oriented measures include use and user studies, document delivery studies, shelf availability tests, circulation studies, in-house use studies, and various qualitative measures of use. Collection-oriented measures include verification studies and citation analysis. All of these methods have their disadvantages and drawbacks; the recommended approach is to use several to complement each other.

Overall, the emphasis is shifting from collection building to collection management, as librarians seek to use their collections to meet the service priorities of their readers. The key five elements in this are the size, utilization, access, age and condition of the collection.

Where to now?

After you review the focus questions at the beginning of this chapter, you may wish to consider the following issues:

- To what extent is the evaluation of a collection different to carrying out a library-based research study of another kind? Perhaps there has been some such study carried out in your library – you may even have been a member of the project team. Can you identify the stages we described above, in 'Steps in conducting an evaluation', in the execution of that study?
- Approaching the same issue from the other direction, obtain a copy of a standard social sciences research methods text (such as one of those we recommend in note 6). Can you relate their recommendations to our description of a well-executed collection evaluation?
- Search the library literature for a library user study that included a collection assessment component, or made recommendations regarding the collection. Can you identify all the steps we recommend in that study? Using our categories, what type (or types) of user study was it?
- Finally, find and examine a collection-oriented study. What steps, if any, did the authors take to minimize the various disadvantages we noted above?

Further reading

Collection evaluation has been a concern of collection managers for some decades, and this is reflected in the substantial corpus of literature on the topic. It is advisable to read selectively in this field, perhaps combining general reviews with up-to-date summaries of developments. One of the most comprehensive general reviews is Geoffrey Ford, *Review of methods employed in determining the use of library stock*, BNB Research Fund Reports 43, British Library, 1990. The regular bibliographies by Thomas Nisonger (see note 5) point to more recent writings on collection evaluation, many of which are worth reading.

Among the more current summaries of recent developments is the chapter by G. E. Gorman and R. H. Miller, 'Changing collections, changing evaluation'. In G. E. Gorman (ed.), *International yearbook of library and information management 2000–2001: collection management*, Library Association Publishing, 2000, 309–38. This includes not only a summary of the present situation but also suggestions for future developments in evaluation procedures.

For a blow-by-blow account of how to evaluate a collection using traditional methods, there is nothing better than B. H. Hall, *Collection assessment manual for college and university libraries*, Oryx Press, 1985, but this is now out of print. A new work being released as we go to press is G. E. Gorman and R. H. Miller's *Evaluating library collections*, Aslib, 2000, which takes a more realistic approach to evaluating collections when budgets and staff time are limited.

More than once in this chapter we have advocated a somewhat critical approach to the traditional, time-consuming methods of collection evaluation and would like to conclude by recommending a book that takes this same view. This is Howard White's 'brief tests' methodology explained in detail in H. D. White, *Brief tests of collection strength: a methodology for all types of libraries*, Contributions in Librarianship and Information Science 88, Greenwood Press, 1995.

Notes

1   R. M. Magrill and M. East, 'Collection development in large university libraries'. In M. H. Harris (ed.), *Advances in librarianship*, vol. 8, Academic Press, 1978, 1–54, at p.39. The most influential work on collection size as a measure of collection adequacy has been that by Clapp and Jordan. They developed a formula that began with the statement of a base number of volumes to which are then added more volumes, the additional number being calculated according to quite specific factors. They used lists of required titles, produced by academics in each discipline area, to establish the base of 42,000 volumes, which

they argued was the minimum number needed regardless of factors such as subjects taught or student numbers. They then calculated additional volumes to be added as follows: 60 volumes per full-time member of teaching staff, ten volumes per full-time student, 2400 volumes for each subject area in which work is done at Master's level, and 16,000 for areas in which doctoral work takes place. V. W. Clapp and R. T. Jordan, 'Quantitative criteria for adequacy of academic library collections', *College & Research Libraries*, **50** (2), 1989, 154–63, a reprint of a *College & Research Libraries* article originally published in 1965.

2   S. Bohme and D. Spiller, *Perspectives of public library use 2: a compendium of survey information*, Loughborough University, Library and Information Statistics Unit, 1999; D. Spiller, *Providing materials for library users*, Library Association Publishing, 2000, 69–84.

3   R. M. Magrill and J. Corbin, *Acquisitions management and collection development in libraries*, 2nd edn, American Library Association, 1989, 234.

4   A. Bookstein, 'Sources of error in library questionnaires', *Library Journal*, **4**, 1982, 85–94. See also J. S. Kidston, 'The validity of questionnaire responses', *Library Quarterly*, **55** (2), 1985, 133–50.

5   B. Lockett (ed.), *Guide to the evaluation of library collections*. Collection Management and Development Guides 2, American Library Association, 1989; B. H. Hall, *Collection assessment manual for college and university libraries*, Oryx Press, 1985; T. E. Nisonger, *Collection evaluation in academic libraries: a literature guide and annotated bibliography*, Libraries Unlimited, 1992; T. E. Nisonger, 'The collection development literature of 1996: a bibliographic essay', *Collection Building*, **17** (1), 1998, 29–39; T. E. Nisonger, 'A review of the 1997 collection development and management literature', *Collection Building*, **18** (2), 1999, 67–80.

6   There are many useful texts in this area, and more are being published every year. A standard work in library science is the widely available, comprehensive volume by C. H. Busha and S. P. Harter, *Research methods in librarianship: techniques and interpretation*, Library and Information Science series, Academic Press, 1980. Also worthwhile are R. R. Powell, *Basic research methods for librarians*, 3rd edn, Ablex Publishing Company, 1997; P. D. Leedy, *Practical research: planning and design*, 5th edn, Macmillan, 1993; E. R. Babbie, *The practice of social research*, Wadsworth, 1990; and Natalie L Sproull, *Handbook of research methods: a guide for practitioners and students in the social sciences*, 2nd edn, Scarecrow, 1995.

7   P. L. Alreck and R. B. Settle, *The survey research handbook*, 2nd edn, McGraw-Hill/Irwin, 1994.

8 J. Barton and J. Blagden, *Academic library effectiveness: a comparative approach*, British Library Research and Innovation Centre, 1996; Joint Funding Councils' Library Review Group, *Report* (Follett Report), HEFCE, 1993.

9 Spiller, loc. cit.

10 S. J. Slote, *Weeding library collections: library weeding methods*, 4th edn, Libraries Unlimited, 1997.

11 F. W. Lancaster, 'The tip of the iceberg', *Bulletin of the American Society for Information Science*, **4** (3), 1978, 32.

12 R. A. Trueswell, 'A quantitative measure of user circulation requirements and its possible effect on stack thinning and multiple-copy determination', *American Documentation*, **16**, 1965, 20–5.

13 M. Day and D. Revill, 'Towards the active collection: the use of circulation analyses in collection evaluation', *Journal of Librarianship and Information Science*, **27** (3), 1995, 149–57.

14 W. E. McGrath, 'Correlating the subjects of books taken out of and books used within an open-stack library', *College & Research Libraries*, **32** (4), 1971, 280–5; G. Ford, 'Stock relegation in some British university libraries', *Journal of Librarianship*, **12** (1), 1980, 42–55.

15 K. G. Altmann and G. E. Gorman, 'Density of use as a criterion in the deselection and relegation of serials', *New Library World*, **101** (1155), 2000, 112. See also K. G. Altmann and G. E. Gorman, 'Anatomy of a serials collection and its usage: case study of an Australian academic library', *Library Collections, Acquisitions and Technical Services*, **23** (2), 1999, 149–61.

16 A. N. Brandon and D. R. Hill, 'Selected list of books and journals for the small medical library', *Bulletin of the Medical Library Association*, **83** (2), 1995, 151–75; 'Selected list of nursing books and journals', *Nursing Outlook*, **42** (2), 1994, 247–64; and 'Selected list of books and journals in allied health', *Bulletin of the Medical Library Association*, **82** (3), 1994, 71–82.

17 A recent example was provided by Lake Superior State University, Michigan, which developed its own listing of multicultural works in order to assess the adequacy of its collection – and then proceeded to fill the gaps identified: M. J. Delaney-Lehman, 'Assessing the library collection for diversity', *Collection Management*, **20** (3/4), 1996, 29–37.

18 Bradford's law states that if scientific journals are arranged in order of decreasing productivity of articles on a given subject, they can be divided into a nucleus, which contains the journals specifically devoted to the subject, surrounded by a number of zones or groups, each with a significantly smaller

number of relevant articles. See S. C. Bradford, *Documentation*, Crosby Lock-wood, 1948, 116.

19 K. G. Altmann and G. E. Gorman, 'The relevance of "cited by leading jour-nal" to serials management in Australian university libraries', *Australian Library Journal*, **48** (2), 1999, 101–15; K. G. Altmann and G. E. Gorman, 'Can impact factors substitute for the results of local use studies? Findings from an Australian case study', *Collection Building*, **18** (2), 1999, 90–4.

20 S. Herner and M. Herner, 'Information needs and uses in science and tech-nology', *Annual Review of Information Science and Technology*, **2**, 1967, 2.

21 M. E. D. Koenig, 'Citation analysis for the arts and humanities as a collection management tool', *Collection Management*, **2** (3), 1978, 249.

10
Preservation and weeding

Focus questions

- What environmental conditions are appropriate to facilitate the long-term preservation of library resources?
- What strategies have libraries adopted to ensure increased usage of materials does not place them at increased risk of damage?
- How might digital materials be preserved?
- Why is disaster planning important, and how might it be undertaken?
- What is the generally accepted basis of weeding?
- How might one go about deciding which serials to cancel?
- Should electronic media also be considered for weeding?

It may seem strange to deal consider together both preservation, arranging for the long term retention of information sources, and weeding. Are not these alternatives? However, both deal with decisions about the long-term value of materials: is this an item which we will always require? Or is it something which was acquired to meet a specific need, now past?

These two areas thus share a common core of professional decision making about the value of materials. Unfortunately, this in turn means they also share a common problem with the cost in terms of staff time of undertaking these activities. Weeding, in particular, can be daunting for librarians whose whole professional ethos is to gather, rather than discard – and at the end of it, what do you have? Only a few spaces on shelves, quickly filled. For this reason, too many libraries find it easier to leave materials, once acquired, generally available. The longer-term effect of this neglect is that material of continuing value may not be adequately protected, while a mass of items of little or no enduring value crowd the library's shelves and catalogues, making it harder to find current material. The library ends up looking like a bibliographic scrapheap.

Both preservation and weeding come at the end of the library information life cycle (see Figure 10.1). They are the final processes involved in managing information resources in libraries.

One of the core functions of libraries is to preserve real access to the documentary record. This is an activity that will give them, in common with archives, an enduring role in the wired world of the 21st century.

Preservation

Here, we need to start with some definitions. *Preservation* is the generic term, and includes all activities associated with the maintenance of resources and the preservation of information content. This is contrasted with *conservation*, which refers to the treatment of the physical items themselves in order to extend their usable life (and *restoration*, which involves treating damaged material to return it as close as possible to its original state). Thus preservation is both the wider term, and the

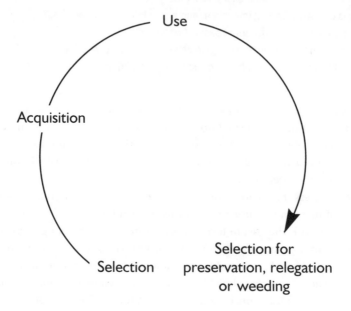

Fig. 10.1 *The library information life cycle*

area we consider here. By contrast, conservation is a more specialist area, coverage of which would require something like a companion volume to this, and one whose basis in organic chemistry presents a substantial barrier to many librarians.

As with collections management as a whole, preservation does not simply *happen*, by default. It must be managed. And the key problem in this area has not changed in the last hundred years: it is that the more successful we are in acquiring and promoting our rare and valuable items, the more readers will want to access them, and the more these items are used, the more vulnerable they are to damage. To prevent this, we need to adopt a range of appropriate management strategies.

Environmental strategies

For some years, it has been widely accepted that library materials should be preserved in air-conditioned stacks with a temperature of 20° Celsius, plus or minus 2°, and at 50% relative humidity, plus or minus 5%. While these conditions are undoubtedly suitable for most collections, that blanket recommendation masks the underlying principle that environmental conditions need to be stable to ensure long term preservation. Major changes or fluctuations in temperature or relative humidity will do more damage to organic materials like paper than consistent storage outside these limits.

Take air-conditioning. In many institutions, if air-conditioning is provided it is for the comfort of staff, not for the sake of the materials. Hence it is likely to be too warm and too humid, for people sitting working will get cold at only 20° (and indeed, this suggested temperature is already a compromise: a case could be made that 18° would be preferable for paper-based materials). Most people also find 50% relative humidity too dry. Worse, if an air-conditioned building is unoccupied over periods of time, such as during weekends or holidays, the air-conditioning may be turned off to save money. One of us worked in an Australian university library where the air-conditioning was always turned off during the break between Christmas and New Year in the middle of the Australian summer. Had that substantial building not been air-conditioned at all, the longer-term seasonal fluctuations in temperature and humidity would have been far less damaging to the collection.

Another example known to us is the new national library of a developing country. This replaced a traditional colonial period building which permitted the unhindered circulation of air, essential in that humid climate. But the new library is an air-conditioned glass box, unlivable for staff and readers when (not if) the power supply fails. There is now a growing literature on the desirability of shifting from artificial environmental control to passive environmental control.[1]

Protection from sunlight is another concern. Few of us do not own books whose covers have faded from excessive sunlight. *Any* light will damage material, so the ideal is to store items in the dark and only turn on lights when they are being used – another example of the tension between preservation and access. Photographic materials, in particular, should be stored in the dark to maximize their life. This includes slides, negatives, microforms and, most vulnerable of all, prints.

Because human comfort is not what is important with materials preservation, environmental monitoring is desirable. While the instruments may be hired, the preferable course is clearly to employ a conservator to undertake an assessment of the library, or at least its stack areas. Particular problem areas may then be identified, and strategies developed to address these. In the longer term, if a new building is contemplated it would make sense to consider the collection requirements alongside the requirements of staff and readers.

Preservation options

Since the demands of usage and preservation are so frequently at variance, one alternative is to copy material into another format, such as microfilm, and make that available in lieu of the original, which can be stored under ideal conditions. The classic example of this approach is, of course, newspapers. Since these are printed on cheap, high-acid paper and certain to be damaged if used in the original, most libraries provide their readers with microfilm copies instead. This has several advantages:

- One microfilm master can be made of each paper thought worth retaining, and copies inexpensively duplicated from that.
- Copies damaged through use can readily be replaced.
- Microfilm is known to have quite an extended life if stored appropriately.
- The technology involved in reading and copying microfilms is relatively simple, and unlikely to be affected greatly through technological change.
- Few readers actually need to consult the originals (even if none of us like using microfilm), which then can be stored under ideal conditions.

As a result, microfilm has been long established as the principal strategy for the preservation of information *content*, especially where – as with newspapers – the artefactual value of the original is limited.

Newer technologies, such as CD-ROM, are much more subject to technological obsolescence. Archivists, in particular, are well aware of this, and the library profession has much to learn from the archival. Some of the problems associated with digital preservation are noted below. Despite greater technological vulnerability, however, there are obvious possibilities for making available digital copies of fragile, at-risk or rare originals. This seems an obvious strategy to adopt with an institutional website, for example, as several libraries have demonstrated.[2] In future we will increasingly see such digital copies – offering advantages of instant global availability and multiple concurrent access – take the place of the hated microfilm.

Digital preservation

Paper's ubiquity should not be surprising. We have nearly two thousand years experience in making paper by hand and, for the last two hundred years or so, making paper by machine. When kept in cool and dry conditions, high quality paper that is also moderately alkaline and made from purified cellulose pulp is likely to remain flexible, durable and last for several hundred years. Due to its demonstrated permanence and durability over time, the life expectancy of high quality paper has become the benchmark for information resources of enduring value.[3]

Digital materials are different. Not only are the media upon which the data are written – magnetic tape, metal discs, plastic discs – themselves inherently less stable, they are also more affected by any lack of perfect cleanliness. Most of all, however, they are affected by machine dependency. We all know how rapid technological development has been in the area of personal computers; in our rush to keep reasonably in touch with the current standard, we buy and use newer and newer equipment. As a result data written only a few years ago use formats and machines long obsolete. Both the authors of this book used punched paper cards as a first offline computer storage device: does anyone still have a paper card reader? The first home computer one of us owned took 5¼ in. disks; neither of us can now read these (I migrated my data, including a thesis, from 5¼ to 3½ in. disks). In only 30 years' time, how many of us will be able to read 3½ in. disks? Or the current generation of CD-ROMs?

Behind the issue of the carrier format is the issue of the data format. Just as I cannot now read a 5¼ in. disk, my current word-processor cannot read Appleworks files created only 15 years ago. Yet I own and can read many of my grandparents' books. Digital data not only has to be *refreshed* (recopied digitally using various error detection and correction techniques) but also *migrated* (transferred from one generation of hardware and software to a later). The appearance and context of this migrated data changes along with the means of accessing it: in migration, we are preserving the memory but hardly the substance of the original – although, of course, in some cases this does not matter greatly. The cost of continued migrations is another matter, and may be difficult to justify if an object is not being used consistently:

> Migration requires a unique new solution for each new format or paradigm shift [in computing technology] and each type of document that is to be converted into that new form. Since every paradigm shift entails a new set of problems, there is not necessarily much to be learned from previous migration efforts, making each migration cycle just as difficult, expensive, and problematic as the last.[4]

The use of standard formats, such as ASCII, is one way in which the problems of migration might be minimized. However, at least with ASCII, this is at the very real cost of discarding much of the information associated with an original (such as most formatting).

Another proposed preservation strategy is *emulation*. Here, an electronic publication or document is captured along with its 'metadata'. The *Free online dictionary of computing* defines metatdata as:

> Data about data. In data processing, meta-data is definitional data that provides information about or documentation of other data managed within an application or environment. For example, meta-data would document data about data elements or attributes, (name, size, data type, etc) and data about records or data structures (length, fields, columns, etc) and data about data (where it is located, how it is associated, ownership, etc.). Meta-data may include descriptive information about the context, quality and condition, or characteristics of the data.[5]

In addition, specifications for the hardware and software system that produced or managed the record are added, so that in future it should be possible to build software that 'emulates' (or mimics) the hardware environment and the creation or management software. This may mean that electronic documents could be preserved with at least some of their original functionality (which may be important). Jeff Rothenberg has carried out a pilot project to test the feasibility of emulation as a preservation strategy for digital publications.[6] This was for NEDLIB, a collaborative project of European national libraries which hopes to create the basic infrastructure upon which a networked European deposit library can be built. While Rothenberg's report is promising, it is still too soon to know if this approach will be successful in the longer term – all of this is very much at the cutting edge of technological experimentation. As noted, this is an area in which archivists share many of the problems of librarians, and keeping a watching brief across both professions would seem essential.[7]

These are real problems facing the profession today. Many libraries, especially state and national libraries, are attempting to preserve the content of websites which incorporate material that, if published conventionally, would have been collected following their collection development policy. These resources are selected and acquired, agreement is reached with their rights owners on archiving and access, and then persistent access to their content is needed, even when the digital files change location. Once again, taking a co-ordinated national or international perspective and facilitating co-operation between libraries seems to be the only way in which such a vision may be realized.[8]

If all else fails, we can always print out a facsimile on paper.

Appropriate handling of material

Finally, whether materials will be retained in the long term or are merely expected to meet current needs, it is simply good housekeeping to have them handled properly. Prevention is better than cure. One of us uses a public library where all material must be returned through drop-in chutes outside the library. Books, magazines and the plastic cases of music CDs are routinely damaged both by the fall, and in turn by having other material fall upon them. Libraries need to:

- design systems and equipment that do not damage materials
- encourage and train staff to handle material appropriately, and in doing so set an example to readers
- encourage readers to handle material appropriately.

Several libraries have produced leaflets or rules for the guidance of their readers. Some years ago, those in the British Library were those shown in Figure 10.2.

Of course, some readers (and staff) will always accidentally or carelessly damage materials, but by reducing this and taking the sort of measures suggested above, maximum value can be obtained from the funds provided to a library. The aim should be to replace material when its information is no longer current, or weed it when it is no longer needed, and not because its life has been prematurely shortened.

BRITISH LIBRARY RULES

WARNING

The Reading Rooms exist to provide readers with the means for research. So far as possible, all books and manuscripts are made available. This in turn depends on proper conservation of the collections. All readers are asked to help by handling material carefully. The regulations for admission include the following prohibitions:

- Do not put a book or anything else on top of an open book.
- Do not fold any page.
- Do not straighten out creased or dog-eared pages; you may only damage the book further.
- Do not lean on books while reading.
- Do not drop books or handle them roughly.
- Do not put books on the floor.
- Do not bend books back, lay them face downwards, or otherwise damage the binding.
- Do not write in or mark books in any way.
- Do not write on paper resting on a book, open or closed.
- Do not bring any materials that can harm a book into the Library. These include: Food, Paste or glue, Ink in bottles, Adhesive tape of any sort, Scissors & knives.

Nicolas Barker
Head of Conservation
British Library

Fig. 10.2 *Former British Library rules*

Disaster planning

For some reason, this always sounds strange: who would *plan* for a disaster? Perhaps the better term would be 'disaster preparedness', as Thomas suggests.[9] Regardless of the terminology, however, only a manager who did not see the library as essential to the organization would risk being unprepared for a major disaster.

Disasters do happen. Readers will recall fires at the Bibliothèque Nationale in Paris and the public library in Norwich, and the flooding of the off-site store of the University of Sussex. A fire at the National Library of Australia in 1985 at one point threatened the whole building. The then Director General of the Library was watching the fire when he was approached by the chief of the Fire Brigade: 'We don't know whether we can save the building,' he was told. 'Is there anything in particular you'd like to save?' Fortunately, the Fire Brigade was able to save the building with only relatively minor damage to the collections. (However, the Library's services were affected for many months.) The University of Auckland Library was without power for over a week in 1998 when a power cable failed.[10] The more recent experience of libraries in countries such as Kosovo and Bosnia suggests that terrorism and cultural genocide must also be considered.[11] The one thing survivors from a disaster or near disaster no longer question is the importance of adequate planning.

The essence of risk management is to estimate the likelihood of a disaster taking place, and then consider the magnitude of the impact if it did. By simply multiplying these two factors together, it is possible to rank potential threats and address the more serious.

As with any management process, disaster planning should itself be the result of a conscious planning process, ideally involving a project team comprised of staff chosen to reflect several areas within the library as well as individual expertise, the development of procedure manuals and resources, a training programme so that every member of staff knows what is expected of them in the event of a disaster, and explicit provision to review and update these procedures and training programmes. There are a few clear guidelines here:

- Disaster manuals should be kept off-site as well as on.
- Staff lists with full out-of-hours contacts details should similarly be available off-site – and kept up to date.
- Computer back-up files must also be off-site.
- Lists of experts to whom to turn for assistance, suppliers of restoration equipment and supplies and so on, preferably local, need to be developed.
- Collection priorities should be set: what treasures does the library own which should be saved first? However, here the bottom line must be that human life is the first priority. Preparedness to give up one's life for the library appears on few job descriptions.

It should go without saying that all of these lists and manuals must be kept off-site as well as on, readily available, in multiple copies and certainly in the homes of senior and responsible staff. Since keeping these up to date will require ongoing attention, this must be the responsibility of a particular member of staff who is given the opportunity and resources to do it.

Perhaps one of the less visible outcomes of effective disaster preparedness planning is that the process of identifying and preparing to cope with potential disasters also raises general awareness of the whole area. Some potential causes of disaster can be identified and guarded against – the possibility of water entry, for example. It is perhaps ironic that a library better able to cope with such a disaster may also be less likely to be called upon to do so.

Weeding

It should be evident that there is no direct and simple correlation between the number of volumes on the shelves and the worth of a collection to its users. As noted, excessive numbers of outdated, little-used older materials are more likely to serve as a barrier to readers, than a welcome supplement to more recent acquisitions.[12] Comparative library statistics really do only say, 'My library is bigger than your library', not 'My library is *better* than your library'.

Weeding is the process of removing material from open access and reassessing its value. It is a generic term, which includes both relegation and discarding. Once an item has been removed it can be *relegated* or transferred to storage in another area under the control of the library, designed for less regular use, perhaps one operated jointly with partner institutions.[13] Other material may be sold, or *discarded*: permanently removed from the stock of the library (and with the catalogue and other records updated to reflect this).

Why weed?

Positive reasons for weeding (apart from lack of space) may include a belief that there is an optimum size beyond which the collection should not be allowed to grow and, more importantly, a conviction that with the passage of time some at least of the items on the shelves of any library lose some or all of whatever value they originally had, and become a distraction to users rather than an asset. That even good libraries are likely to contain much material of limited value hardly needs demonstration. Assessment of German research libraries damaged in World War II showed that in some cases as much as 40% of the collection was not worth replacing, and in other cases that 99% of the circulation requirements of a particular library could be met by between 25 and 40% of the stock.[14] Of course, 'circulation requirements' are only of limited value as indicators of value.

It is probably true that most librarians can always find a valid reason for keeping material they want to keep, and that weeding is distasteful to many. Archivists are accustomed to the concept of 'appraisal': they examine unique items, choose only a minority of these and discard the remainder. Librarians, on the other hand, appear uncomfortable with discarding material even when it is held widely in other libraries. One also should remember that many readers may feel the same way, so it is sensible not to overlook the political ramifications of any kind of operation designed to remove stock from open access. To suggest to a user that his or her favourite material is in some way second class or unimportant or out of date, and so can be relegated or discarded, may be unwelcome at the least.

A good deal has been written about weeding and there are several practical guides to the process available, but because of the staff time involved and the predilections of many members of our profession, this very practical matter remains one of the most neglected tasks in libraries of all kinds. We should weed our collections because:

- The material and the information is out of date.
- The material is physically damaged or worn out.
- Better editions are available.
- Duplicate copies are no longer required.
- Community needs have changed.
- Institutional objectives have changed so that library objectives must change also.
- The item should not have been bought in the first place.
- Unwanted material can get in the way: it has a 'hindrance effect'.
- Open-access storage is more expensive and cannot be justified for low-use items.
- The overall costs of collection storage and maintenance are ongoing.

To these we should perhaps add why most libraries do not weed (despite their policies saying that they do):

- It takes too much time.
- Bigger still seems better to librarians (but not to readers).
- Our professional culture is one of collecting, not discarding.
- Mistakes are permanent.
- Readers may be resistant to the process.
- It's a dirty, physically demanding job.

Our policies and procedures, then, have to address as many of these concerns as possible. The alternatives are that we microfilm everything, convert everything to digital form, or simply keep everything.

The bases of weeding

The classic rule is that the criteria for weeding should be essentially those used in the first place for selection – in fact, weeding has often been referred to as 'deselection'. This, of course, immediately suggests that weeding belongs in a collection development policy (as recommended in Chapter 2), but it will probably also be useful to complement this with written procedures. Because weeding is by its nature a time-intensive process, it makes sense to attempt as much as possible to make it a process that may be undertaken by lower-level, unqualified (and so less expensive) staff.

Back in Chapter 5 we noted Ranganathan's famous laws, including that:

- Books are for use.
- Every book its reader.
- Save the reader's time.

This immediately suggests that books that are not used, books that no longer have readers and unwanted books that get in the way of readers are prime candidates for weeding. In fact, most practical approaches to weeding rely on certain basic assumptions which follow on from these, at least in part:

- The use of a book is a measure of its value.
- Past use of books is a valid indicator of likely future use.
- Circulation figures are an indication of the actual 'use' of an item.
- Measurements of 'use' outside the library are indicators of use within the library, which can be significantly higher than circulation figures would suggest.[15]
- The effect of browsing should at least be taken into account, even if it cannot be measured.

It seems to be a basic assumption underlying methods of analysis of use or user statistics that value is directly proportionate to use, but both common sense and studies in the field suggest that the availability of material, rather than perceived ideas of value, is probably the most significant factor affecting material use. Actual known usage is merely one of the factors that need to be taken into account.

Approaches to weeding

The ultimate aims of weeding must be to increase accessibility, to improve efficiency and to reduce costs. There are several possible approaches to this. The most common approach is based on rules, guidelines, principles and the exercise of a minimal amount of professional expertise. It relies on a series of decisions being made about titles on the basis of their age and the length of time they have been on the shelf since the last loan, which is known as the 'shelf-time period'. Its drawbacks stem from the apparent difficulties regarding the definition of 'use' and, some would say, the limited value of past use as an indicator either of what ought to have been done in the past, or of what should be done in the future.

Various mathematically based formulae have been proposed in efforts to make weeding less subjective, but these formulae have tended to be rather too complex and of questionable validity. The approaches based on them have not yet been shown to be better than the straight 'shelf-time period' method. Combined to some degree with techniques that take into account the age of materials, the shelf-time method can be said to produce a cheap and effective approach to weeding. Whatever methods are used, cost is going to be one of the most important factors – cost of identifying material, removing it, altering location records, disposing of the material or storing it elsewhere, retrieving it when necessary, and rectifying the inevitable mistakes.

In the early 1960s a weeding system was set up at Yale University which seems to have worked fairly well.[16] Besides shelf-time period the Yale system made use of other weeding criteria, the operation of which required subjective judgement on the part of the weeder. Monographs were selected for weeding if:

- they dealt essentially with scientific or technical subjects, and their treatment was out of date
- they were on highly specialized topics that were treated more effectively in other works
- they were primarily concerned with the lives of obscure people.

At the end of their project Yale staff had found that it was easier to choose specific titles rather than specific small groups within a subject field, that it was not possible to specify large groups, either by subject or by form, and that it was best for librarians to make the initial choice which was later checked by academics. Projects completed in other institutions, while agreeing essentially with these results, have shown that there are considerable differences in the agreement rate between librarians and academics in different subject discipline areas. The highest rate of agreement appears to be in the sciences, falling away to the lowest rate of agreement in the humanities, which only emphasizes that different methods are needed for different situations. While most of these studies have been carried out in academic libraries, there emerge important guidelines that any weeding programme could do well to follow:

- that the likelihood of future use be the sole criterion for weeding, and
- that the best method of establishing likely future use is 'shelf-time period', defined as the time the material has remained on the shelf since last issue or, in the case of very recently bought material, since accession.

Increasingly, the most influential approach to weeding is that known as the 'Slote method' after its inventor, Stanley Slote, whose book, *Weeding library collections*, is now in its fourth edition.[17] Slote's approach is clear, practical and based on common sense. He eschews subjective methods, as the following advice suggests: 'Do not make a subjective judgement about keeping a book because you think the author, subject or title is important. If the book card indicates it should be removed, remove it. Do not do subjective weeding!'

His 'method' (which is in fact a collection of basically similar methods, to be chosen as library circumstances or preferences dictate) is based squarely on shelf-time period, and on the proposition that past use is the best indicator of future use. Theoretically, past use is not an absolute predictor of future use. But practically, in library after library where the assumption of predictability has been tested, it has been shown that past use has been a reliable, valid predictor of future use. Furthermore, in every case where shelf-time period has been used for weeding, contrary to expectations, usage was found to increase. Thus, this variable as a predictor of future use can be applied without fear of reducing the value of the collection.

The Slote method, as outlined in detail in his text, does not demand highly trained personnel and seems suitable for all kinds of libraries. Though Slote's approach may be too common sensical and too mechanical to satisfy all librarians in all circumstances, it has clearly earnt its place as an eminently workable solution to the problem of weeding.

What not to weed

One of the reasons why professional staff must be involved to some extent in the deselection process is that there will always be standard or classic works of enduring value to a library's collection, however little current use they may appear to have received. They are the kind of books that should be available in a public library, or a university library, even if only one borrower every three years wants them. In a national library, of course, there will be much more concern to build a collection of record – a collection at Conspectus Level 5, or close to it.

Some expertise is needed to know what authors are 'standard', especially as these include not only obvious people such as Charles Dickens and Jane Austen, but good contemporary writers such as Maeve Binchy, Vikram Seth or, most recently, Michael Chabon. Distinguished non-fiction writers such as Barbara Tuchman, A. J. P. Taylor and Alan Bullock should also be considered. The greater the knowledge of books staff members have the less likely they are to go wrong, but there is, unfortunately, no simple formula for knowing what to discard.

When this kind of material becomes worn or damaged, it should be replaced if still in print. If it is out of print the old copies should be repaired or re-bound if they are not too badly damaged. Here, too, such signs of use are an indicator of value.

Periodicals and serials

In recent years one of the truisms of librarianship has been that the cost of periodicals has been rising so swiftly and inexorably that the subscription bill seemed likely to take up the entire book-vote allocation. This has been particularly true for academic libraries. It is apparent that what we are seeking in collection development is balance: balance between monographs and serials, and also balance between print and electronic information sources. But when expenditure on one component is growing much more quickly than on others, balance can only be re-established by pruning. Indeed, in some libraries we know, reductions in the serials budget could more properly be described as 'slash and burn'.

The processes of deciding on the titles for cancellation are usually long and tortuous. In an academic library the most important factors to be taken into account are usually:

- the question of who should make the decisions, with the answers ranging from leaving them all to librarians, through involvement of the teaching staff, to sole responsibility being left to academics
- the relative importance of the results of citation analysis and use studies[18]
- factors specific to the individual titles, such as price, language of publication, coverage by indexing services, availability for borrowing elsewhere and relationship to the teaching curriculum.

Other factors that have been mentioned are the reputation of the publisher, predicted future use, and a calculation of cost per shelf-unit or per item use. Possibly the only area of agreement in the whole discussion is that no one factor can be relied on solely, even to the same extent as perhaps 'past use' can be for monograph weeding. Much talk has been expended on the possible assignment of weightings to the various widely differing criteria in order to allow for a final points score to be awarded. Once again, it is important to involve all parties concerned. Even though the use of detailed decision models may not result in a more accurate final decision in terms of cost or space savings, the fact that stakeholders have been asked for their opinions and listened to will have significant political value.

Librarians in school, public and national libraries will conclude that here, at least, their academic colleagues have it easy. With no subject experts readily to hand, and answerable instead to lay committees or the general community, all the decisions have to be internal. Hence, proportionately more weight will be given to such statistics as are available, including citation analysis and usage. Even though it may be accepted that there exists a fairly high correlation between borrowing of monograph volumes and their use in the library, and thus that circulation figures could be regarded as a proxy for in-library use, it is quite likely that a different situation exists with periodicals. They are used in-library to a much greater extent than monographs; each volume is part of a set rather than an individual work; and photocopying probably distorts what might otherwise have been a 'normal' use pattern.

There is also the 'impact factor', the ratio between the number of articles published in a journal and the number cited (or the number of uses noted). A large monthly with many articles is likely to be cited, read or photocopied more than a small quarterly. There is also little doubt that problems of differential access to articles through indexing and abstracting journals will affect citation rankings to such an extent that analysis of citations can be of very little use in comparing journals that have been covered by the indexing services with those that have not. In addition, as so many of these tools are North American in origin, national patterns of usage elsewhere are almost certain to differ. A further point is that such studies may be of very little use in collection management if they measure only raw use, and ignore various factors such as subscription costs, the staff costs of claiming for lost issues, and the normal costs of receiving, processing, binding and storage.

For practical purposes it is also essential to take into account factors such as gaps in the holdings of any specific title, the known availability of titles in nearby libraries (or in other members of a consortium), and likely availability on interlibrary loan. Inevitably, given the complexity of such decisions, they will consume a great deal of staff time.

Electronic media

Despite their relative newness, electronic media are also candidates for deselection. One reason for this is that, if a library has to pay an annual licence fee for a product or service, continuing usage has to justify that expenditure – in exactly the same way as serials are only renewed if demand for each title is there. Other possible reasons for weeding electronic resources will include if they duplicate or are superseded by more recent material, along with experience suggesting that ease of use is not adequate, hardware has changed – or indeed, that the library's vendor has changed. Of course, when a library subscribes to an electronic indexing or abstracting service, it should also reconsider its subscriptions to print equivalents if these are now duplicated.[19] Increasingly, users will prefer the electronic alternative because of its enhanced search capabilities.

Deselection or weeding is of enhanced importance in an electronic environment because of the notorious tendency of internet sites to become hopelessly outdated, disappear, or move from the address at which they were first located. It is arguably much *more* important for websites and portals to be kept up to date. There are, of course, software tools which check that web links are still current; checking the currency and value of the content to which they lead is less easily automated.

Procedures

If staff costs and the time of professional librarians and, perhaps, of readers prepared to review weeding decisions are to be contained, then as much use as possible will need to be made of support staff. A possible procedure will be:

1 Following established guidelines, support staff select possible candidates for weeding.
2 Professionals in the collections management area examine these titles.
3 Readers examine remaining titles. Only titles that all parties agree are redundant are removed.
4 Support staff undertake the clerical procedures associated with writing off deselected items.

Some years ago, one of us developed guidelines based upon just such an approach. These appear here as Case Study 10.1.

Case Study 10.1

Weeding policy for a university library

1. Aims

The Library's collection needs to be weeded on a regular basis to achieve the following aims:

- removal of out-of-date or potentially misleading material from the open shelves, so ensuring a higher relative proportion of up-to-date, recent or relevant material is available to the browser
- optimization of shelving and floorspace to house the collection.

2. Responsibility for weeding

The *Academic policy for the Library* provides that the Faculties have responsibility for determining priorities in the allocation of the book vote, for anticipating new or changed course needs, and for working as a team with Library staff on collection development.

Similarly, while a weeding programme will be initiated and managed by Library staff, the Faculties will have the responsibility for advising the Library which items should be removed from the collection and which retained. This Faculty-oriented policy recognizes that academic staff have:

- specialist subject knowledge and expertise in their areas
- in-depth knowledge of present and likely future teaching-related use of the collection
- in-depth knowledge of present and likely future research-related use of the collection
- responsibility under the *Academic policy for the Library* for determining priorities for collection building in their particular areas.

At the same time, Library staff also have specialist knowledge and expertise which should be drawn upon, including knowledge of the use of the collection. Accordingly, responsibility for weeding is allocated as follows:

Library staff select material proposed for weeding, according to the following guidelines which have been established in discussion with Faculties and endorsed by the Library User Group of the Information and Communication Services Committee.

Academic staff will then be given the opportunity to review items selected by Library staff for weeding.

3. Weeding guidelines: monographs

The Library is not and cannot serve as a permanent repository for materials unlikely to receive present or future use unless the retention of items is formally part of the Library's academic policy. That role properly belongs to other institutions, such as the National Library. In general, only publications concerning the University, or written by University staff, should be preserved without reference to likely use. In these cases the Library is maintaining an 'archive' collection of such items.

As the former Library Committee has already agreed that unwanted duplicate copies should be removed from the general collection, these guidelines are concerned only with items of which the Library holds a single copy.

Library staff will select monograph material for weeding, taking into account the following factors:

3.1 Age of item

- Scientific and technical material over ten years old will be considered for weeding.
- Social science and humanity material over 20 years old will be considered for weeding.

3.2 Nature of item

The following categories of material will normally be retained:

- original research reports
- primary source material (e.g. statistics, government publications)
- dissertations not published by commercial publishers
- classic or seminal works, identified as such by academic and/or Library staff
- literary works
- other special subject areas as defined in the attached schedule.

The following categories of material will normally be discarded:

- superseded textbooks, school textbooks and secondary compilations
- non-scholarly, popular treatments
- short pamphlets.

3.3 Language

- Material in English, or in languages taught at the University will be retained if appropriate.
- Material in other languages may be considered for weeding.

3.4 Usage

- Material which appears to have been consistently used will be retained, as numerous studies have shown past usage is the best predictor of future use.
- Items seldom or never used will be considered for weeding.

3.5 Physical condition

- Where poor physical condition is a result of consistent use repair or rebinding will be undertaken as a byproduct of the weeding programme.
- Poor physical condition of little-used material may suggest the costs of repair and retention are unjustified.

3.6 Subject

Where Library staff are aware that the University no longer teaches or undertakes research in a particular subject area, the collection may be reduced to those items considered desirable to provide basic information about that area. In such cases, the University may consider transferring the collection to a university teaching in the area or to another appropriate organization. Such a transfer could be as a gift or as a temporary or permanent loan.

If there is genuine doubt about the likely future value of any item, the decision should be to retain it.

4. Weeding guidelines: serials

Library staff will select serial titles for weeding, taking into account the following factors:

4.1 Current subscription status of title

Bibliometric studies have suggested that back issues of cancelled or ceased titles are less likely to be consulted than the back issues of titles of equivalent age to which a current subscription is maintained. Therefore:

- Backsets will be retained of titles to which the Library currently subscribes.
- If a title has been cancelled or has ceased publication, consideration will be given to weeding the complete set.

4.2 Nature of title

- Titles containing research findings, historical information, statistics or similar prime source material will be retained.
- Titles with directory information, newsletters and other ephemeral publications will be considered for weeding.

4.3 Extent of use

Usage will be determined from loan records, photocopy and interlibrary loan requests, and reshelving required.

- Titles consistently used will be retained.
- Titles seldom or never used will be considered for weeding.

4.4 Completeness of set

A very incomplete set may be discarded.

4.5 Physical condition

A set which is unbound or in poor physical condition may be discarded. If there is evidence of high usage, replacement volumes or microforms may be considered as an alternative.

4.6 Subject

Where Library staff are aware that the University no longer teaches or undertakes research in a particular subject area, holdings of serial titles may be reduced to those considered basic to providing information about it.

4.7 Holdings in other libraries

- A title not held elsewhere in the country will be retained, as a matter of principle, in support of scholarship and research.
- A title not held elsewhere in the region will be retained unless the case for disposing of it is very strong.
- If a title of doubtful value is widely held within the region, this will be a factor suggesting it should not be retained.

4.8 Discard, storage or alternative formats

Decisions on whether to discard an item, store an item or replace printed copies with microforms or electronic products will be made by Library staff on the basis of consultations with the appropriate faculties.

If there is genuine doubt about the likely future value of any title, the decision should be to retain it.

In considering this case study, we suggest you ask yourself:

- What are the underlying principles behind this policy?

- What adaptation would be needed to make these guidelines relevant and usable in a public library?
- Could – or should – weeding of electronic resources be handled in a similar way?

The concept of the 'self-renewing library'

This approach to the management of academic libraries arose as a result of the report of the Working Party of the University Grants Committee set up in Britain in 1975 with the specific task of looking into 'the minimum essential capital requirements of university libraries (excluding copyright libraries) in regard to reader places and storage, in the light of current limitations on UGC capital resources, with particular reference to possible ways of providing for the remote storage of books and periodicals in repositories to avoid the necessity for a continual expansion of central library facilities'.[20] The intention was to make certain that any future building expansion went into low-cost storage rather than into the usual high-cost library building, and to exempt the copyright libraries, Oxford and Cambridge, from these restrictions. The Committee, referred to ever since by the name of its chairman as the Atkinson Committee, recommended the 'self-renewing library': one that would not grow beyond a certain size because it balanced its new accessions by the withdrawal of 'obsolete or unconsulted material' each year. However, some allowance was to be made for a slight overrun because of the increase in the amount being published each year, and the need for permanent retention of at least some of each year's publications. The principle was that of a library of a certain limited size, maintaining itself at very close to that size by discarding each year as much material as it took in. At the time, that concept attracted a considerable amount of criticism. Most was directed at the proposition that the optimum size established for each library would be tied to student numbers, a suggestion that appeared then and now to ignore the very real need for more than merely adequate library services in order to ensure that university-based research in all fields can continue.

The Atkinson Committee's report is of interest in this volume for at least three reasons:

- It challenges the role of the library as depository, suggesting instead the library as active service facility. What is important in library service is the ability to satisfy users, not the numbers of books.
- In a digital age, physical holdings are now no longer at the core of information

provision. If we are to take the idea of access complementing ownership seriously, then the core material required for permanent, on-site physical storage may well be more nearly constant than seemed possible a quarter of a century ago.

- The Atkinson model almost perfectly reflects the concept advanced at the beginning of this chapter of a library information life cycle (see Figure 10.1). To realize the model would require the kind of collection management policies we have been advocating throughout.

Despite its theoretical attractions, however, it is an argument that makes practical sense only if a library already has adequate collections and access to a full range of appropriate electronic information sources. As a device to justify saving taxpayers' money, it is as threadbare a proposition as the suggestion that the internet can substitute for proper library provision.

Review of Chapter 10

This chapter was based on the final stages of the library information life cycle. It introduced preservation, the long-term retention of information sources, and considered the appropriate environmental conditions that might facilitate this: controlled temperature, relative humidity and lighting control, noting that long-term stability is of most importance and that in some circumstances air-conditioning may be quite inappropriate.

The traditional approach to preservation has been to microfilm material, thus providing access copies while the originals are preserved. This avoids the traditional conflict between access and preservation. Newer digital technologies promise similar benefits, while at the same time offering wider availability. But digital media are machine dependent, and constant changes in both storage media and software require not merely data refreshment but data migration if long-term access is to be possible. This is an area in which librarians are working with archivists, and where the answers are not yet known. Finally, common-sense handling procedures and appropriately designed equipment can help prevent everyday damage to materials in current use.

Library disasters are all too familiar. There are several straightforward steps that every library should take to anticipate possible disasters and minimize their impact.

If some materials merit long-term preservation, others should be relegated or discarded once their immediate usefulness has passed. There are a long list of reasons this should take place, both to save storage costs and facilitate reader access to useful items, yet staff costs and professional prejudices have too often led to the deferral or abandonment of weeding programmes. The criteria used for weeding should be related to those of selection, and appear in the library's collection development policy. Most experts agree with Slote, in his *Weeding library collections,* that past use indicates potential future usage, and the 'shelf-time period' is the single most useful method of determining this. However, some standard and classic works should always be retained.

With serials, consultation with readers supplemented by usage and citation analysis statistics will suggest possible titles for cancellation, but the local availability of titles should also be taken into account. Electronic media should also be subject to continuing appraisal of their relevance and value. Finally, the concept of the 'self-renewing library', once much criticized, may in fact be more relevant today than when first put forward. Physical holdings are now no longer at the core of information provision.

Where to now?

For the final time, we suggest that you review the focus questions at the head of this chapter. Many of the preservation issues we raise are readily observable by the non-expert when visiting any library:

- Are the environmental conditions apparently designed to suit the collection or its readers? Is there any sign of environmental monitoring of rare or valuable items? Can sunlight fall on material?
- Examine the book return arrangements. Are these designed to minimize handling damage? Is any guidance routinely provided to readers on looking after library materials?

Similarly, if a weeding programme is active, there should be some visible evidence of this:

- Is there an appropriate balance between newer and older (but still useful) material on the open shelves? Are older duplicates offered for sale to readers?

However, much that was covered in this chapter will be known only to staff. Whether there is a disaster plan, for instance, and if so whether it is kept up to date and with copies off-site may only become publicly known if a disaster occurs.

If *you* are working in a library, however, you may well wish to enquire about the existence of any disaster plan, and how up to date it may be.

Further reading

A chapter such as this could not hope to cover several specialist technical areas in real depth. Those wishing to know more about preservation issues might first consult M. L. Ritzenthaler, *Preserving archives and manuscripts*, Society of American Archivists, 1993. J. Feather, G. Matthews and P. Eden, in *Preservation management: policies and practices in British libraries*, Gower, 1996, surveyed preservation management practices in British libraries; Chapters 1 and 7 provide the most useful starting place. Also useful is R. Harvey, *Preservation in libraries: principles, strategies and practices for librarians*, Bowker-Saur, 1993. A very recent bibliography of the area is provided by R. E. Schnare, S. G. Swartzburg and G. M. Cunha, *Bibliography of preservation literature, 1983-1996*, Scarecrow, 2001.

For readers seeking more practical information, the Northeast Document Conservation Center produces *Preservation of library and archival materials: a manual*, which is available in both hard copy (1992) and online at **www.nedcc.org/plam3/newman.htm**. This has sections on the environment, storage and handling, and conservation procedures. In the UK, the National Preservation Office provides some assistance on the Frequently Asked Questions page of its site, at **www.bl.uk/services/preservation/faq/html**, but the information is not as comprehensive as that supplied by the Northeast Document Conservation Center.

It will also have been apparent that the preservation of digital objects is very much a current hot topic. In Australia, a recent special issue of *Australian Academic & Research Libraries* (**31** (4), December 2000), included five articles on the topic. In the USA the Council on Library and Information Resources (**www.clir.org**) takes an active interest in this field, and its *Preservation and Access International Newsletter* regularly lists new publications related to the preservation of digital information. The European Commission on Preservation and Access, and its European Conservation Information Centre (**www.knaw.nl/ecpa**), have a similar interest, but with less prolific output. Other current material may be found in archival journals such as those cited in note 7.

Disaster planning is well covered by such works as H. Anderson and J. E. McIntyre, *Planning manual for disaster control in Scottish libraries & record offices*, National Library of Scotland, 1985; J. Ashman, *Disaster planning for library and information services*. Aslib Know How Guides, Aslib, 1995; and G. Matthews and P. Eden,

Disaster management in British libraries: project report with guidelines for library managers, British Library, 1996.

For weeding the obvious starting point is S. J. Slote, *Weeding library collections: library weeding methods*, 4th edn, Libraries Unlimited, 1997. For an alternative perspective, which places Slote's work in the wider context of an extensive literature on weeding, see R. Williams, 'Weeding library collections: conundrums and contradictions'. In G. E. Gorman (ed.), *International yearbook of library and information management 2000–2001: collection management*, Library Association Publishing, 2000, 339–61. As noted, there is also a very substantial literature on journal citation analysis, some of which will indeed be of value to the serials librarian or collections manager. Appropriate starting points here might be the bibliographic pointers in T. E. Nisonger, *Collection evaluation in academic libraries: a literature guide and annotated bibliography*, Libraries Unlimited, 1992, 97–119; and K. G. Altmann and G. E. Gorman, 'Usage, citation analysis and costs as indicators for journal deselection and cancellation: a selective literature review', *Australian Library Review*, **13** (4), 1996, 379–92.

Notes

1 C. Pearson and S. King, 'Passive environmental control for small cultural institutions in Australia', *Australian Academic & Research Libraries*, **31** (2), 2000, 69–78; R. L. Kerschner, 'A practical approach to environmental requirements for collections in historic buildings', *Journal of the American Institute for Conservation*, **31**, 1992, 65–76; S. Rowoldt, 'Going archivally green: implications of doing it naturally in Southern African archives and libraries', *South African Journal of Library and Information Science*, **66** (4), 1998, 141–7.

2 See, for example, the British Library with its online Gutenberg Bible: **http://prodigi.bl.uk/gutenbg/default.asp** [27 April 2001].

3 A. Howell, 'Perfect one day – digital the next: challenges in preserving digital information', *Australian Academic & Research Libraries*, **31** (4), 2000, 121–41, at p. 122.

4 J. Rothenberg, *Avoiding technological quicksand: finding a viable technical foundation for digital preservation*, Council for Library and Information Resources, 1998, 13–16, available at **www.clir.org/pubs/reports/rothenberg/contents.html**.

5 *Free online dictionary of computing* **http://wombat.doc.ic.ac.uk/foldoc/index.html** [27 April 2001].

6 J. Rothenberg, *An experiment in using emulation to preserve digital publications,*

Koninklijke Bibliotheek, 2000, available at **www.kb.nl/coop/nedlib/home-flash.html** [27 April 2001].

7　See such journals as *American Archivist, Archivaria* and *Archives and Manuscripts*, and preservation journals such as *Advances in Preservation and Access* and *International Preservation News*.

8　See A. Wise, 'Managing national distributed collections: reflections on the British experience'. In G. E. Gorman (ed.), *International yearbook of library and information management 2000–2001: collection management*, Library Association Publishing, 2000, 267–90 for an overview of the British experience here; C. Webb, 'Because it belongs to all of us: national arrangements for digital preservation in Australian libraries', *Australian Academic & Research Libraries*, **31** (4), 2000, 154–72 for an Australian perspective.

9　C. F. Thomas, 'Preservation management: something old, something new'. In G. E. Gorman (ed.), *International yearbook of library and information management 2000–2001: collection management*, Library Association Publishing, 2000, 365–80.

10　A. Grant, 'Benighted! How the University Library survived the Auckland power crisis', *Australian Academic & Research Libraries*, **31** (2), 2000, 61–9.

11　A. Stipcevic, 'The oriental books and libraries in Bosnia during the war, 1992–1994', *Libraries and Culture*, **333** (3), 277–82.

12　A point made eloquently in a school library context by P. Manning, 'When less is more: cultivating a health collection', *School Library Journal*, **43**, 1997, 54–5.

13　For details, see L. Payne, 'Library storage facilities and services.' In G. E. Gorman (ed.), *International yearbook of library and information management 2000–2001: collection management*, Library Association Publishing, 2000, 291–306.

14　J. P. Danton, *Book selection and collections: a comparison of German and American university libraries*, Columbia University Press, 1963; R. A. Trueswell, 'A quantitative measure of user circulation requirements and its possible effect on stack thinning and multiple-copy determination', *American Documentation*, **16** (January), 1965, 20–5.

15　See, for example, P. Metz and C. A. Litchfield, 'Measuring collections use at Virginia Tech', *College & Research Libraries*, **49** (6), 1988, 501–13.

16　L. Ash, *Yale's selective book retirement program*, Archon Books, 1963.

17　S. J. Slote, *Weeding library collections: library weeding methods*, 4th edn, Libraries Unlimited, 1997.

18　K. G. Altmann and G. E. Gorman, 'Anatomy of a serials collection and its usage: case study of an Australian academic library', *Library Collections, Acquisitions and Technical Services*, **23** (2), 1999, 149–61; K. G. Altmann and G. E. Gorman,

'The relevance of "cited by leading journal" to serials management in Australian university libraries', *Australian Library Journal*, **48** (2), 1999, 101–15.

19 O. G. Norman, 'The impact of electronic information services on collection development: a survey of current practice', *Library HiTech*, **15** (1–2), 1997, 123–31.

20 Great Britain, University Grants Committee, *Capital provision for university libraries: report of a working party*, HMSO, 1976.

The literature of collection management

Adela Clayton

Coverage

This select and annotated bibliography covers the area of collection management, largely as defined by the scope of this volume. It is limited to material published since 1990, as there are several excellent bibliographies covering earlier material (see, for example, the bibliographies of Thomas Nisonger listed below in 'Collection evaluation and review'). Within this time span, the primary focus is upon more recent material as with the increasing introduction of electronic resources change has been so marked.

Arrangement

A conscious decision was taken not to arrange the material included here in the sequence of the chapters in this volume. This was for two reasons: first, each chapter already lists 'Further reading' as its final section. Second, there are some topics – such as copyright or government publications – which are discussed in several chapters. It seemed more useful to bring material on these topics together.

Following the general material which appears immediately below, items are grouped into broad subject areas, arranged alphabetically.

Collection management journal titles

Acquisitions Librarian
Against the Grain
   www.against-the-grain.com/
The Bottom Line
Collection Building

Collection Management
Library Collections, Acquisitions and Technical Services
Library Resources and Technical Services
Serials

The following titles are also worth checking for collection management articles.

Ariadne
   www.ariadne.ac.uk
Australian Academic & Research Libraries
College & Research Libraries
D-Lib
   www.dlib.org/
Electronic Library
Information Technology & Libraries
Journal of Academic Librarianship
Journal of Library Administration
Journal of Library and Information Science
Library Admin and Management
Library Hi Tech
Library Trends

General

AcqWeb
   http://acqweb.library.vanderbilt.edu/acqweb/lis_cd.html [22 April 2001].
   Provides comprehensive links to information and resources of interest to acquisitions or collection development librarians. Includes listservs. International in scope.
Atkins, S. (1996) Mining automated systems for collection management. *Library Administration and Management,* **10** (1), 16–19.
   Describes the way that data from library automated systems may be used for collection development planning and management, urging librarians not to waste this capacity.
Baker, D. (ed.) (1997) *Resource management in academic libraries,* Library Association Publishing.
   Includes chapters on academic libraries, resource management, old and new universities and colleges of advanced education, total quality management, per-

formance indicators, costing, fund allocation and formulae, research collections, IT, operating costs and space planning. Four of the 16 chapters are by Baker.

Biblarz, D. (1997) The role of collection development in a teaching library, *European Research Libraries Cooperation*, **7** (2), 397–422.

The teaching library is one that supports the curriculum of its parent academic institution. Outlines the coverage of a collection development policy and the justification for expressing it in writing. Explains how to perform collection assessment, outlining established techniques including the use of Conspectus. Two appendices list collection assessment measures and collection depth indicators.

Branin, J. J. (1998) Shifting boundaries: managing research library collections at the beginning of the 21st century, *Collection Management*, **23** (4), 1–17.

A concise overview of the collection management practices and issues of US research libraries. Reviews three significant issues – the rapid expansion of education, scholarship and library collections; the shift from collection development to collection management; and attempts at co-operative collection development that influenced collection management during this period.

Branin, J. J., Groen, F. and Thorin, S. (2000) The changing nature of collection management in research libraries, *Library Resources & Technical Services*, **44** (1), 23–32.

Well-written by recognized authors, the article makes good observations about the changing scene. Demonstrates that procedures regularly used in the past no longer work.

BUBL LINK, *Catalogue of internet resources: collection development*, **http://bubl.ac.uk/link/c/collectiondevelopment.htm** [10 April 2001].

An annotated list of websites covering all fields.

Buckland, M. (1995) What will collection developers do?, *Information Technology & Libraries*, **15**, 155–9.

Defines the role of collection management in the electronic environment, advising librarians to focus on content rather than format.

Butler, M. A. and Kingma, B. R. (eds) (1996) *The economics of information in the networked environment*, Association of Research Libraries.

These conference papers cover diverse funding sources, collaboration, ownership vs access, and volunteerism, and conclude that the publisher–library relationship needs reinventing.

Carrigan, D. P. (1995) Toward a theory of collection development, *Library Acquisition: Practice and Theory*, **19** (1), 97–106.

Argues that a library collection should be seen as an investment. Senior library managers have an obligation to ask whether benefits to patrons justify the investment.

Cassell, K. A. and Futas, E. (1991) *Developing public library collections, policies, and procedures: a how-to-do-it manual for small and medium sized public libraries*, How-To-Do-It Manuals for Libraries 12, Neal-Schuman.

Offers step-by-step help with preparing for collection development, gathering and evaluating information about the community the collection serves, writing a policy, and ongoing collection development. It also offers a model policy and selection tools, plus worksheets and other visuals.

Chu, F. T. (1997) Librarian–faculty relations in collection development, *Journal of Academic Librarianship*, **23** (1), 15–19.

Addresses the relationship between librarians and faculty regarding collection development. Data are examined in light of existing studies on lateral relations and faculty–librarian interaction.

Crawford, W. and Gorman, M. (1995) *Future libraries: dreams, madness and reality*, American Library Association.

A reasoned, thorough defence of the book, libraries and librarianship in the context of the electronic environment.

Creth, S. (1991) The organization of collection development: a shift in the organization paradigm, *Journal of Library Administration*, **14** (1), 67–85.

Discusses the place of collection development in the traditional organization of the university library. Suggests a new model for organization, that integrates rather than segments work and staff. Collection development should not be carried out in isolation from other library activities; a team-based approach should yield positive results.

Demas, S. (1994) Collection development for the electronic library: a conceptual and organizational model, *Library Hi Tech*, **12** (3), 71–80.

Outlines the conceptual framework and organizational model developed at the Albert R. Mann Library to guide them in systematic selection of electronic media for the library. Traditional procedures for printed books and periodicals have become adapted to suit the electronic media.

DeWitt, D. L. (ed.) (1998) *Going digital: strategies for access, preservation and conversion of collections to a digital format*, Haworth Press.

Although dated in some aspects, the book raises important and current issues and the volume is worth reading by anyone involved in planning for digital library projects, particularly in the research libraries context.

eLib (1998) *Introduction to eLib: the Electronic Libraries Programme*, Electronic Libraries Programme, available at **www.ukoln.ac.uk/services/elib/** [26 April 2001].

This programme has explored the ways in which IT could assist libraries. A number of projects were carried out investigating such issues as preservation, electronic reserves, digitization (JSTOR) and document delivery. New material continues to be added to this page.

Evans, G. E. and Zarnosky, M. R. (2000) *Developing library and information center collections*, 4th edn, Libraries Unlimited.

Latest edition of a standard text. Covers topics such as censorship, book reviews, writing a collection development policy, serials, electronic resources, government documents, etc.

Forsman, R. B. (1998) Electronic resources transforming research libraries: challenges in the dynamic digital environment. In F. C. Lynden and E. A. Chapman (eds), *Advances in Librarianship*, **22**, Academic Press.

Provides a thoughtful literature survey that covers the information professional, library licensing, fiscal management and a look to the future.

Futas, E. (ed.) (1995) *Collection development policies and procedures*, 3rd edn, Oryx.

Part 1, the opening introduction and survey of the state of play, is valuable and stimulating. Parts 2 (full policy statements from two academic and two public libraries) and Part 3 (selections from a range of policies) are of value primarily to students and to librarians who are writing or revising their policies.

Gabriel, M. R. (1995) *Collection development and collection evaluation: a sourcebook*, Scarecrow Press.

Contains comprehensive bibliographies on collection development, collection evaluation and acquisitions (up to 1991) as well as examples of US collection development policies and US national guidelines and standards on collection development and collection evaluation, plus a glossary of terms.

Gessesse, K. (2000) Collection development and management in the twenty-first century with special reference to academic libraries: an overview, *Library Management*, **21** (6 and 7), 365–72.

The collection development policy for an academic library must include selection criteria and collection parameters covering new media formats. Examines some of the concepts and problems that an academic library must consider in order to align its collection development activities with the changing environment of digital librarianship in the 21st century.

Gorman, G. E. (ed.) (2000) *International yearbook of library and information management 2000–2001: collection management*, Library Association Publishing.

Comprehensive coverage of this topic by eminent authors in the light of the electronic environment. Arranged in five parts: overall view, access and acquisitions, co-operative collection management and storage, evaluating and weeding, preservation and archives.

Gorman, G. E. and Miller, R. H. (eds) (1997) *Collection management for the 21st century: a handbook for librarians,* Greenwood Press.

A thoroughly indexed collection of essays by a wide range of knowledgeable authors that will be of considerable interest to those responsible for collections in libraries of all kinds, but particularly large research and special libraries. Covers areas such as practical aspects, professional issues and results of research.

Gregory, V. L. (2000) *Selecting and managing electronic resources: a how-to-do-it manual for librarians,* Neal-Schuman.

A concise guide to policies, selection, budgeting, organization and access, evaluation, copyright and preservation with many practical features – worksheets, examples or resource sheets in almost every chapter. Excellent selection criteria are suggested.

Handman, G. P. (1994) *Video collection development in multi-type libraries: a handbook,* Greenwood Library Management Collection, Greenwood Press.

First and highly successful attempt to focus on video collections issues in a thorough and scholarly manner.

Harloe B. and Budd, J. M. (1994) Collection development and scholarly communication in the era of electronic access, *Journal of Academic Librarianship,* **20,** 83–7.

Defines the aim of electronic collection development in the academic environment as provision of efficient electronic access to scholars: the collection manager becomes the 'connection manager'.

Internet library for librarians

www.itcompany.com/inforetriev [30 April 2001].

Under 'Libraries' subheading has a range of useful links for collection development and serials (including vendors). Includes collection development policy statements, some full-text reviews, links to publishers' catalogues and also listservs and newsgroups.

Janes, J. and McClure, C. R. (1999) The web as a reference tool: comparisons with traditional sources, *Public Libraries,* **38** (1), 30–9.

This exploratory study offers a preliminary view of the success with which quick fact reference questions can be answered using resources in freely available websites. It suggests that the same level of accuracy and timeliness can be obtained as with traditional print-based resources. Implications for collection development, resource sharing and budgets are discussed.

Jenkins, C. and Morley, M. (eds) (1999) *Collection management in academic libraries,* 2nd edn, Gower Publishing.

This edition contains several new chapters on electronic resources, learning support, document delivery strategies, preservation and disaster planning, as well as revised chapters on organization, finance and budgeting, performance measurement, serials management, stock retention and relegation. US and British authors.

Johnson, P. and Macedon, B. (eds) (1999) *Virtually yours: models for managing electronic resources and services,* ALCTS Papers on Library Technical Services and Collections 8, Association for Library Collections and Technical Services.

Describes the best practices and current strategies for managing electronic resources from acquisitions to patron use. Experts in collection development and acquisitions from both academic and public libraries, including Ross Atkinson, Clifford Lynch and Karen Schmidt, cover the fields of selecting, acquiring and circulating electronic resources and information. Also examined are innovative, positive and practical management models that were tested in a range of libraries. Includes two chapters on licensing.

Joint Information Systems Committee, *Networks and innovative services for higher education web site*

www.jisc.ac.uk [10 April 2001].

JISC funds a wide range and growing number of national services for the benefit of the UK higher education and research communities. It is developing the Distributed National Electronic Resource (DNER), which is intended to provide a managed national collection of electronic resources.

Lancaster, F. W. (1994) Collection development in the year 2025. In P. Johnson and S. S. Intner (eds), *Recruiting, educating, and training librarians for collection development,* New Directions in Information Management 33, Greenwood Press.

Electronic sources may not be very different from print, but processes involving remote sources may be where greater changes lie.

Larsgaard, M. L. (1998) *Map librarianship: an introduction,* 3rd edn, Libraries Unlimited.

The new edition of this standard work provides information on spatial data in digital format.

Lee, S. H. (ed.) (1999) *Collection development in a digital environment,* Haworth Press. Also published as *Journal of Library Administration,* **28** (1).

Includes 'Chaos breeds life: finding opportunities for library advancement during a period of collection schizophrenia' (James G. Neal); 'Collection development and professional ethics' (Kenneth Frazier); 'Building the global collection – world class collection development: scenario planning and collection development' (Joan Giesecke); 'Digital information and the subscription agent as information coach' (Kit Kennedy).

Lee, S. H. (2000) What is a collection?, *Journal of the American Society for Information Science*, **51** (12), 1106–13.

Examines tangibility, ownership, a user community and an integrated retrieval mechanism. The emergence of non-traditional media poses two specific challenges: to question the necessity of finite collections and contest the boundaries of a collection. A critical analysis of these issues results in a proposal for an expanded concept of collection.

Martin, K. F. (1996) Managing the CD-ROM collection development process: issues and alternatives, *Collection Management*, **21** (2), 77–102.

Useful article on this specific type of resource covering selection and budgeting issues, evaluation, policies, licensing and networking.

Morley, M. and Woodward, H. (eds) (1993) *Taming the electronic jungle: electronic information: the collection management issues*, National Acquisitions Group and United Kingdom Serials Group.

These conference papers provide a meaningful debate of the broad issues – such as licensing and prices, networked services, print vs electronic resources. Another feature is the exploration of the debates between librarians and publishers.

Nisonger, T. E. (2000) Collection development in an electronic environment, *Library Trends*, **48** (4), 639–941.

Special issue begins with a historical overview from 1980 to 2000. The papers by Curt Holleman and Paul Metz on criteria for selection are particularly worthwhile.

Nolan, C. W. (1999) *Managing the reference collection*, American Library Association.

Includes useful criteria for creating and implementing reference collection development policies and procedures, selecting and managing print and electronic reference services, and evaluating and weeding reference collections. It places the question of information technology within the broader context or reference services.

OCLC

www.oclc.org/home/ [29 April 2001].

OCLC is a non-profit membership organization serving almost 40,000 libraries around the world. It aims to further access to the world's information and reduce library costs by offering services for libraries and their users. Services include resource-sharing tools and preservation services.

Osburn, C. B. and Atkinson, R. (1991) *Collection management: a new treatise*, Foundations in Library and Information Science 26, parts A and B, JAI Press.

Provides extensive background on past, current and future issues as well as an overview by prominent contributors. Of use to practitioners and students although published at a time when electronic resources were not as central. Dan Hazen's chapter, 'Selection: function, models, theory', has a thorough review of theoretical models for selection. Joseph Branin's chapter on co-operative collection development is an excellent survey.

Owens, G. S. (ed.) (1996) *Electronic resources: implications for collection management*, Haworth Press. Published simultaneously as *Collection Management*, **21** (1).

Discusses the strengths and weaknesses of electronic resources, as well as the implications these resources have on collection management. It also provides guidance on incorporating electronic resources into library collections.

Pastine, M. (1996) *Collection development: past and future*, parts 1 and 2, Haworth Press. Also published as *Collection Management*, **21** (2) and **21** (3/4).

Some of the chapters are 'Competition, collaboration, and cost in the new knowledge environment' (Kathryn Hammell Carpenter); 'Collection issues in the new library environment' (Curt Holleman); 'Integrating electronic resources into collection development policies' (Kristin D. Vogel); 'Managing the CD-ROM collection development process: issues and alternatives' (Katherine F. Martin and Robert F. Rose); 'Collecting bits: the internet as a library resource' (Robert Skinner).

Pastine, M. (1997) *Collection development: access in the virtual library*, Haworth Press. Also published as *Collection Management*, **22** (1/2).

Deals realistically with effects that new communication technologies are likely to have in the future. Two large bibliographies are included. Curt Holleman's article on electronic tools for collection management is especially useful.

Price, D. J. (1998) The hybrid library and collection development, *The New Review of Information and Library Research*, **4**, 129–39.

Covers aspects of rights management, financial models and licensing agreements, as well as key technological issues.

Sandelands, E. (1998) Creating an online library to support a virtual learning community, *Internet Research*, **8** (1), 75–80.

Describes how an independent business school has created a virtual library in partnership with database publisher Anbar Electronic Intelligence. Outlines the virtual business school model being developed and used. Examines the relationship between the partner organizations. Analyses the benefits being experienced by faculty and student's investment to date and anticipated.

Schaefer, M. T. (1998) Critical examinations of problems in electronic information dissemination and storage, *Information Retrieval and Library Automation*, **34** (5), 1–6.

Examines the value and the problems of electronic information dissemination and storage.

Sellen, B. and Curley, A. (eds) (1992) *The collection building reader*, Neal-Schuman. Reprint of 30 articles from the journal *Collection Building*, grouped in four sections: 'Management issues', 'Selection/deselection', 'Evaluation' and 'Resource sharing'. Authors include Paul Mosher, Elizabeth Futas and Bill Katz.

Shaw, S.H. (1995) A symposium on collection management in the electronic environment, *Library Acquisitions: Practice and Theory*, **19** (1), 107–10.
Covers the following papers: 'Managing the old and the new: collection development in an expanding information environment'; 'Emerging trends in scholarly communication: impact on libraries'; 'Collection development for the electronic library: mainstreaming the selection and acquisition of electronic resources'; and 'Sharing resources in the CIC (Committee for Institutional Cooperation): implications of CICNET, electronic literature and the virtual library'.

Sweeney, J. (1998) Collections. In M. B. Line (ed.), *Librarianship and information work worldwide*, Bowker-Saur.
State-of-the-art review of literature published about library collections and stock issues worldwide. Issues covered include: financial problems and how to cope with them; collection development; problems with periodicals; user interaction; library automation; collection management, evaluation and retention and disposal issues; preservation and disaster management; security; the digital library; electronic periodicals; the internet and world wide web; and particular collections.

Thomsen, E. (1996) *Reference and collection development on the internet: a how-to-do-it manual*, Neal-Schuman.
This is a practical guide with a well-organized approach to effectively integrating internet resources into reference services and collections, but is has not gone as far as thinking about more current issues such as integrating electronic resources into the catalogue.

Washington Research Libraries Consortium
www.wrlc.org/ [10 April 2001].
WRLC is a regional resource-sharing organization established by seven universities in the Washington DC metropolitan area. The site includes good examples of resource-sharing policies, objectives and plans.

Wilkie, C. (1999) *Managing film and video collections*, Know How Guide, Aslib.
This series is intended to give practical advice from experts on current issues to practitioners and in this volume the expert's view comes through on every page. The book covers issues about film formats and equipment, preservation,

documenting and cataloguing holdings; searching; security and staff training.

Wilson, M. C. and Edelman, H. (1996) Collection development in an interdisciplinary context, *Journal of Academic Librarianship*, **22** (3), 195–200.

This paper examines the growing trend of interdisciplinary research, and reports on a case study in one US academic library.

Access vs ownership

Beam, J. (1997) Document delivery via Uncover: analysis of a subsidized service, *Serials Review*, **23** (4), 1–14.

An analysis of journal use at one US academic library and impacts on budgets and staff. Results from several years' data indicated that subsidized unmediated delivery was cost effective when compared with the purchase of additional serial subscriptions.

Beardman, S. (1996) The cost-effectiveness of access versus ownership: a report on the Virtual Library Project at the University of Western Australia Library, *Australian Library Review*, **13** (2), 173–81.

Outlines research into document delivery costing and service issues over a two-and-a-half-year trial.

Brin, B. and Cochran, E. (1994) Access and ownership in the academic environment: one library's progress report, *Journal of Academic Librarianship*, **20** (4), 207–12.

Discusses the methodology used at the University of Arizona Library to tackle the access/ownership issue and to determine options to guide the library in decision making, policy formulation, and the provision of services.

Connolly, P. (2000) Interlending and document supply: a review of recent literature, *Interlending and Document Supply*, **28** (1), 40–7.

Examines the impact of world wide web delivery, the increasing number of periodicals being published electronically and the creation of digital libraries. Discusses some of the projects undertaken by higher education institutions to deliver electronic material to researchers and students. Includes articles on various resource-sharing activities highlighting the usual access versus ownership issues.

Hawbaker, A. C. and Wagner, C. K. (1996) Periodical ownership versus fulltext online access: a cost-benefit analysis, *Journal of Academic Librarianship*, **22** (2), 105–10.

Compares the costs and benefits of periodical ownership against online access of a full-text periodicals database in one US academic library. For a 15% increase in expenditure a full-text database allows the library to offer more than twice as many journals as it does currently.

Higginbotham, B.B. and Bowdoin, S. (1993) *Access versus assets: a comprehensive guide to resource sharing for academic librarians*, American Library Association.
Explores a broad range of cost-effective and efficient approaches to providing patrons with information from outside the local library.

Kane, L. T. (1997) Access vs ownership, *College & Research Libraries*, **58** (1), 59–67.
Proposes a third option to the traditional 'warehouses of information' and the modern 'providers of access to information' models. This is an 'access and ownership' model which would involve libraries identifying the most-used materials and purchasing only those. All other materials would be obtained by interlibrary loans, document delivery, full-text databases, CD-ROM databases and internet resources.

Lee, S. H. (ed.) (1996) *Access, ownership and resource sharing*, Haworth Press. Published simultaneously as *Journal of Library Administration*, **22** (4).
Collection of articles based on a 1994 conference, grounded entirely in the US experience and most relevant to academic libraries. Articles explore the role of libraries in acquiring, storing and disseminating information in different formats to help in using technology to share scarce resources and connect library users with library collections.

Pastine, M. (1997) Ownership or access to electronic information: a selective bibliography, *Collection Management*, **22** (1/2), 187–214.
Bibliography of US articles, monographs and conference proceedings on ownership or access to electronic information covering material published up to 1996. Not annotated.

Pedersen, W. and Gregory, D. (1994) Interlibrary loan and commercial document supply, *Journal of Academic Librarianship*, **20** (5/6), 263–72.
Examines the cost and performance of six commercial document suppliers accessible via OCLC and compares their service to that of traditional interlibrary loan. Results indicated that, while commercial firms cannot be recommended as a wholesale replacement for ILL, they can add much-needed flexibility to a library's overall plan for document delivery.

Sundt, C. L. (1998) The quest for access to images: history and development. In F. C. Lynden and E. A. Chapman (eds), *Advances in Librarianship*, vol. 22, Academic Press.
Examines the history of access to image collections focusing on the recent use of electronic resources to overcome difficulties and challenges usually associated with image access.

Truesdell, C. B. (1994) Is access a viable alternative?, *Journal of Academic Librarianship*, **20** (4), 200–6.

Three performance criteria can be used to evaluate the effectiveness of access: costs, turnaround time and success rate. Truesdell concludes from a review of the literature of the past decade that consistency and reliability are the most usual obstacles to substituting ownership for access.

Tyckoson, D. (1991) Access vs ownership: changing roles for librarians, *Reference Librarian*, **34**, 37–45.

The library can no longer function solely as a warehouse of information. In order to survive as information professionals for the future, librarians must shift their emphasis from one based on ownership to one based on access. Examines the factors behind the need for such changes and looks at their impact on the role of the librarian as an information professional.

Acquisitions

Alessi, D. L. (2000) Raising the bar: book vendors and the new realities of service, *Journal of Library Administration*, **28** (2), 25–40.

Changes in continuations, firm orders, value-added services, approval plans, retrospective collection development, and database creation and maintenance are being made to keep current library users and to attract new ones.

Black, D. (1998) In search of out-of-print books: the past, the present and the future, *Georgia Library Quarterly*, **35**, 11–17.

Reviews the historical methods used to acquire out-of-print and out-of-stock material. A comparison is made between these methods and new technological approaches available via the internet. Includes a short description of online databases available for searching and investigates future developments in book acquisitions and the impact that the changes will have on libraries and administration.

Bluh, P. (1996) The winds of change: acquisitions for a new century, *Law Library Journal*, **88** (1), 90–5.

Identifies major issues that will influence the nature of acquisitions work and the change in role for the acquisitions librarian.

Bosch, S, Promis, P. and Sugnet, C. (1994) *Guide to selecting and acquiring CD-ROMs, software and other electronic publications*, American Library Association.

Concisely written guide provides direction and suggestions for selecting and acquiring electronic materials. The steps involved in the process of purchasing most of the electronic formats presently available are clearly delineated. Issues from policy concerns, through access or ownership, to leasing and rental agreements are all covered.

Brennan, P., Hersey, K. and Harper, G. (1997) *Licensing electronic resources: strate-gic and practical considerations for signing electronic information delivery agreements,* Association of Research Libraries, available at **www.arl.org/scomm/licensing/licbooklet.html** [29 April 2001].
Practical advice and questions to consider when signing agreements. Includes several useful links.

Chapman, L. (2001) *Managing acquisitions in library and information services,* Library Association Publishing.
Provides clear, sensible and practical up-to-date advice for the novice covering topics from pre-order checking, publishers, suppliers, ordering (including standing orders, out-of-print, etc.) and checking on orders supplied, to finance and budgets.

Duchin, D. and Wagner, C. S. (1996) Trials and tribulations: out-of-print, *Library Acquisitions: Practice and Theory,* **20** (3), 341–50.
Describes how vendors and book dealers address the special needs of libraries and their methods for finding out-of-print books. Search strategies include adver-tising, using reference works, using vendors and dealers, and searching internet and web databases.

Eaglen, A. (2000) *Buying books: a how-to-do-it manual for librarians,* How-To-Do-It Man-uals for Librarians, 99, 2nd edn, Neal-Schuman.
Covers vendor selection and ordering in the electronic age, bibliographic tools, acquisitions and automated systems, bookstores, future of the publishing industry, etc. Includes glossary.

Flowers, K. A., Keck, K. A. and Lindquist, J. L. (1995) Collection development and acquisitions in a changing university environment, *Library Acquisitions: Practice and Theory,* **19** (4), 463–9.
Some time constraints have affected procedures used in acquisitions.

Gold, H. (2000) Acquisitions, the internet and the academic library, *Acquisitions Librarian,* **23**, 71–80.
Presents an overview of how librarians and library staff are using electronic tools, which tools and what benefits and drawbacks they present. Websites, OPACs, listservs, and direct library–vendor links are some of the electronic resources that aid acquisition departments in their choices and ordering decisions. Includes specific examples and useful websites.

Harris, M. H. and Hannah, S. A. (1996) 'The treason of the librarians': core com-munication technologies and opportunity costs in the information era, *Journal of Academic Librarianship,* **22** (1), 2–8.
Initial article in a special symposium addressing the role of academic libraries

in the digital era. Librarians advocating a conservative, even reactionary, stance relative to the emerging integrated digital communication environment place the future of library and information services at risk.

Henderson, T. (1996) Weaving the web: using the world wide web in library acquisitions, *Library Acquisitions: Practice and Theory*, **20** (3), 367–74.

A concise outline of the ways in which internet resources can be used for bibliographic verification, ordering and current awareness. Gives practical examples of how an acquisitions librarian might carry out daily tasks using the internet.

Johnson, S. D. (1997) Library acquisitions pages on the world wide web, *Library Resources and Technical Services*, **21**, 195–224.

Thirty-one acquisitions and collection development pages were examined. While design rather than content was the focus, it shows how design is an important part in providing information.

Kraft, N. O. (1996) The acquisitions module: stepchild of the IOLS, *The Electronic Library*, **14** (3), 211–14.

Questions whether integrated online library systems provide acquisitions modules of sufficient quality. Discusses problems and options.

Leiserson, A. B. (1997) AcqWeb: book-buying in the age of the internet, *Library Hi Tech*, **15** (3/4), 39–44, 55.

Beginning with an outline of the development of *AcqWeb*, the editor describes its structure and features. This is a site that has continued to develop and is a valuable tool for the collection management professional.

Martin, M. S. (1994) Acquisitions: long distance, *Collection Management*, **20** (1/2), 3–13.

Buying library materials for a country far distant from the principal sources of publication presents specific problems, financial and procedural. This report of responses to the problems by the National Library Service of New Zealand in the 1960s is relevant to some of the difficulties presently facing third-world countries.

Morris, A. (2000) E-commerce, document delivery and academia, *Vine*, **120**, 18–27.

Examines the range of options available for libraries and researchers to obtain or access documents electronically. Lists suppliers and discusses selection criteria, both informed by the results of the Electronic Libraries Programme (eLib)-sponsored FIDDO (Focused Investigation of Document Delivery Options) project completed in 1999.

Muir, A. and Davies, J. E. (2000) Legal deposit of digital material in the UK: recent developments and the international context, *Alexandria*, **12** (3), 151–66.

A UK government working party developed recommendations on how to achieve a comprehensive national archive including non-print material. Recommended a statutory and distributed system for deposit. The government accepted the need for legislation and asked the working party to carry out further work on definitions, the impact on business and an interim voluntary code of practice for some types of non-print material. The code of practice came into operation at the beginning of 2000.

Scheschy, V. M. (1999) Publishers on the web: from Addison to Ziff, *Library Collections, Acquisitions, and Technical Services*, **23** (1), 73–8.

Argues there will be fundamental changes in the methods libraries use to acquire material, as acquisitions staff and collection development librarians move on from restricting online ordering to items that are required urgently or are out-of-print.

Schmidt, K. A. (ed.) (1999) *Understanding the business of library acquisitions,* 2nd edn, American Library Association.

Highly recommended, authoritative summary of the current library acquisitions scene. It covers the publishing industry and the library supply business, practical issues of acquisitions and some thoughts on management issues, as well as licensing.

Secor, J. R and Shirk, G. M. (2000) The coming restructure of library book vending, *Libri*, **50** (2), 104–8.

Reviews models vendors have operated with over the last three decades. New business goals must emphasize co-operation.

Soete, G. J. (1999) *Managing the licensing of electronic products*, SPEC Kit 247, Association of Research Libraries.

This SPEC survey sought to discover how research libraries have organized the licensing of electronic products and how they approach the associated problems.

Stanford University Libraries, *Copyright and fair use*, available at **http://fairuse.stanford.edu** [29 April 2001].

This site is sponsored by the Council on Library Resources, FindLaw Internet Legal Resources and the Stanford University Libraries and Academic Information Resources. Provides links to primary materials (legislation and judicial opinions, treaties), cases and issues, internet resources and overview of copyright laws, naturally with a US perspective.

Toub, S. E. (1997) Adding value to internet collections, *Library Hi Tech*, **15** (3/4), 148–54.

Discusses when librarians should develop their own internet collections and provides strategic guidance for those who choose to do so. Concludes that there are two key ways of adding value to collections of internet resources: by ensuring the findability of internet resources via well-planned organization, navigation, labelling and learning systems, and by carefully selecting, evaluating and describing the resources in their internet collections.

White, G. W. and Crawford, G. (1998) A cost-benefit analysis of electronic information, *College & Research Libraries*, **59** (6), 503–10.

Reports on a study of BPO (the ABI/Inform Business Periodicals On Disc CD-ROM database) at Pennsylvania State University, which found that the costs of purchasing full-text CD-ROMs were more than offset by the reduction in interlibrary loans.

Wilkinson, F. C. and Thorson, C. C. (1998) *The RFP process: effective management of the acquisition of library materials*, Libraries Unlimited.

Sections on approval plans, standing orders, serials and electronic services from vendors are especially useful. Part 4 covers vendor perspectives and also evaluation.

Budget management

Ford, G. (1999) Finance and budgeting. In C. Jenkins and M. Morley (eds), *Collection management in academic libraries*, 2nd edn, Gower Publishing, 39–69.

Concentrates on materials allocation budgets including examples of formulae. Does not discuss electronic resources.

Johnston, B. J. and Witte, V. (1996) Electronic resources and budgeting: funding at the edge, *Collection Management*, **21** (1), 3–16.

Offers a view of the careful balancing required as libraries budget for both traditional and emerging information sources. Documents the budgetary shifts taking place in a research library at Washington University over a ten-year period.

Kiger, J. E. and Wise, K. (1996) Auditing an academic library book collection, *Journal of Academic Librarianship*, **22** (4), 267–72.

Illustrates how academic and research libraries might apply attribute sampling techniques to editing principles to determine specifically prescribed information about the collection.

Martin, M. S. (1995) *Collection development and finance: a guide to strategic library-materials budgeting*, American Library Association.

The budgeting cycle is completely covered in a practical and flexible way for public, special and academic libraries. Recommended for librarianship students and the new library manager. Has chapters on collections and finance, preparing and writing a budget, various types of budgeting, serials and databases, allocation procedures and budget monitoring.

Snyder, H. and Davenport, E. (1997) *Costing and pricing in the digital age: a practi-*

cal guide for information services, Library Association Publishing.

A clearly written and authoritative introduction to budgeting with explanation of budgeting terms; however, not focused on collection development.

Tebbetts, D. R. (2000) The costs of information technology and the electronic library, *Electronic Library,* **18** (2), 127–36.

Discusses the impact of information technology requirements on the costs of electronic libraries. Poses key questions concerning hardware, software and network installation and upgrades and provides strategies for dealing with the essential needs for continuous funding and long-term financing.

Censorship

American Library Association, Office for Intellectual Freedom (1996) *Intellectual freedom manual,* 5th edn, American Library Association.

A primary, authoritative source on intellectual freedom policy, procedures and application for public, academic, special and school libraries in the USA, offering practical opinions for anticipating and responding to censorship attempts. Compendium of ALA intellectual freedom policies. Covers how to handle complaints and how to write effectively to a legislator. Includes such tasks as developing a materials selection programme and dealing with the political strategies of organized pressure groups.

Emery, J. (1994) A critique of the principles of censorship, *Collection Management,* **18** (3/4), 63–9.

Argues that it is essential for librarians to understand the impact of censoring materials and the danger of suppressing information regardless of the validity of ideas expressed in these materials. Asserts that librarians, rather than seeing themselves as guardians of the truth, should ensure the provision of unrestricted access to materials needed by library users.

Higgins, S. E. (2000) Information, technology and diversity: censorship in the 21st century. In G. E. Gorman (ed.), *International yearbook of library and information management 2000–2001: collection management,* Library Association Publishing, 99–117.

Looks at issues such as human rights, censorship and the internet, the information poor, privacy, diversity, social context and globalization as they apply to censorship and outlines relevance of censorship to collection development.

Moorcroft, H. and Byrne, A. (1996) Intellectual property and indigenous peoples' information, *Australian Academic & Research Libraries,* **27** (2), 87–94.

Discusses the complex issues in cultural documentation, primary and moral rights to which libraries and archives must respond.

Owen, U. (2000) Gateways to freedom: libraries and the new millennium, *Libri*, **50** (1), 6–13.

Begins with brief overview of classic censorship. Suggests that concentration of media ownership has affected the extent to which minorities are heard and outlines the important part libraries can play in maintenance of free expression.

Williams, C. L. and Dillon, K. (1993) *Brought to book: censorship and school libraries in Australia*, ALIA Thorpe.

Provides a thorough review of the literature on the topic related to Australia and to a lesser extent overseas. Has chapters covering definition of censorship, legislation, philosophic aspects and role of literature and education. Based on survey of 145 teacher-librarians.

Collection development policies

AcqWeb *Collection development resources*, available at
www.library.vanderbilt.edu/law/acqs/libsci.html#colldev [21 April 2001].
Links to online collections of policies.

Anderson, J. S. (ed.) (1996) *Guide for written collection policy statements*, 2nd edn, Collection Management and Development Guides, American Library Association.
A step-by-step plan for creating policy statements. Includes guidelines for preparing policies for co-operative arrangements, interdisciplinary coverage, electronic collections, and the use of preservation in collection management. An expanded selection of Conspectus materials and a bibliography categorized by library type are also included.

Association of Research Libraries (1998) Checklist for drafting electronic information policies, *ARL Newsletter*, **196**, available at
www.arl.org/newsltr/196/checklist.html [29 April 2001].
A brief guide followed by a large number of links to sample electronic information policies.

Ferguson, A. W. (1995) Interesting problems encountered on my way to writing an electronic information collection development statement, *Against the Grain*, **7** (2), 16–19.
Summary of problems and questions arising during the writing of a collection development statement.

Frank, D. G. et al. (1993) The relevance of collection development policies: definition, necessity, and applications, *RQ*, **33** (1), 65–74.

A good summary including analysis, policy-making advice and a basic annotated bibliography of which the most recent item is dated 1992.

Maple, A. and Morrow, J. (2001) *Guide to writing collection development policies for music*, Music Library Association Technical Reports Series 26, Scarecrow Press. Specifically devoted to music collections, this guide refers not only to the process of planning a music library's information resources collection but also to other related activities incorporated into or co-ordinated with the collection development policy: collection management activities and resource-sharing programmes.

Snow, R. (1996) Wasted words: the written collection development policy and the academic library, *Journal of Academic Librarianship*, **22** (3), 191–4.
Instead of writing policies that quickly become irrelevant and outdated, bibliographers should concentrate on selection and evaluation of their collections.

Van Zijl, C. (1998) The why, what, how of collection development policies. *South African Journal of Library and Information Science*, **66**, 99–106.
Discusses the importance of the collection development policy in the contemporary library and the information that should be included as well as the criteria that could be applied in selection of materials. It concludes with a brief guide to the writing of policies.

White, G.W. and Crawford, G. A. (1997) Developing an electronic information resources collection development policy, *Asian Libraries*, **6** (1), 51–6.
Instead of focusing on how well a given item supports the collection, the policy gives general guidance on the selection of electronic resources. Covers many criteria.

Wood, R. J. and Hoffmann, F. W. (1996) *Library collection development policies: a reference and writers' handbook*, Scarecrow Press.
Part 1 covers policy rationale, implementing a policy and policy components. Part 2 is a collection of collection development policies divided into sections by type of library, e.g. academic, public, school, etc.

Collection evaluation and review

Altmann, K. G. and Gorman, G. E. (1996) Usage, citation analysis and costs as indicators for journal deselection and cancellation: a selective literature review, *Australian Library Review*, **13**, 379–92.
Looks at the literature devoted to the serials crisis that has been developing in the past 30 years, focusing on the three categories of indicators most often discussed as appropriate for making deselection and cancellation decisions: usage,

citation analysis and costs, including worth. It concludes that no single method or indicator on its own is adequate for making informed decisions in academic libraries.

Altmann, K. G. and Gorman, G. E. (1999) Anatomy of a serials collection and its usage: case study of an Australian academic library, *Library Collections, Acquisitions and Technical Services*, **23** (2), 149–61.

Reports the results of a serial usage study conducted at an Australian academic library, indicating what can happen to holdings if collection development staff do not have access to usage data.

Altmann, K. G. and Gorman, G. E. (1999) The relevance of 'cited by leading journal' to serials management in Australian university libraries, *Australian Library Journal*, **48** (2), 101–15.

Highlights the importance of Australian scientific journals to overall serial usage in a variety of disciplines in an Australian university library. Examination of journal citation reports demonstrates that there is a high degree of cross-citation between major Australian science journals.

Altmann, K. G. and Gorman, G. E. (2000) Density of use as a criterion in the deselection and relegation of serials, *New Library World*, **101** (3), 112–22.

Demonstrates that density of use favours the retention of used titles that occupy a small amount of shelf space compared with titles occupying a large amount of shelf space. While the paper presents an easy method for identifying titles possessing a high total use but having a comparatively low density of use, the strategy fails to identify titles having a high density of use but which also have some scope for partitioning between open and closed access. It therefore outlines a simple method of partitioning these titles between open and closed access to increase the density of use of the open access collection.

Baker, S. and Lancaster, F. W. (1991) *The measurement and evaluation of library services*, 2nd edn, Information Resources Press.

This second edition of a standard work combines material from the first edition (1977) with extracts from another Lancaster work, *If you want to evaluate your library* . . . (University of Illinois Press, 1988), adding some evaluative studies. Provides detailed information on the evaluation of academic, public, school and special libraries.

Butkovich, N. J. (1996) Use studies: a selective review, *Library Resources and Technical Services*, **40**, 359–68.

Reviews the major approaches for analysing use of library materials including surveys, reshelving studies, non-use studies, circulation, patron observation, citation analysis and interlibrary loan data.

Carrigan, D. P. (1996) Collection development: evaluation, *Journal of Academic Librarianship*, **22** (4), 273–8.

Argues for a distinction between evaluation of the collection and evaluation of the collection development activity. Discusses issues such as overselection, circulation statistics, interlibrary loan use and use of internet.

Delaney-Lehman, M. J. (1996) Assessing the library collection for diversity, *Collection Management*, **20** (3/4), 29–37.

Describes a project undertaken by the library at Lake Superior State University to assess the cultural diversity of its collection by comparing library holdings to a standard bibliography of multicultural works. Since such a bibliography did not exist the library developed its own bibliography in subject areas appropriate for a small academic or public library focusing on American cultures. The library held only 10%.

Eager, C. and Oppenheim, C. (1996) An observational method for undertaking user need studies, *Journal of Librarianship and Information Science*, **28** (1), 15–23.

The problem of designing user studies that reliably measure user needs has hampered the study of information needs. Major constraints quoted in research are time and money. This article describes a new research tool in this field.

Ennis, K. (1995) *Guidelines for college libraries: recommendations for performance and resourcing*, 5th edn, Library Association Publishing.

Addresses the quality, resource and service issues of library provision within the UK further education sector, covering strategic management, resource and service management, quality management and evaluation and inspection and marketing.

Ford, G. (1990) *Review of methods employed in determining the use of library stock*, BNB Research Fund reports 43, The British Library.

A comprehensive review of types of evaluation.

Harrell, J. (1992) Use of the OCLC/AMIGOS collection analysis CD to determine comparative collection strength in English and American literature: a case study, *Technical Services Quarterly*, **9** (3), 1–14.

In 1989 OCLC and AMIGOS Bibliographic Council released a new product called *Collection Analysis CD* which was developed to assist OCLC libraries in measuring the adequacy of their collections as compared with peer institutions. The CD-ROM database, which provides statistical data as well as lists of titles in specified categories, is evaluated and possible uses in a collection development setting described.

Kelland, J. L. and Young, A. P. (1994) Citation as a form of library use, *Collection Management*, **19** (1/2), 81–100.

Reviews the citation analysis literature selectively over the previous 20 years for articles that address the relation between citation and library use in academic libraries. In spite of limitations because of the many variables, it concludes that citation analysis remains a useful tool for evaluation of library collections and subject literatures.

Lancaster, F. W. (1993) *If you want to evaluate your library . . .,* 2nd edn, Library Association Publishing.

A detailed review of and practical advice on the methods available and their appropriateness.

Nisonger, T. E. (1992) *Collection evaluation in academic libraries: a literature guide and annotated bibliography,* Libraries Unlimited.

This standard work has been kept up to date by the following literature reviews.

Nisonger, T. E. (1998) The collection development literature of 1996: a bibliographic essay, *Collection Building,* **17** (1), 29–39.

Nisonger, T. E. (1999) A review of the 1997 collection development and management literature, *Collection Building,* **18** (2), 67–80.

Nisonger, T. E. (2000) Use of the journal citation reports for serials management in research libraries: an investigation of the effect of self-citation on journal rankings in library and information science and genetics, *College & Research Libraries,* **61** (3), 263–75.

Explores the use of the Institute for Scientific Information's 'Journal Citation Reports' (JCR) for periodical management in academic libraries. A literature review summarizes reported uses of these data by libraries and scholars. Concluded that librarians can use JCR data without correcting for periodical self-citation, although self-citations do exert a major effect on the rankings for a small number of periodicals.

Osareh, F. (1996) Bibliometrics, citation analysis and co-citation analysis: a review of literature, *Libri,* **46,** 149–58.

Presents a background of bibliometrics and citations analysis, and applications, as well as document and author co-citation analysis, journal-by-journal and country-by-country analysis as a research method. Limitations, problems, and reliability and validity of citation analysis as a research method are discussed. Has a bibliography of 66 items.

Roy, L. (1993) Displays and displacement of circulation, *Collection Management,* **17** (4), 57–77.

Studies of displays have mainly been limited to examining the effect of display on the items on display. This study of eight small US public libraries tested the broader effect of displays on turnover rate and total circulation. It found that, while books on display may circulate more often, this circulation is displaced from other areas of the collection.

Ventress, A. (1991) Use surveys and collection analyses: a prelude to serials rationalization, *Library Acquisitions: Practice and Theory*, **15** (1), 109-18.
Examines the evaluation of a serials collection in a large Australian research library prior to instituting a programme of cancellations.

White, H. D. (1995) *Brief tests of collection strength: a methodology for all types of libraries,* Contributions in Librarianship and Information Science, Greenwood Press.
Takes a critical approach to the usual time-consuming methods of collection evaluation. The author claims that results can be obtained quickly and carefully demonstrates applications, validity and usefulness of his tests.

Conspectus

Blake, V. L. P. and Tjoumas, R. (1994) The Conspectus approach to collection evaluation: panacea or false prophet?, *Collection Management*, **18** (3/4), 1-31.
Covers the history and development, benefits and problems of this strategy and highlights some questions for research in the area.

Davis, B. (1998) How the WLN Conspectus works for small libraries, *Acquisitions Librarian*, **20**, 53-72.
Part of a thematic issue devoted to public library collection development in the information age. Looks at some of the benefits of using the Conspectus in small libraries and suggests appropriate adaptations of the Conspectus structure. In particular demonstrates the efficiency of WLN Conspectus software as a tool for assessing small collections in public libraries.

Davis, B. (1998) Using local marketing characteristics to customize the Conspectus for fiction assessment, *Acquisitions Librarian*, **19**, 29-44.
There are several possible ways to assess fiction, biography and biographical fiction collections using accepted Conspectus methods. Recommends that the choice of method be guided by the meaningful collection groupings that are used by a local library to provide access to its resources. Since these arrangements are usually related to the ways customers use the library and to the methods the library uses to market its collection, they suggest ways to organize assessment data and relate the data to acquisitions activities. Notes the flexibility of WLN Conspectus software which enables librarians to produce customized assessment results by adapting techniques and tools to local collection arrangements.

Wolf, M. T. (1999) By the dawn's early light, *Journal of Library Administration*, **28** (1), 19-32.

Argues that there is a well-entrenched, global commercial monopoly on the distribution and approval of ideas, characterized by 'bottom-line thinking' and 'content' that is already predetermined by distributors. Relates this to collection development, having regard to the threatened viability of the traditional library. Stresses the need for co-operation and 'accelerated resource sharing'. Librarians should develop 'a national/international conspectus for our global library' and develop 'cooperative just in case repositories to serve the just in time needs of our clientele'.

Wood, R. J. (1996) The Conspectus: a collection analysis and development success, *Library Acquisitions: Practice and Theory*, **20** (4), 429–53.

Despite a great deal of criticism levelled at the Conspectus, it is the most widely used collection development and co-operative collection development methodology to date. Explains why it is regarded as an effective tool of its type for a multi-type library consortium or network, and for many large public and academic libraries on an institutional basis. Discusses history and various aspects of the Conspectus.

Wood, R. J. and Strauch, K. (eds) (1992) *Collection assessment: a look at the RLG Conspectus*, Haworth Press. Also published as *The Acquisitions Librarian*, **7**.

Articles cover what the RLG Conspectus is, how it is used and misused, and its strengths and weaknesses.

Co-operative collection development and resource sharing

Alexander, A.W. (1999) Toward 'the perfection of work': library consortia in the digital age, *Journal of Library Administration*, **28** (2), 1–14.

Motives for library co-operation, along with potential obstacles and keys to success, are identified, and a connection between service quality improvement and library co-operation is noted. The role of library consortia in the current electronic environment is described, with particular emphasis on the 1990s, and prospects for the future of library consortia are outlined, with a description of key environmental factors that will affect them.

Allen, B. M. (1999) Consortia and collections: achieving a balance between local action and collaborative interest, *Journal of Library Administration*, **28** (4), 85–90.

Addresses the questions: why should collection managers embrace collaboration as a tool for effective management of collections, and how are local needs balanced against the collective needs of a consortium? Reviews the factors that are forcing change, increasing budget and service pressures, copyright and licensing issues, and preservation and the creation of permanent archives of information.

Baker, S. K. and Jackson, M. E. (eds) (1995) *The future of resource sharing*, Haworth Press. Also published as *Journal of Library Administration*, **21** (1/2).
   Articles emphasize resource sharing, interlibrary loan and document delivery, and also cover co-operative collection development, economic decision models, consortia arrangements and copyright.
Carpenter, B. (2000) A field guide to collaborative collection development, *Computers in Libraries*, **20** (6), 28–30, 32–3.
   The Outagamie Waupaca Library System (OWLS), a 16-member public library system with access to the internet, shares their network with the Nicolet Federated Library System (NFLS), creating a larger network called OWLSnet. The problem of how to guide users of the OWLSnet libraries in the efficient use of the internet was approached through the design of a library system website. The website design process and the main features of the site are described and the way in which the provision of a free web-based service enabled the libraries to determine clearly what services could be charged for.
Cummings, A. M. et al. (1996) Resource sharing: collection development and document delivery, *Journal of Library Administration*, **23** (3/4), 169–77.
   The availability of text and data in electronic form, whether so produced in the first instance or converted retrospectively from print products, in principle permits a degree of resource-sharing among institutions that was unimaginable in the past. The extent to which institutions will practise it, however, will depend upon a host of other considerations. Considers the characteristics of some of the resource-sharing and document delivery arrangements various consortia have already attempted, including Conspectus, UnCover, Ariel and Faxon Finder.
Dwyer, J. (1999) Consortial review and purchase of networked resources: the California State University experience, *The Bottom Line*, **12** (1), 5–11.
   Outlines the history and organization of this system, its principles for the acquisition of electronic information resources, and the criteria and recommendations for an initial core collection. The system's advantages and disadvantages and future directions are discussed.
Electronic Libraries Programme (eLib)
   www.ukoln.ac.uk/services/elib/ [21 January 2001].
   This programme, an initiative of the Joint Information Systems Committee, has funded UK higher education co-operative projects.
Foskett, D. J. and Perry, S. (1993) The Consortium of University Research Libraries: an experiment in resource sharing in the United Kingdom, *Library Acquisitions: Practice and Theory*, **17** (3), 303–10.

Describes the CURL co-operative scheme for the provision of machine-readable bibliographical records.

Hacken, R. (1992) The RLG Conoco Study and its aftermath: is resource sharing in limbo?, *Journal of Academic Librarianship*, **18** (1), 17–23.

The 1985 Conoco Study assessed certain theoretical judgements of collection decision makers focusing on the areas of geology and German literature. In practice, however, selectors still rely much more heavily on institutional self-interest than on an idealistic notion of national interaccessibility.

Hannesdottir, S. K. (1992) *The Scandia Plan: a cooperative acquisition scheme for improving access to research publications in four Nordic countries*, Scarecrow Press.

Reasons suggested for the failure of this ambitious scheme (1956–80) were its primary commitment to collecting peripheral material and the lack of centralized administrative support.

Harloe, B. U. (ed.) (1994) *Guide to cooperative collection development*, Collection Management and Development Guide 6, American Library Association.

Guide to assessing viability and identifying issues that need to be addressed in co-operative collection development, while helping librarians and administrators initiate the co-operative collection process and develop the principles, policies and operating procedures that are essential to successfully maintaining a co-operative collection development programme. Covers practical and conceptual issues; especially useful for staff training or for students.

Henty, M. (1993) Resource sharing among Australian libraries: a distributed national collection, *Library Acquisitions: Practice and Theory*, **17** (3), 311–17.

Resource sharing among Australian libraries is long-standing and takes a number of forms including interlibrary lending, the sharing of bibliographic information, shared storage facilities and reciprocal borrowing schemes. The Australian library community has developed the concept of a distributed national collection.

Holley, R. P. (1998) Cooperative collection development: yesterday, today and tomorrow, *Collection Management*, **23** (4), 19–35.

An overview of the issues of collection development in the pre-internet and then in the internet era. The future may lie in providing financial subsidies to fund large storehouses of digital records.

Information policy: copyright and intellectual property (1999) IFLA, available at **www.ifla.org/II/copyright.htm** [26 May 2001].

One of the Electronic Collections on IFLA's website. Provides links to a wide range of articles, copyright statements and international instruments, not only for the US but worldwide.

Kachel, D. E. (1996) Improving access to periodicals: a cooperative collection management project, *School Library Media Quarterly*, **24** (2), 93–103.

Rare report of this type of research in school and public libraries where collection usage was studied to make better, more cost-effective decisions about periodical collections.

Kleiner, J. P. and Hamaker, C. A. (1997) Libraries 2000: transforming libraries using document delivery, needs assessment, and networked resources, *College & Research Libraries*, **58** (4), 355–74.

Describes three projects designed to use document delivery and electronic access to expand collections, identify faculty periodical needs and share resources among Louisiana libraries.

Landesman, M. and van Reenen, J. (1997) Consortia vs. reform: creating congruence, *Journal of Electronic Publishing*, **6** (2), available at **www.press.umich.edu/jep/06-02/landesman.html** [14 May 2001].

Research libraries face two possible solutions to addressing their users' needs: the rapidly growing consortial movement, and the movement to advocate and support reforms in scholarly communication. These two solutions may, at least partially, cancel one another out. Reforms in the system of scholarly communication are seen as the most critical piece of the long-term solution. Specific case studies.

McLean, N. (1999) The evolution of information resource sharing infrastructure: an Australian perspective, *Library Hi Tech*, **17** (3), 256–64.

Examines the characteristics underpinning resource sharing among university libraries in Australia and describes a series of projects aimed at improving the technical infrastructure of interlibrary lending. Has a summary of challenges inherent in creating global information infrastructure.

Prabha, C. and Danelly, G. N. (eds) (1997) Resource sharing in a changing environment, *Library Trends*, **45** (3).

Issue devoted to this theme, with papers on selection, acquisition, access and archiving of information and materials and the potential role of co-operation by authors such as E. Shreeves, C. A. Lynch, B. Kingma.

Pye, J. and Ball, D. (1999) *Library purchasing consortia in the UK: activity, benefits and good practice*, Library and Information Commission Research Report, The British Library.

Reports results of a survey of UK library consortia and their use by libraries for purchasing library materials. A range of key factors shaping recent developments in four library and information science sectors (further education, higher education, medical and health libraries, public libraries). The structure and markets of the UK book and periodical publishing industry in the UK are reviewed, with attention paid to historical as well as more recent practice that has had an impact on library supply.

Pye, J. and Ball, D. (1999) Purchasing consortia: trends and activity in the UK, *The Bottom Line*, **12** (1), 12–18.

Bournemouth University Library and Information Services investigated the activities of library purchasing consortia in four types of library (further education, higher education, medical and health libraries, public libraries). Focuses on the context that has encouraged their promotion and presents early findings.

Schad, J. G. et al. (1992) The future of collection development in an era of fiscal stringency: a symposium, *Journal of Academic Librarianship*, **18** (1), 4–16.

Includes the following papers: 'Moving toward concrete solutions in fundamental values' (M. A. Keller); 'Steady as she goes: moving from print to electronic forms of information with budget reductions' (D. M. Goehner); 'Collection development is just one of the service options' (H. S. White); 'Don't get mired in it: make some bricks' (K. Strauch); 'Is money the issue? Research resources and our collections crisis' (D. C. Hazen); 'Rationing resources in a reconceptualized environment' (J. F. Williams).

Smith, K. W. (1998) *OCLC 1967–1997: thirty years of furthering access to the world's information*, parts 1 and 2, Haworth Press. Also published as *Journal of Library Administration*, **25** (2/3) and (4).

Shaughnessy's chapter on successful co-operation among 13 US libraries is of special interest.

Soete, G. J. (1998) *Collaborative collections management programs in ARL libraries*, SPEC Kit 235, Association of Research Libraries.

The most common form of collaborative programme focuses on the acquisition of electronic resources. Collaboration in printed resources, because of the low-use, high-cost materials, requires more ongoing attention, is frequently visible to only a small number of users, and often does not save money. Preservation agreements were common.

Thornton, G. A. (2000) Impact of electronic resources on collection development, the roles of librarians, and library consortia, *Library Trends*, **48** (4), 842–56.

As the purchase of virtual resources accelerates, particularly through consortial agreements, the autonomy of the local library will fade and the roles of librarians will change drastically. This rapid transformation is illustrated by a discussion of OhioLINK and its effects, both positive and negative, on one member library.

Wise, A. (2000) Managing national distributed collections: reflections on the

British experience. In G. E. Gorman (ed.), *International yearbook of library and information management 2000–2001: collection management*, Library Association Publishing, 266–90.

Largely based on experiences of the Joint Information Systems Committee, it describes this and associated projects, outlining developments in 2000. It also looks at international initiatives including giving a brief overview of the International Coalition of Library Consortia. Concludes with a list of the essentials for managing distributed collections effectively and efficiently.

Wolf, M. and Bloss, M. (1998) Without walls means collaboration, *Information Technology and Libraries*, **17** (4), 212–15.

Reports over the past decade show that many research libraries are collecting much of the same materials and are becoming more homogeneous. Discusses probable reasons for this. Cites the experience of the Center for Research Libraries in co-operative collection development and concludes with notes on what action can be taken to halt and eventually reverse this trend

Copyright

Cornish, G. (2001) *Copyright: interpreting the law for libraries, archives and information services,* 3rd rev. edn, Library Association Publishing.

A standard work, authoritative and easy-to-read guide.

Pedley, P. (2000) *Copyright for library and information service professionals*, 2nd edn, Aslib.

Comprehensively researched information. It discusses all major licensing schemes, gives advice on practical issues such as dealing with an employer who wishes to break the law. The lack of an index is a severe handicap to its use as a working manual.

Schockmel, R. B. (1996) The premise of copyright, assaults on fair use, and royalty use fees, *Journal of Academic Librarianship*, **22** (1), 15–25.

If publishers focus on maximizing revenues, the balance inherent in copyright toward economic incentive and against the promotion of fundamental public needs are likely to result in user fees making access more costly than ownership.

Strong, W. S. (1999), Copyright in a time of change, *Journal of Electronic Publishing*, **4** (3), [8]pp.

A very readable paper discussing the changing relationships between publishers and readers as a result of electronic publishing, including the flexibility in meeting reader needs and the legal issues. The purpose of copyright is discussed. Not a purely US view.

Disaster management

Ashman, J. (1995) *Disaster planning for library and information services,* Aslib Know How Guides, Aslib.

Concise but comprehensive with clear layout. Covers disaster prevention, disaster preparedness, salvaging water-damaged library materials and conservation. Includes staff training.

Baillie, J., Doig, J. and Jilovsky, C. (eds) (1994) *Disaster in libraries: prevention and control,* 2nd edn, CAVAL.

Well adapted for Australian conditions from National Library of Scotland's *Planning a manual for disaster control in Scottish libraries and record offices.* Concise.

Doig, J. (1997) *Disaster recovery for archives, libraries and records management systems in Australia and New Zealand,* Centre for Information Studies.

A good practical guide and reference tool for a broad range of institutions, including guidance on developing a disaster plan.

Kenney, A. R. (1998) From analog to digital: extending the preservation tool kit, *Collection Management,* **22** (3/4), 65–79.

Provides a theoretical and practical framework for the use of digital technology for preservation.

Matthews, G. and Eden, P. (1996) *Disaster management in British libraries: project report with guidelines for library managers,* The British Library.

Overviews current disaster management practice in UK libraries and produces guidelines on disaster management based on good practice for library and information service management. Details the methodology followed, and discusses the findings.

Smith, W. (1998) Lost in cyberspace: preservation challenges of Australian internet resources, *LASIE,* **29** (2), 6–25.

Examines practical issues in the preservation of internet resources, providing an outline of the National Library of Australia's PANDORA (Preserving and Accessing Networked Documentary Resources of Australia) Project. Although only a small percentage of resources is being examined, it can be inferred that a wide range of materials is at long-term risk.

Sturgess, P. and Rosenberg, D. (eds) (1999) *Disaster and after: the practicalities of information service in times of war and other catastrophes,* Taylor Graham.

Based on papers at a conference held to discuss impacts of fire, flood and war on the provision and preservation of information, it is a definitive volume in the area. Highlights aspects such as the value gained from internet-based media for information exchange at such times.

Electronic reserve collections

Christoff, C. (1999) *Electronic reserves operations in ARL libraries*, SPEC Kit 245, Association of Research Libraries.

Intellectual property discussions have been prominent in most discussions of electronic reserves and have in some cases, led to the development of university-wide copyright statements or policies. Electronic reserves copyright issues, however, await resolution. Found that most libraries chose to develop their own 'home-grown' systems rather than purchase a commercial product.

Dugdale, C. (1998) Managing short loan collections in academic libraries: print and electronic alternatives for the new learning environment, *Journal of Librarianship and Information Science*, **30** (2), 133–40.

Problems are examined through the various approaches to print short-loan collections adopted by a UK university reflecting specific responses to the needs of users at different campuses. Considers the increases in efficiency that might be achieved through the introduction of an electronic reserve collection system designed to address the issue of the 'peak demand periods' and to meet the needs of each user group.

Muir, A. (1998) Publishers' views of electronic short-loan collections and copyright clearance issues, *Journal of Information Science*, **24** (4), 125–229.

A point of view from the publishers rather than librarians.

Soete, G. J. (1997) *Issues and innovations in electronic reserves,* Transforming Libraries Issue 1, Association of Research Libraries, available at **www.arl.org/transform/eres/eres.html** [30 April 2001].

Gives an overview of the situation at the time, discusses copyright issues and likely future developments together with links to sample documents from four libraries that were involved and to vendors of systems and copyright clearance agencies.

Gifts

Carrico, S. B. (1999) Gifts in academic and special libraries: a selected bibliography, *Library Collections, Acquisitions, and Technical Services*, **23** (4), 421–31.

An annotated bibliography of the most useful and informative sources on the various aspects of this topic.

Corson, F. A. (2000) Cybergifts, *Library Trends*, **48** (3), 619–33.

The world wide web may attract visitors but it is electronic mail that can be the library's most powerful fundraising tool.

Denning, C. (1999) Gifts and exchanges: problems, frustrations, . . . and triumphs,

Acquisitions Librarian, **22**, 1–190.

Thematic issue devoted to gifts and exchanges with current articles on policies, trends, automation, soliciting and practical suggestions for handling gifts.

Denning, C. et al. (1999) *The gifts and exchange function in ARL libraries*, SPEC Kit 241, Association of Research Libraries.

Re-examination of gift policies has taken place. World events, budgetary and personnel changes have had an impact on exchange activity.

Government publications

Butcher, D. (1991) *Official publications in Britain*, 2nd edn, Library Association Publishing.

Unfortunately now ten years old and hence starting to become out of date. Covers scope and structure of official publishing in Britain, bibliographic control, selection resources, availability. Chapters on parliamentary publications, publications of government departments, national and regional bodies, and local government.

Cheverie, J. F. (ed.) (1998) *Government information collections in the networked environment: new issues and models*, Haworth Press. Published simultaneously as *Collection Management*, **23** (3).

Contents include: 'Government information today: the dilemma of digital collections' (Jennifer L. Souza and Ellen M. Dodsworth); 'New tools for collection development: the Internet Scout Project' (Susan Calcari and Amy Tracy Wells); 'Building digital collections of government information: the Mann Library/USDA partnership' (Gregory W. Lawrence).

Morehead, J. (1996) *Introduction to United States government information sources*, 5th edn, Libraries Unlimited.

Latest edition of a standard work. The first chapter, 'Public access in the electronic age', covers legal aspects of information provision and electronic sources of government information. Other chapters cover the Government Printing Office; checklists, indexes, and guides to government information; sources of federal government information; statistical sources; reports of government research activities; and geographic data.

O'Mahony, D. P. (1998) Here today, gone tomorrow: what can be done to assure permanent and public access to electronic government information. In F. C. Lynden. and E. A. Chapman (eds), *Advances in librarianship*, vol. 22, Academic Press.

The discussion of the issues surrounding government documents can easily be extended to address all non-print information – if permanence issues are not addressed they ultimately become access issues.

Pond, C. (2000) British official publishing in the internet age, *Aslib Proceedings*, **52** (6), 200–6.

Examines the state of UK official internet publishing in 2000. Discusses issues of design, content, archiving, electronic communication and copyright, and points out areas where action would be desirable.

Outsourcing

Benaud, C. L. and Bordeianu, S. (1999) Outsourcing in academic libraries: a selective bibliography, *Reference Services Review*, **27** (1), 78–89.

An annotated bibliography addressing the broad issues of outsourcing, especially in academic libraries, although of some relevance to public, special and federal libraries. The list is divided into books on outsourcing in libraries; general articles on the history, theory and impact of outsourcing on libraries and librarianship; opinion pieces; and articles that relate to individual libraries' experiences with outsourcing.

Broadmeadow, S. (1997) Outsourcing document supply: the BT experience, *Interlending and Document Supply*, **25** (3), 108–12.

Describes the design and implementation of an automated document request system in a UK library. It allows users to enter requests for documents from their own workstations. The requests are transmitted to the British Library Document Supply Centre (BLDSC). Documents are supplied direct to the users and returned by them directly to the BLDSC. This allows library staff to provide an efficient document delivery service without tying up staff time with routine tasks such as photocopying and filing. Looks at user reaction to the system and possible future developments.

CPI Ltd (1999) *Outsourcing book selection: supplier selection in public libraries. A report to the BNB Research Fund*, Library and Information Commission.

Covers theoretical principles as well as presenting a thorough examination of the Westminster and Hertfordshire projects, their potential outcomes and implications of supplier selection together with a useful costing model.

Oder, N. (1997) Outsourcing model – or mistake: the collection development controversy in Hawaii, *Library Journal*, **122**, 28–31.

This is followed by another article by J. Charles and S. Mosley, 'Keeping selection in-house', outlining traits of effective selectors. It is written in the context of the Hawaii and other US outsourcing experiences.

Propas, S. W. and Johnson, S. E. (1998) Outsourcing, quality control, and the acquisitions professional, *Library Acquisitions: Practice and Theory*, **22** (3), 279–85.

Based on outsourcing experiences at Stanford University Libraries. Argues that the need for experienced technical services librarians increases rather than decreases in a library that outsources some of its technical service operations. Quality control, once built into routines carried out at the clerical level, becomes a major factor for the success of the outsourced operation. Describes the quality control programmes developed for monitoring a no-return approval plan and vendor-supplied cataloguing.

Strickland, S. A. (1999) Outsourcing: the Hawaiian experience, *Journal of Library Administration*, **29** (2), 63–72.

The outsourcing of technical services in the Hawaii State Public Library System is an example of management's failure to consider all the interrelated services performed by on-site library staff. Recounts the events surrounding the Hawaii outsourcing experiment in order that library managers, as well as librarians, can fully understand its ramifications before embarking on a similar course of action.

Willett, C. (1998) Consider the source: a case against outsourcing materials selection in academic libraries, *Collection Building*, **17** (2), 91–5.

Argues that outsourcing approval plans to vendors creates a prejudice against the alternative press. Argues that library managers have a duty to make alternative materials available for use and to secure the independence, integrity and accountability of libraries.

Preservation

Banks, P. and Pilette, R. (2000) *Preservation: issues and planning*, American Library Association.

An important contribution to the preservation literature, it provides a complete overview of three major preservation challenges: caring for collections with artefactual value, managing the preservation of paper-based collections with primarily informational value, and managing digital information.

Bellingham, K. and Lavrencic, T. (1995) Copyright impediments to the preservation of Australia's documentary heritage, *Australian Library Review*, **12** (4), 381–8.

The avenues that enable one to copy material for preservation without infringing copyright are considered and suggestions made for reform.

Dewitt, D. L. (1998) *Going digital: strategies for access, preservation, and conversion of collections to digital format*, Haworth Press. Simultaneously published as *Collection Management*, **22** (3/4).

Articles on local or remote access, preservation and access, issues of choice and use of digital-imaging technology, selection strategies for determining what material to digitize.

Eden, P. (1997) Concern for the future: preservation management in libraries and archives, *Journal of Librarianship and Information Science*, **29** (3), 121–9.

Combines the results of two questionnaire surveys of preservation policies, to compare the ways in which librarians perceive and carry out preservation management and how their perceptions and activities compare with those of archivists. Issues discussed include attitudes to preservation, selection for preservation, resources available, external funding, increasing use of library and archive collections, photocopying demand, past neglect, and digital technology. Concludes that there needs to be a coherent and comprehensive UK national preservation strategy.

Eden, P. et al. (1999) Developing a method for assessing preservation needs in libraries, *Library Management*, **20** (1), 27–34.

Describes development and testing of a standard method for assessing preservation needs of paper-based and photographic materials. Discusses core preservation management issues and inclusion of questions on these in the assessment.

Feather, J., Matthews, G. and Eden, P. (1996) *Preservation and the management of library collections*, 2nd edn, Library Association Publishing.

Very readable volume on aspects of preservation including electronic matters and digitization of library materials. Administrative information useful. Chapter 1 gives a good summary of the preservation problem and contrasts modern and outdated approaches to handling it.

Forgas, L. (1997) The preservation of videotape: review and implications for libraries and archives, *Libri*, **47** (1), 43–56.

Discusses reasons for deterioration of videotapes, steps that can prolong their life and various reformatting options.

Gehret, C. L. (1999) Preservation from a collection development perspective, *Acquisitions Librarian*, **21**, 115–24.

Discusses the role of the collection developer as integral to the preservation of library materials in material selection, collection maintenance, staff and user education and budgeting.

Graham, P. S. (1997) *Building the digital research library: preservation and access at the heart of scholarship*, Follett Lecture series, UKOLN, available at **www.ukoln.ac.uk/services/papers/follett/graham/paper.html** [29 April 2001].

Preservation must be managed from the earliest point possible in digital library item selection. The challenge of intellectual preservation is to guarantee integrity of malleable electronic information over long periods of time.

Harvey, R. (1993) *Preservation in libraries: a reader*, Bowker-Saur.

Although not easy to read, this is a good introduction providing sensible ideas with less depth, but more breadth of opinion than his other volume, listed below.

Harvey, R. (1993) *Preservation in libraries: principles, strategies and practices for librarians*, Bowker-Saur.

Presents a detailed review of all aspects relating to the preservation of library materials including: an overview of problems, causes and solutions; why library materials deteriorate; surveying and controlling the library environment; careful handling of library materials; disaster preparedness; book maintenance, repair procedures and binding; preservation of the intellectual content by reformatting to other media; technological and corporate strategies and the development of library preservation programmes.

Hazen, D., Horrell, J. and Merrill-Oldham, J. (1998) *Selecting research collections for digitization*, Council on Library and Information Resources. Also available at **www.clir.org/pubs/reports/hazen/pub74.html** [7 May 2001].

An excellent resource for those planning digitization projects who want to ensure that all issues are covered. The book's focus is on the decision-making process, raising questions dealing with the intellectual nature of the materials, the users, the nature of use, and how the project will be described, delivered, and retained, as well as cost–benefit analysis.

Helfet, J. (1996) The use of recordable CDROMs as an electronic archiving medium for librarians, *The Electronic Library*, **14** (3), 221–4.

Libraries should not adopt a complacent attitude to their archived information. Discusses reasons why conventional archival storage methods are unlikely to be totally satisfactory. CD-ROMs can offer many benefits as electronic archiving media.

Howell, A. (2000) Perfect one day – digital the next: challenges in preserving digital information, *Australian Academic & Research Libraries*, **31** (4), 121–41.

Compares and contrasts some of characteristics of information in paper-based format and in digital format, particularly those that affect their preservation. Leading ideas on why digital information is short-lived, current best thinking on how digital information may be preserved and some recent initiatives in Australian libraries are also included. This whole issue of *AARL* is devoted to digital preservation.

Merrill-Oldham, J. (1999) *Library storage facilities, management, and services*, SPEC Kit 242, Association of Research Libraries.

This SPEC survey focuses on the physical characteristics of library storage facilities, the management issues inherent in their operation, and the services they provide. Suggests electronic document delivery will be employed increasingly to offset diminished on-site access and appropriate environmental conditions will give libraries time to undertake long-range preservation reformatting and conservation programmes.

Payne, L. (2000) Library storage facilities and services. In G. E. Gorman (ed.), *International yearbook of library and information management 2000–2001: collection management*, Library Association Publishing, 291–306.

Covers purpose, design and types of library storage and storage facilities' role in library co-operation and future development.

Ritzenthaler, M. L. (1993) *Preserving archives and manuscripts*, Society of American Archivists.

This highly recommended volume addresses preservation as a management function. Core elements in an archives preservation programme are defined; the nature of archival materials and the factors that affect their long-term keeping are broadly discussed. Includes extensive illustrations, glossary, bibliography, advice on setting up a workspace, basic preservation procedures and supplies and equipment.

Schnare, S. G., Schwartzburg, S. G. and Cunha, G. M. (2001) *Bibliography of preservation literature, 1983–1996*, Scarecrow Press.

Includes organizations and other resources for collection preservation. Suggests strategies and sources of advice.

Sitts, M. K. (ed.) (2000) *Handbook for digital projects: a management tool for preservation and access*, Northeast Document Conservation Center, available at **www.nedcc.org/digital/dighome.htm** [25 April 2001].

Intended as a management tool for institutions concerned with preservation and access issues. Assists with informed decision making on timing of digitization, integrating preservation needs with scanning projects, selecting materials for scanning, working with outside vendors, maintaining quality control, developing indexing and navigation tools, and building databases, as well as providing network access.

Waters, D. and Garrett, J. (1996) *Preserving digital information: final report and recommendations*, Commission on Preservation and Access and the Research Libraries Group, available at **www.rlg.org/ArchTF/index.html** [25 April 2001].

The Committee was appointed by the Research Libraries Group to investigate and recommend means to ensure 'continued access indefinitely into the future of records stored in digital electronic form'.

Selection and selection resources

Alexander, J. E. and Tate, M. (1999) *Webwisdom: how to evaluate and create information on the web*, Lawrence Erlbaum Associates.

A good guide but not as readable as Cooke mentioned below.

Arlen, S. and Lindell, A. (1998) Web tools for collection managers, *Collection Building*, **17** (2), 65–70.

Very good review of sites that contain useful tools and resources for selectors.

Bosch, S., Promis, P. and Sugnet, C. (1994) *Guide to selecting and acquiring CDRoms, software, and other electronic publications*, Acquisitions Guidelines 9, American Library Association.

A concise guide including a discussion of material types, selection criteria, and acquisitions issues. It includes definitions, glossary, bibliography and index.

Bybee, H. et al. (1998) A net full of tools for collection development and technical services, *Choice*, **35**, Supp., 39–51.

An excellent and concise review of major sites that provide useful tools and resources for selectors. Part 1 lists internet tools for materials selection and acquisition; Part 2 internet tools for serials, including vendor sites; Part 3 cataloguing sites.

Ciolek, T. M. and Goltz, I. M., *Information quality WWW virtual library*, available at **www.ciolek.com/WWWVL-InfoQuality.html** [29 April 2001].

An excellent collection of links which covers all aspects of information quality. It is thorough and frequently updated. The sections on 'Building quality WWW resources' and 'Evaluation of information resources' are the most useful for collection managers.

Cooke, A. (1999) *A guide to finding quality information on the internet: selection and evaluation strategies*, Library Association Publishing.

Authoritative and easy-to-use guide to evaluating information, definitions, strategies, quality, search facilities, discussion lists and e-journals. Includes a glossary and excellent annotated bibliography. Based on extensive research for Cooke's PhD thesis.

Dannelly, G. N. (1999) 'Uneasy lies the head': selecting resources in a consortial setting, *Journal of Library Administration*, **28** (2), 57–68.

Provides a brief history of library co-operation in America, with emphasis on the latter half of the 20th century. Motives for library co-operation, along with potential obstacles and keys to success, are identified. The role of consortia in the current electronic environment is described and prospects for the future of library consortia outlined.

Davis, T. (1997) The evolution of selection activities for electronic resources, *Library Trends*, **45** (3), 391–403.

Sets out the legal and technical context (access methods and licensing) in which selection of resources takes places at the local institution, which must then be taken into account in sharing resources with other institutions.

Demas, S., McDonald, P. and Lawrence, G. (1995) The internet and collection development: mainstreaming selection of internet resources, *Library Resources and Technical Services*, **39** (3), 275–90.

Presents methods for developing systematic identification, evaluation and selection of internet resources. Identifies key collection policy issues and includes an excerpt from a collection policy statement.

Hastings, S. K. (1998) Selection and evaluation of networked information resources, *Acquisitions Librarian*, **2**, 109–22.

Discusses appropriate methods for selection for public libraries and the different tools available to evaluate the use and effectiveness of a collection of networked electronic resources.

Hirshon, A. et al. (1998) *Statement of current perspective and preferred practices for the selection and purchase of electronic information*, International Coalition of Library Consortia, available at **www.library.yale.edu/consortia/statement.html** [25 April 2001].

Provides an international perspective on consortial licensing and purchasing of electronic information. Addresses current and future electronic information environment issues such as the increasing expectations of library users, fair use, archiving of information, pricing strategies, and electronic information delivery measurement. The preferred practices section covers contract negotiations, pricing, data access and archiving, system platforms, licensing terms, information content and its management, and user authentication.

Kim, F. Y. (1997) Selecting internet resources: experience at Hong Kong University of Science and Technology (HKUST) Library, *The Electronic Library*, **15** (2), 91–8.

Describes the composition, goals, selection guidelines and process, problems and achievements of this library's Selection of Internet Resources Group.

Kovacs, D. K. (2000) *Building electronic library collections: the essential guide to selection criteria and core subject collections*, Neal-Schuman.

Has a more policy-oriented approach than other works on this topic. Some material is quite basic, useful for the beginner. It has a companion website which is intended to keep URLs up to date.

Kovacs, D. K. and Elkordy, A. (2000) Collection development in cyberspace: building an electronic library collection, *Library Hi Tech*, **18** (4), 335– 61.

Offers a practical discussion of some guidelines and practical strategies on where and how to find, identify, evaluate and select appropriate web-based information resources. Focuses on web-based information resources rather than other electronic information resources such as CD-ROM or fee-based databases. Includes a literature review and extensive 'webliography' of collection development sites and listservs.

Lin, Y. P. (1999) *Web page development and management*, SPEC Kit 246, Association of Research Libraries.

Concludes that building a well-balanced library website is a complex task that involves the user community as well as the information provider. Library web development demands professional expertise, networking and web-authoring skills, and artistic creativity. A high-profile library website should incorporate easy navigation, strong graphics, substantial content, multimedia formats, a well-indexed search engine and fast communication.

McAdam, S. (1999) Selection/acquisition of non book materials: videos, CD-ROMS, tapes, etc., *Acquisitions Librarian*, **21**, 125–45.

Covers licensing, copyright, the legal ramifications of donations, censorship and budgeting, and offers suggestions for non-book sources.

Milnor, N. (1998) Cyberselection: the impact of the internet on collection development in public libraries, *Acquisitions Librarian*, **20**, 101–7.

Based on interviews with working librarians, explores four ways in which use of the internet is impacting selection in public libraries: selection tools and information, providing alternative sources of information, information access and currency, and impact on materials budgets.

Morville, P. et al. (1999) *The internet searcher's handbook: locating information, people and software*, 2nd edn, revised by G. A. Decandido, Neal-Schuman.

For the beginner. Aims to provide 'an understanding of the principles of Internet searching and a detailed knowledge of currently available research tools'.

Pearson, J. W. (1999) Building a new undergraduate library collection, *College and Undergraduate Libraries*, **6** (1), 33–45.

Examines problems and successes with finding the best sources for a 'core' collection for a new undergraduate library, covers methods for selecting types of material – monographs, serials, media and electronics – and discusses budget issues and material.

Poulter, A., Hom, D. and Tseng, G. (2000) *The library and information professionals guide to the internet*, 3rd edn, Library Association Publishing.
Skilfully concise guide. Part 1 covers the history and functions of the internet; Part 2 explains how it provides access to people and information resources; Part 3 has practical tips and etiquette; Part 4, which covers half of the book, is a broadly classified guide to resources. The links are listed on the publisher's special purpose website at
www.lapwing.org.uk

Rabine, J. L. and Brown, L. A. (2000) The selection connection: creating an internal web page for collection development, *Library Resources and Technical Services*, **44** (1), 44–9.
Contains a useful literature review and web tools of use to acquisitions and collection development.

Richards, D. T. (1991) By your selection criteria are ye known, *Library Acquisitions: Practice and Theory*, **15** (3), 279–85.
Brief review of the range of criteria used in the library selection process.

Robinson, W. C. (1995) Price of materials and collection development in larger public libraries, *Library Acquisitions: Practice and Theory*, **19** (3), 299–312.
Price is always a consideration but not the most important one in the selection decision.

Spiller, D. (2000) *Providing materials for library users*, Library Association Publishing.
Highly recommended for students and information processionals. Covers policy and provision, assessing user requirements, budgeting, evaluation and weeding, and serials.

Stielow, F. (1999) *Creating a virtual library: a how-to-do-it manual for librarians*, Neal-Schuman.
Aimed at managers, stressing administration, content and policy making.

Timmons, M. E. (2000) The internet and acquisitions: sources and resources for development, *Acquisitions Librarian*, **23**, 1–127.
Articles include using the internet in acquisitions generally and in acquiring materials such as for young adults; book publishers' websites; and the acquisition of electronic journal resources. Each reviews relevant websites.

Toub, S. E. (1997) Adding value to internet collections, *Library Hi Tech*, **15** (3/4), 148–54.
Advises on appropriate time and how to develop a library's own internet col-

lection. Emphasizes well-planned organization, navigability, labelling and systems, as well as the careful selection evaluation and description of resources. Internet guides to evaluation included.

Van Orden, P. (2000) *Selecting books for the elementary school library media center*, Neal-Schuman.

Thirteen chapters devoted primarily to selection guidelines for specific genres, such as picturebooks, folk literature, etc.

Yochelson, A. et al. (1997) *Collection development and the internet: a brief handbook for recommending officers in the Humanities and Social Sciences Division at the Library of Congress*, Library of Congress (links updated to February 2000), available at

http://lcweb.loc.gov/acq/colldev/handbook.html [22 April 2001].

Aims to provide practical guidance in using the internet to extend the techniques traditionally used in the area of collection development.

Serials

ALCTS (1997) *ALCTS guide to performance evaluation of serials vendors*, ALCTS Acquisitions Guidelines 10, American Library Association.

Maintains that evaluating serials vendors is the best way to ensure quality service at an affordable cost. This guide provides the tools for measuring vendor systems and services including subscription agents and standing order vendors, and explains how to collect and analyse vendor performance data for comparison. It also covers how to incorporate vendor evaluation into regular work activity so that choices are not made under crisis conditions.

Arms, W. Y. (2000) Preservation of scientific serials: three current examples, *Microform and Imaging Review*, **29** (2), 50–6, available at

www.press.umich.edu/jep/05-02/arms.html [4 May 2001].

Three approaches to archiving electronic texts are described in the form of case studies: the ACM Digital Library, the Internet RFC series, and *D-Lib Magazine*. Discusses the major issues surrounding the long-term preservation of electronic scientific information.

Burrows, T. and Kent, P. G. (eds) (1993) *Serials management in Australia and New Zealand: profile of excellence*, Haworth Press.

Well-written essays from a hands-on perspective, exploring the decision-making processes in detail, though lack of index makes it difficult to use for reference.

Cargille, K. (ed.) (2000) Digital archiving: whose responsibility is it?, *Serials Review*, **26** (3), 50–68.

Presents a range of perspectives on digital archiving of serials, highlighting the problems and offering views on who should solve them.

Chadwell, F. A. and Brownmiller, S. (1999) Heads up: confronting the selection and access issues of electronic journals, *Acquisitions Librarian*, **21**, 21–35.

Examines how collection development and acquisitions librarians can best adapt their policies and procedures to face the challenges of selecting and providing access to electronic journals. Emphasizes the necessary changes that should be incorporated into collection development policies, and provides an overview of the benefits and disadvantages of electronic journals.

Duranceau, E. F. (1998) Electronic journal forum. Archiving and perpetual access for web-based journals: a look at the issues and how five e-journal providers are addressing them, *Serials Review*, **24** (2), 110–15.

Reviews the archiving and perpetual access approaches of five full-text e-journal providers (Blackwell's Electronic Journals Navigator, Highwire Press, JSTOR, OCLC's Electronic Collections Online, and Project Muse), placing these approaches in the broader context of archiving issues for web-based journals.

Elsevier (1996) *TULIP final report*, Elsevier, available at

www.elsevier.nl/homepage/about/resproj/trmenu.htm [21 January 2001].

TULIP (The University Licensing Program) was a scheme in which Elsevier delivered electronically the contents of its materials science journals to nine US university libraries for a period of five years.

Farrington, J. W. (1997) *Serials management in academic libraries: a guide to issues and practices*, Greenwood Press.

Contains detailed advice on the preparation of an operational specification, types of systems, functions and standards for serials automation.

Gusack, N. and Lynch, C. A. (1995) [The TULIP Project], *Library Hi Tech*, **3** (4), 7–74.

Special issue devoted to The University Licensing Program or TULIP, which was a co-operative research project testing systems for networked delivery and use of journals. Articles cover different aspects of the project, which involved Elsevier Science and a number of major US universities.

Hawbaker, A. C. and Wagner, C. K. (1996) Periodical ownership versus fulltext online access: a cost–benefit analysis, *Journal of Academic Librarianship*, **22** (2), 105–10.

Compares the costs and benefits of periodical ownership against online access of a full-text periodicals database in one US academic library. A full-text database allows the library to offer more than twice as many journals as it does currently for a 15% increase in expenditure.

Kidd, T. and Rees-Jones, L. (eds) (2000) *Serials management handbook: a practical guide to print and electronic serials management*, Library Association Publishing.

Covering budgeting, processing stock management, exploitation and usage analysis, this book provides a useful concise overview for the student or beginner professional.

Kingma, B. R. and Irving, S. (1997) *The economics of access versus ownership: the costs and benefits of access to scholarly articles via interlibrary loan and journal subscriptions*, Haworth Press. Also published as *Journal of Interlibrary Loan, Document Delivery, and Information Supply*, **6** (3).

Presents an economic model to conduct analyses of relying on interlibrary loan rather than purchase for access to journal articles.

Klemperer, K. (2000) *Electronic journals: a selected resource guide*, Harrassowitz, available at

www.harrassowitz.de/ms/ejresguide.html [7 May 2001].

Links to general sources of information: overviews, bibliographies and collections of papers; e-journal lists and directories; electronic journal providers, definitions; usage studies of electronic journals; standards, legal and business issues; academic issues; preservation and archiving of electronic material, and journals and discussion lists.

Leathem, C. A. (1998) Issues in electronic journals selection and management, *Internet Reference Services Quarterly*, **3** (3), 15–28.

Discusses selection criteria, access, cost factors, cataloguing treatment and copyright issues.

Lightman, H. and Manilov, S. (2000) A simple method for evaluating a journal collection: a case study of Northwestern University Library's economics collection, *Journal of Academic Librarianship*, **26** (3), 183–90.

Reports on process and benefits of an evaluation process which combined citation analyses with non-statistical techniques.

MacLennan, B. *Serials in cyberspace: collections, resources and services*, available at **www.uvm.edu/~bmaclenn#ejour** [15 May 2001].

Has links to the following categories of resources: selected sites with electronic journal collections and services (international), selected e-journal titles, associations, societies organizations programs etc., other useful sources (not e-journal specific).

Metz, P. (1992) Thirteen steps to avoiding bad luck in a serials cancellation project, *Journal of Academic Librarianship*, **18** (2), 76–82.

Academic librarians need to plan carefully and involve faculty throughout the process to avoid excessive damage to the collection or the library's relationship with the rest of the institution.

Nisonger, T. E. (1998) *Management of serials in libraries*, Libraries Unlimited.

A very comprehensive volume including chapters on citation analysis, studies of periodical use, electronic journals, and serials automation as well as practical management issues. Appendix 3 is select annotated listing of WWW sites that are relevant to serials. Bibliographies are provided for each chapter in addition to the general bibliography at the end of the volume.

Roberts, E. (1992) PILL: document delivery as an alternative to local ownership of seldom-used scientific journals, *Journal of Academic Librarianship*, **18** (1), 30–4.

One way that libraries can continue to support researchers' literature needs, despite increasing costs, is by developing effective document delivery systems. Reports on a survey of physics, chemistry, and biochemistry academics of their use of and attitudes to interlibrary loans. Recommendations based on the survey are made for a more effective service.

Rooks, D. C. (1993) Electronic serials: administrative angst or answer, *Library Acquisitions: Practice and Theory*, **17** (4), 449–54.

Considers budgeting and staffing resources, collection development implications and patron reactions, as well as internal and external political realities.

Russell, R. (ed.) (2000) *Making sense of standards and technologies for serials management*, Library Association Publishing.

This edited collection of studies by well-known strategic and technical professionals covers key standards and technologies for serials management and access. Chapters include descriptive standards for serials management, standards for the terms of availability metadata, standards for serials holdings and for document requesting.

Sanville, T. J. and Winters, B. A. (1998) A method out of the madness: OhioLINK's collaborative response to the serials crisis. In C. N. Simser and M. A. Somers (eds), *Experimentation and collaboration: creating serials for a new millennium*, Haworth Press, 125–39.

Examines the way in which OhioLINK community and individual libraries are trying to leverage their collective resources to dramatically reverse the trend of decreasing subscriptions due to increased serial prices and decreasing budgets.

Simser, C. N. and Somers, M. A. (1998) *Experimentation and collaboration: creating serials for a new millennium*, Haworth Press. Published simultaneously as *The Serials Librarian*, **34** (1/2) and (3/4).

Covers a wide range of issues, from the practical outline by Trisha Davis and John Reilly on understanding license agreements for electronic products to Bruce Kingma's economic analysis of library consortia and Andrea Keyhani's discussion of whether creating an electronic archive should be the role of libraries.

Snowley, I. (1995) Tendering for periodical supply: how librarians can manage the process, *Serials*, **8** (3), 227–30.

Covers the main aspects that should be included in a tender document.

Werner, A. (1996) Serials acquisition: selection – an overview of criteria, *Serials Librarian*, **29** (1/2), 153–61.

Reviews the traditional criteria for print serials.

Woodward, H. (1994) The impact of electronic information on serials collection management, *IFLA Journal*, **20** (1), 35–45. Also published in *Serials*, **7** (1), 29–36.

Examines the various types of electronic periodicals currently available and discusses issues relating to storage, access, selection, acquisition, bibliographic control, training and resource allocation. Defines the factors that need to be assessed in developing a collection management policy for electronic periodicals and surveys the various current awareness services and document delivery services.

Theft prevention

Foster, C. (1996) Determining losses in academic libraries and the benefits of theft detection systems, *Journal of Librarianship and Information Science*, **28** (2), 93–104.

A study in a small college library found that statistical sampling techniques used for determining the number of books missing from the library collection produced results acceptably close to actual inventories of the full collection. Different ways of allocating a monetary value on replacing lost material were compared and used as the basis for a cost–benefit analysis of the introduction of library theft detection systems. This study showed that the first year's operating costs would be met by savings in replacement costs.

Johansson, D. (1996) Library material theft, mutilation, and preventive security measures, *Public Library Quarterly*, **15** (4), 51–66.

An entertaining description of the methods used by libraries throughout history to reduce or prevent material theft and mutilation, which have ranged from use of curses to electronic security systems.

O'Neill, R. K. (ed.) (1998) *Management of library and archival security: from the outside looking in*, Haworth Press. Also published as *Journal of Library Administration*, **25** (1).

Contains much practical advice and discusses such issues as dilemmas of theft by staff.

Soete, G. R. (1999) *Management of library security*, SPEC Kit 247, Association of Research Libraries.

A broad, well-documented collection of ideas and examples on the management of library security. The bibliography is short but current. Sample documents are included that cover almost every aspect of security: theft, patron relations, misuse of electronic resources, evacuation procedures, package bomb indicators and emergency blackouts. Also useful is the wide variety of incident report forms included. Adaptable to most library situations.

Weeding

Engeldinger, E. A. (1999) Weeding 'naturally', *College and Undergraduate Libraries*, **6** (1), 47–51.

Argues that, as college libraries are not research libraries, they should abandon the notion that size has some relationship to value.

Joswick, K. E. and Stierman, J. P. (1993) Systematic reference weeding: a workable model, *Collection Management*, **18** (1/2), 103–16.

Describes one library's weeding project which included a committee, and reflects on the benefits and negative aspects of the result.

Mathews, E. and Tyckoson, D. A. (1990) A program for the systematic weeding of the reference collection, *Reference Librarian*, **29**, 129–43.

The authors maintain that weeding is considered an integral part of the collection development programme by the authors of standard collection development texts, but it is not often put into actual practice.

Roy, L. (1994) Weeding. In A. Kent and H. Lancour (eds), *Encyclopedia of library and information science*, **54** (17), 352–98, published by M. Dekker.

Described by R. Williams (see below) as a 'monumental survey of the weeding literature'.

Slote, S. J. (1997) *Weeding library collections: library weeding methods*, 4th edn, Libraries Unlimited.

Regarded as the key work on the methodology of collection review for weeding. His methodology has been revised in the light of research that challenges the belief that circulation reflects in-library use of materials.

Williams, R. (2000) Weeding library collections: conundrums and contradictions. In G. E. Gorman (ed.), *International yearbook of library and information management 2000–2001: collection management*, Library Association Publishing, 339–61.

Up-to-date, critical evaluation of the literature in this field.

Williams, S. (1999) Stock revision, retention and relegation in US academic libraries. In C. Jenkins and M. Morley (eds), *Collection management in academic libraries*, 2nd edn, Gower Publishing, 205–24.

Covers history, review of other literature in the field, collection review and a case study.

Index

Page numbers in *italics* refer to figures